circles of
compassion

essays connecting issues of justice

circles of
compassion

essays connecting issues of justice

 Vegan Publishers™

edited by **Will Tuttle, PhD**

Published by:
Vegan Publishers, Danvers, MA, www.veganpublishers.com

Cover and text design: ©Robin H. Ridley / parfaitstudio.com
Watercolor art: ©Madeleine Tuttle / madeleinetuttle.com
Farm Sanctuary goats: ©Jo-Anne McArthur / weanimals.com
Road: ©Avohitatevs; Hands: ©Dolgachov / dreamstime.com

Printed in the United States of America on 100% recycled paper
Third Printing
3 4 5 6 7 8 9 10

ISBN 978-1-940184-06-7

Table of Contents

Foreword: Connecting the Dots

by Carol J. Adams

What is *intersectionality?* The concept was developed as a critical race theoretical intervention in anti-discrimination law. It has also subsequently been employed as a method for analyzing and combating oppressive structures and practices beyond discrimination law.

Feminists have been among the activists and scholars analyzing mutually reinforcing logics of domination and drawing connections among the varied implications of power relations. Many of these writers have identified ecofeminism as an important resource for discussing intersectionality.

Ecofeminism posits that the domination of the rest of nature is linked to the domination of women, and that both dominations must be eradicated. To the issues of sexism, racism, classism, imperialism, and heterosexism that concern feminists, ecofeminists add environmental exploitation. Analyzing mutually reinforcing logics of domination, and drawing connections among practical implications of power relations, has been a core project of ecofeminism, and we've benefitted from insightful writings by Marti Kheel, Greta Gaard, Lori Gruen, Deborah Slicer, pattrice jones, and others.

Others who write on this subject often acknowledge the influence of feminism and ecofeminism in the development of their understanding of interconnected oppressions. Jim Mason's *An Unnatural Order* (1997) is an example of this. Mason argues that all human oppression originates in the domestication and subsequent oppression of animals. Mason coined the term *misothery* (from the Greek words for *hatred/ contempt* and *animal*) to denote speciesist derogation of animals, which he views as parallel to *misogyny*, hatred and contempt for women.

The theory that the oppression of women, animals, and other subjugated groups are interrelated has proven to have practical implications. For instance, it has brought about the recognition that companion animals are often targets of abusers as well as the human victims of domestic violence.

As feminists were developing what we now call "ecofeminism" in the 1970s, the contemporary animal rights movement was beginning to take shape. By the early 1980s, as more and more animal advocacy groups emerged, it was becoming clear that the budding movement, though rhetorically attuned to sexism and racism was not as inclusive as it should have been. This meant that while we were fighting against some social injustices, we were simultaneously promoting them in our daily actions.

This book originally began with the vision of two feminist-animal activists who wanted to help others make sense of the intuition that how we respond to animals is connected to and is a part of social justice in the world. In 2006, Ashley Maier and Stacia Mesleh created "Connect the Dots," an organization whose mission was to promote and build capacity to address the connections between human, animal, and environmental well-being.

In 2008, they decided to edit a collection of essays that addressed the commonality of oppression. Their call for papers explained that they wanted

> to illustrate that a pervasive mindset, conscious or unconscious, underlies most human-caused violence, exploitation, and oppression. This mindset is "Me and those like me are better and more important than others. Our feelings, wants, needs, desires, and very lives are worth more than 'theirs.'" This mindset persists in most cultures and reveals itself in

manifestations that are both socially sanctioned (i.e. animal consumption, land use, inequitable pay) and non-socially sanctioned (i.e. abuse of companion animals, toxic waste dumping, rape). These two branches of injustice share the same root system; thus one cannot be watered without causing the other to thrive and grow. The outcomes of this mindset include, but are not limited to: patriarchy, racism, sexism, homophobia, heterosexism, classism, genderism, ageism, environmental destruction, speciesism, consumerism, family violence, sexual violence, the prison industrial complex, war… Though seemingly disconnected, these manifestations are connected by the paradigm of perceived superiority. This mindset endures because it has well-established safe havens within the human social norms of most cultural contexts.[1]

Ashley and Stacia wanted to shine a light on the daily choices that feed and sustain this mindset, allowing it to hide in plain sight. They envisioned that their anthology would contribute to the dialogue and community building they saw as necessary to expand justice beyond the currently accepted borders that offer shelter to a privileged few.

They invited contributors to write about how they see oppression shaping the world, or about their journeys towards connecting the dots of oppression, or defining moments that illuminated the inter-connectedness of oppressions, and/or advice to those who aspire to live a more just life. From the beginning of their project, I discussed with them the progress on the manuscript.

In 2013, a variety of forces caused Ashley and Stacia to realize they had to put "Connect the Dots," the organization, on hold, and that they would not be able to complete the book. They had previously signed on with Vegan Publishers to publish this anthology, and with their permission, the publisher sought out a new editor who embodied the intersectionalist spirit of the collection. Fortunately, Will Tuttle, one of the contributors and author of the influential *The World Peace Diet*, indicated willingness to become the editor, ultimately making this book possible. Eleven of the essays you find here were originally written for *Connect the Dots* (you'll find some references to this term in some of the essays). Will identified other contributors to augment the conversation about intersectionality and brought the book to completion.

As a published author and frequent speaker, Will Tuttle is rightly well-known and admired, but Ashley and Stacia are less well known. I think we should know a little about these talented young women who began the project you hold in your hands. Ashley Jo Maier earned an M.S.W. with a concentration in women's studies, specifically focusing on violence against women, gender inequality, and social change, and recently obtained an M.P.A. As a feminist and vegan, Ashley holds the conviction that we will only end things like gender violence when we recognize the violent context in which we live and we cease to condone the daily acts of violence that take less obvious forms, such as our exploitation of animals and the environment. I am honored that she is one of the contributors to *Defiant Daughters: 21 Women on Art, Activism, Animals, and The Sexual Politics of Meat.*

Stacia Mesleh has worked as a registered nurse in a burn unit and an emergency room, and most recently as the Infection Control Practitioner of a hospital. She has also worked as a Sexual Assault Nurse Examiner and as a volunteer, performing domestic violence exams for a police department. She holds a Bachelor's Degree in Nursing and a Master's Degree in Chemistry and Biochemistry. Through her many life and career experiences, she has come to realize that contributing to the dialogue and actions that strive to make the world more just is a priority and a passion.

With more and more interest in extending the circle of compassion and connecting the dots, the question that arises may be, "Why *don't* we connect the dots?" I've thought about this for many years and have some ideas.

First, I have observed something that I call *retrograde humanism*. This is the idea that our compassion has a finite quality to it; that it is something that can be exhausted and so should be extended to humans first. In fact, compassion is something that grows; compassion offers us an inclusive, not exclusive, vision. Retrograde humanists clearly haven't figured out that you can be both working for social justice for human beings and for animals, and that these causes are interconnected. Like me, many vegans and animal activists have worked in homeless shelters and domestic violence shelters; they're social workers, housing advocates, etc.

Clearly, a fear speciesists have is that they will have to forego one of their pleasures in life: eating animals and animal products. Many people today feel very stressed and quite unhappy. They have few things to look forward to, and these are almost always sensual pleasures. Tasty food gives them one of their few reasons for putting up with life's many unpleasant struggles. They don't realize, because they haven't experienced it, that eating vegan food is a pleasure, not a punishment.

They fear confronting a negative experience: the loss of security and enjoyment, and their identity as benefiting from oppression. They fear losing the power and control associated with being in dominant positions.

They fear change. While change may be hard, not changing is harder; most people just haven't realized this yet.

Finally, they don't connect the dots because historical memory is unstable and influenced by stereotypes, including a gender binary that privileges men and their words over women and theirs. We need to learn our history of connecting the dots and extending compassion. Lori Gruen and I offer a beginning discussion of this in our chapter "Groundwork" in the recently published *Ecofeminism: Feminist Intersections with Other Animals and the Earth.*

While the animal advocacy movement is often said to begin with the 1976 appearance of Peter Singer's *Animal Liberation*, this claim ignores the great amount of grassroots and analytic work that preceded the appearance of this book. His writings on the subject began as a 1973 book review of the 1971 book, *Animals, Men and Morals*, edited by Stanley Godlovitch, Roslind Godlovitch, and John Harris. It contained an essay by Ruth Harrison whose own book, *Animal Machines*, about factory farming, had been published in 1964. In 1965, Brigid Brophy wrote "The Rights of Animals." That essay appeared in *The Sunday Times* in London. It catalyzed the Godlovitches and Harris to begin work on their anthology. Well-known animal advocate Kim Stallwood dates the start of the contemporary animal rights movement to Brophy's essay. I would put its beginning the year before with Harrison's book.

Either way, it is a decade before the publication of *Animal Liberation*. By dating the modern animal movement from Singer's book, women (Harrison and Brophy among others) are lost to view. In addition, the early feminist concern for other animals that can be found in writings from 1972 to 1975 is overlooked. While Singer's work has certainly had significant impact, as has the work of other theorists like Tom Regan, identifying animal liberation as having "fathers" such as Singer and Regan and no "mothers" has generated a few problems.

Some believe that animal rights activism is the teleological fulfillment of human rights activism. It's important to understand the concept of "teleology" because it helps us understand retrograde humanism as well as a phenomenon that can be found in the animal rights movement. *Teleology* identifies *purpose* in nature, finding "final causes." For instance, retrograde humanists believe that humans are the fulfillment of evolution and thus worthy of more consideration than other animals or nature. They see humans as the teleological fulfillment of evolution. But, animal rights activists may hold a teleological belief as well. Some of his readers—who then became animal activists after reading *Animal Liberation*—conclude Peter Singer has made a teleological statement in his preface. To wit: "There's been Black Liberation, Gay Liberation, Women's Liberation. Now let's talk about Animal Liberation." Reading this, some animal activists conclude, "Well, Black Liberation, Gay Liberation, Women's Liberation —that's been done. I need only to focus on animals." Both retrograde humanism and the belief that the animal rights movement is the teleological fulfillment of all other activisms participate in the same false belief system: that there is a ladder of progress, a hierarchy, rather than that we are all interconnected. *Separating animal liberation from feminism and other social justice issues promotes social injustice.*

With teleological fulfillment, the sense of intersectionality is lost. This results in evangelical-like activism rather than a movement that seeks to transform social relations among people as well as between people and the other animals. For instance, during the 1990s, animal advocates proposed that child offenders be tried as adults for animal cruelty. But this proposal failed to take into account any understanding of the prison industrial complex in the United States. Such sentencing would also appear to be a violation of international human rights law.

So, let's consider 1965 as a pivotal year for animal activism. Something else happened that year. "Red Ryder Nails the Hammond Kid," a short story by humorist Jean Shepherd, was published in *Playboy*. That short story was one of several main sources for the movie *A Christmas Story*. At Christmas time, *A Christmas Story* 24-hour marathons are offered on television stations. The story's focus is on a young boy in the 1930s who desires an "Official Red Ryder Carbine Action two-hundred shot Range Model Air Rifle" for Christmas, but various authority figures (the department store Santa Claus, his mother, a female teacher) all warn the young boy that he "will shoot his eye out." His father hears his yearning, and on Christmas Day, after all the gifts are open, gestures toward the corner where the Red Ryder gun is found. But to make the written story a success it needed a foil, and the foil that Shepherd chose was, well, I'll let him describe his first glimpse of her:

"DISARM THE TOY INDUSTRY"
Printed in angry block letters the slogan gleamed out from the large white button like a neon sign. I carefully reread it to make sure that I had not made a mistake,
"DISARM THE TOY INDUSTRY"
That's what it said. There was no question about it.
The button was worn by a tiny Indignant-type little old lady wearing what looked like an upturned flowerpot on her head, and I suspect (viewing it from this later date) a pair of

Ked tennis shoes on her feet, which were primly hidden by the Automat table at which we both sat.

I, toying moodily with my chicken pot pie, which of course is a specialty of the house, surreptitiously examined my fellow citizen and patron of the Automat. Wiry, lightly powdered, tough as spring steel, the old doll dug with Old Lady gusto into her meal. Succotash, baked beans, creamed corn, side order of Harvard beets. Bad news—a Vegetarian type. No doubt also a dedicated Cat Fancier. [2]

He continues with his scene setting: it is a busy Manhattan Automat, before Christmas, and she sits there, "her bright pink and ivory dental plates working over a mouthful of Harvard beets, attacking them with a venom usually associated with the larger carnivores." [3] He informs her that the beet juice is dripping, and she warms to him: "Her uppers clattered momentarily and in an unmistakably friendly manner." [4] Her voice takes on an "Evangelical quaver" as she tells him how toymakers and the government together plot to prepare "the Innocent for evil, Godless war!" [5] She rummages through her burlap handbag—no not rummages, "claws"—and hands him a pamphlet, gathers her stuff, and tells him as she leaves, "Those who eat meat, the flesh of our fellow creatures, the innocent slaughtered lamb of the field, are doing the work of the Devil!" [6]

Looking at the pamphlet, he begins to muse upon his youth, and so unfolds the story of the Christmas he received an Official Red Ryder Rifle.

Why could his Christmas story not stand on its own? Why did it need to be told as a reverie prompted by an interaction with a vegetarian, anti-war, cat-loving, tennis shoe-wearing activist elderly woman? First, it provides contrast—what he desires; what she would have deprived him of. Second—or perhaps this should come first—his readers would find her funny. A humorist must get his magazine readers at first bite, as it were, to guarantee to them that reading the entire story is worth it. But the Red Ryder story itself takes a while to develop in describing the young child's desire for the rifle and the various frustrations of that desire. Through the "humor" right off the bat, it is an invitation and a promise: this story will amuse you.

Here in 1965, before the anti-war movement became populated by middle-class students, is a woman understanding intersectional activism who is painted as unattractive, repulsive, and definitely no Playboy model.

If we trace the animal liberation movement only as far back as Singer's book, there are no old women with tennis shoes who have to be acknowledged as the mothers of the movement and of an intersectional approach. What is lost is not just the women's voices, but also the role of feminism and specifically ecofeminism in addressing intersectionality.

As connecting the dots becomes circles of compassion, let's not stop connecting the dots. And let's remember our foremothers; there's justice in that, too. ◌

Notes

1   Ashley Maier and Stacia Mesleh, call for papers, 2008. Posted with slight rewording at Connect the Dots Movement, accessed September 28, 2014, http://connectthedotsmovement.wordpress.com/about/.

2   Jean Shepherd, "Red Ryder Nails the Hammond Kid," Playboy, December 1965.

3   Ibid.

4   Ibid.

5   Ibid.

6   Ibid.

Introduction: The *Circles of Compassion* Vision
by Will Tuttle

The other evening I tossed a pebble into a pond to observe the beauty of the ripples—the ever-expanding circles—and to contemplate once again how events and actions send reverberations that radiate in every direction, with consequences and intersections far beyond what we might casually realize. This book, *Circles of Compassion*, explores and celebrates this understanding, especially regarding the interconnecting ripples in our culture's web of relations that aren't normally discussed or attended to.

Like every manifestation in our world, this book is a result of an immeasurable variety of ripples that have been created by countless people for thousands of years, bringing this unique expression into existence, and likewise, this book is itself also a pebble tossed into the pond of our shared cultural awareness, and will itself send forth ripples into many lives. The intention we have is that these ripples be radiating circles of increased awareness, leading to more compassion in our hearts and justice in our world.

The unifying idea underlying this book and the *Circles of Compassion* vision is that there are significant connections among the various social justice issues that we face that are both unrecognized and repressed in our shared understanding. Bringing these connections to light is both liberating and empowering in our quest for greater harmony, justice, and wisdom. More specifically, it is our culture's routine mistreatment of animals for food and other products that is like an enormous boulder being thrown continually into the pond of our shared cultural life, creating huge waves that rock everything constantly, and yet are also, somehow, strangely unrecognized and ignored.

Thankfully, increasing numbers of us are both thinking about and discussing the connections between our institutionalized violence toward nonhuman animals and our violence and indifference toward each other and the Earth. This is absolutely essential and one of the healthiest actions we can encourage in ourselves and in our world, helping to raise awareness about the source of our dilemmas and the best way to deal effectively with them.

In *Circles of Compassion*, we have the insights and experiences of authors who have spent years working not just with the liberation of nonhuman animals, but within that context working to raise consciousness about racism, sexism, chronic hunger, ableism, war, heterosexism, environmental devastation, corporatism, and economic inequity. Through these kinds of efforts, an empowering understanding is emerging that helps us see the connections among all these various forms of injustice and violence, and how we can most effectively transform our relationships, our crises, and our cultural situation.

Although there are powerful internal and social factors that work to repress authentic understanding, as more of us discuss the intersection of the issues we face, we are seeing that there is a common core mentality at work. It is also becoming increasingly obvious that the underlying mentality causing our problems is injected into us via our cultural programming, and that it is not innate.

It's animal agriculture. Besides being the driving force behind global climate disruption, rainforest destruction, air and water pollution, soil erosion, desertification, collapse of ocean ecosystems, species extinction, world hunger, chronic disease, economic inequality, and war, animal agriculture is also the driving force in creating the inner mentality that drives conflict, injustice, competition, and the various forms of social injustice that plague our world. Additionally, and importantly, it reduces our innate intelligence and capacities to deal effectively with the problems we're creating.

The good news is that with understanding comes empowerment. The authors contributing to the *Circles of Compassion* vision share their insights into the cultural, spiritual, emotional, and physical transformations they have experienced through their research and their work to heal the wounds that our culture inflicts on all of us growing up and living here. I am delighted to see the long-worked for advent of this unique book and what it represents. I believe there is not a more powerful message we can make an effort to understand and articulate today.

Our natural self-confidence, sensitivity, and self-respect are repressed as we learn to withhold respect and kindness from other living beings. Through our daily meals, and through zoos, rodeos, circuses, hunting, fishing, and many other socially approved practices and products, we are injected with a cultural program of violence toward defenseless and enslaved animals, and the ripples of that radiate as exclusivism, speciesism, and the many forms of separateness and entitlement that we see around us. The good news is that we can awaken from this cultural trance and be a pebble in the pond for justice, equality, and freedom for all, in a way that goes to the roots of the dynamics involved.

Our thoughts, words, and deeds can be transformed by understanding, and we can bring the ripples emanating from our lives into alignment with the values that live in our hearts. We can heal from the culture-induced trauma that numbs and disconnects us from our inherent capacities and from each other, and we can help others as well, by bringing the healing light of awareness to our world.

Thanks for your interest in this area of inquiry and concern, and thanks to all the authors who have contributed their insights to this volume. May the *Circles of Compassion* vision help encourage a movement that understands the interconnectedness of our justice issues and the critical importance of liberating nonhuman animals as essential to our own liberation (and vice versa). May this movement assist in the rebirth of our culture's wisdom and compassion, and may we together transform our individual and collective lives to create a world that honors and reflects not only our potential, but also the beauty, creativity, and abundance of our Earth and the living web of life here. ꩜

Beyond Humanism, Toward a New Animalism

by David Cantor

To understand and promote the radical policy change necessary to institute innate human morality and establish justice, we must understand how animal abuse led early humans to abandon their innate morality and how civilization's overarching animal abuse policy perpetuates violence, injustice, and human misery. Toward those objectives, I submitted to the International Commission on Zoological Nomenclature in 2008 a petition to change our species' zoological name to *Homo complexus*, arguing that humans' hyper-complex imagination, not sapience, distinguishes them from other animals. I use *Homo complexus* because what we call ourselves, like our other practices, affects all animals, including "us." I recommend using *Homo complexus* and avoiding *Homo sapiens*. Establishing a new zoological name depends, in part, on its frequency of usage.

I. Origins of Invidious Distinctions, Violence, Hatred, Terror Culture, and Eliminationism

"What do we fear? What still evokes the most gut-level panic and revulsion?…[T]he hunger of predators for human prey."
—Donna Hart & Robert W. Sussman,
Man the Hunted: Primates, Predators, and Human Evolution

Civilization exists due to the most radical possible change: from living by our species' evolved nature as plant-foraging apes on the African savanna, with a live-and-let-live attitude toward other animals, to living unnaturally according to the most aggressive human beings' imagination, based on animal abuse. Natural prey to large cats, raptors, dogs, and reptiles, with keen eyesight, reflexes, and imagination, and scant bodily defenses, original humans (including hominids) always had to be on the lookout. Social animals confer status on individuals based on service to others, and the most valuable and conspicuous service in the original, natural human way of life was helping fellow humans avoid predation. Matthew Cartmill showed two decades ago in *A View to a Death in the Morning* that the notion of humans as natural "killer apes"—the "man the hunter" concept—originated in flimsy "science."[1] It also contradicts experience and observation, human violence in all of its forms being an intensely salient anomaly, not our species' predominant mode of living. And it ignores our species' herbivore anatomy and physiology, alluded to by eminent archaeologists[2] and detailed from fingernails to intestines in "The Comparative Anatomy of Eating" by Milton R. Mills, M.D.[3]

The violence-rationalizing myth remains popular nevertheless. Donna Hart and Robert W. Sussman lament this fact in the 2009 expanded edition of their 2005 *Man the Hunted*, recipient of the W.W. Howells Book Prize from the Biological Anthropology Section of the American Anthropological Association. The text refutes "man the hunter" so thoroughly that only uncorrected habits of thought sustain it. This, more than cruelty or lack of compassion, perpetuates animal abuse as a way of life. It rains misery and early death on humans along with other animals, drives scores of species extinct on a daily basis, and undermines the natural functioning of the living world as animals have generated, experienced, and adapted to it over hundreds of millions of years.

Prey animals' innate fear of predators does not naturally equate to hatred of them or an organized campaign against them. Predators do not hate "us" or other prey animals any more than "we" hate fruit-bearing trees. Predation and its avoidance coevolved over millions of years. Nearly all prey animals are safe at any given moment as predators mainly capture the young, the old, the ill, the disabled, and the less acute who fail to react to danger promptly. Healthy, quick-witted animals in their prime thrive among predators, sometimes fending them off or even wounding or killing them with horns, antlers, hooves, and other natural defenses. Unbeknownst to prey animals, even to most human beings, by keeping herbivores moving about the landscape, predators help preserve life-supporting vegetation, giving each plant-food source respite from hooves, teeth, and fingers so it can continually regenerate. "Red in tooth and claw," a misleading description of nature so embedded in conventional wisdom that *The Associated Press Guide to News Writing* tells newspersons to use it as a corrective to "Mother Nature," obscures the reality that civilization is far more dangerous than nature.[4] *Homo complexus* is far from the first species equipped by evolution with perception, reason, and morality, so we should assume countless others have the kinds of rich experience such traits afford. In nature undisturbed by humans, viable humans and other animals experienced joy, spirituality, and fulfillment.

From what is known about humans' innate terror of predators[5] and social-primate status-seeking behavior,[6] it is reasonable to deduce that at some prehistoric moment not precisely known, some imaginative members of *Homo complexus* grasped that (1) they could reduce danger and increase feelings of safety and security in their troop (extended-family social-primate society) by killing predators who were not attacking, and (2) killing predators would enhance the killers' status within their troop. Gradually, over thousands of years, a particularly aggressive minority of human beings instituted a de facto eliminationist campaign against predators, establishing the paradigm demagogues still use against targeted human groups today. Early hunters, in a sense, constituted our species' first radical political movement. Radicals promote root policy change. The proto-policy by which original humans lived was to play, couple, forage for plants to eat, meditate (as we now call it), and move on, always alert to animate danger, taking turns on guard duty. Hunting was a radical innovation. And in addition to killing predators, the weaponed class started to imitate them by hunting some of their natural prey, eventually using victims' bodies to make weapons, tools, and clothing.

As compared with wielding rocks or tree branches, rounding up children, and fleeing to avoid predation, turning the tables by hunting predators involved permanent manufactured weapons. The human body lacks killing and defending features like claws, fangs, and tough skin. As reflected in their bodies, humans are naturally peaceable, cooperative, respectful, and perspicacious, with a live-and-let-live attitude toward members of other species that is adaptive as even small animals have sharp teeth, claws, venom, and a will to live.[7] And the more prey animals in an area, the less likely any particular one will be the next victim of predation. Humans' innate affinity for other beings—biophilia[8]—extends even to very distantly related animals, as Elisabeth Tova Bailey shows in *The Sound of a Wild Snail Eating,* in which the author observes a snail in a flowerpot by her bedside during a lengthy convalescence.[9] Our biophilia extends to dangerous animals when they do not pose an immediate threat. Due to our innate empathy, the capacity to experience others' sensations and emotions as our own, harming nonhuman animals arouses sympathy for victims and moral indignation toward perpetrators, as we know from public exposés of atrocities toward other animals. Slowly killing a large animal with spears must have shocked, frightened, and appalled most of the early hunters' fellow troop members.[10] Combine our species' innate morality and biophilia with our natural conservatism—comfort with the familiar and suspicion of novelty—and we can surmise that hunting took hold in part because it involved excursions, as it still does today. Crucially, weapons made with predators in mind could be turned against conscientious objectors, enforcing the emerging might-makes-right paradigm.

A new way of thinking had to take hold for such radical change to become permanently established. Humans learned to consider themselves entitled to safety, and demonized certain animals as being inherently unworthy of life. Thus, speciesism became *Homo complexus'* first harmful invidious distinction, initiating a long series in what would become a violent and oppressive history.[11] The weaponed class appeared to have a legitimate claim to improving troop safety. And to consolidate their increasing status and power, members of the weaponed class taught their troop members to hate the predators they naturally viewed with fear and awe. Thus emerged terror culture, with humans fearing, on the one hand, dangerous nonhuman animals, and, on the other, those humans who killed them. Proto-humanism, a pre-ideological pattern of thought, gelled into humanism over time via religion, secular philosophy, and pseudoscience. Proto-advocates for nonhuman animals would have been easily suppressed. No police, court, or organization could protect an objector from the hunting cabal. Hunters might kill their child or torture a favorite mate to shut them up. By the time humans started living in one place, and growing crops on a significant scale—sowing the seeds of civilization—many predators were extinct due to hunting.[12]

Inculcating a radically new way of life based on misperceiving, misunderstanding, and mistreating nonhuman animals and conferring status and respect based on aggression rather than defense put *Homo complexus* on the destructive course that is so difficult to reverse today. The new way of thinking led inexorably to the following:

- Designating ever more kinds of animals and ever more groups of humans as enemies to maintain the status of the weaponed class and everyone else's allegiance
- Devaluing nonviolent life-affirming social practices such as sharing, caring for others, playing nonviolently, and making love
- Exaggerating problems the ruling class chooses to address and downplaying those it creates, as in
    - devaluing women, children, and nonviolent men as needing rather than providing protection
    - inventing religions and secular philosophies to rationalize aggression and affirm human supremacy over other beings and

violent humans' supremacy over other humans

- Denigrating nonhuman animals as stupid, filthy, ugly, or needing maintenance and training by humans to fulfill their potential
- A preference for innovation separating humans and nature over the natural order
- Esteem for private wealth and power at the expense of nonhuman animals, the living world, and most humans
- Scorn for those who object to animal abuse, violence, or oppression; anticruelty regulations that mask animal-abuse policy
- Over-valuing of meat in the human diet despite lack of an innate taste for it, due to its association with high-status humans
- Denial and repression of knowledge exposing the weaponed class as harmful rather than protective

Thousands of years of habituation to this perversely radical new way of living and thinking helps to explain today's "conservative movement" to undermine a Constitution whose explicitly-stated values—justice, liberty, equality, defense, tranquility, and the general welfare—so strikingly match *Homo complexus'* innate morality and not the might-makes-right regime perpetuated by terror culture.[13]

II. Ramping Up the Misery: Disease, Oppression, War, Genocide, Poverty

> "A cultivated field of maize, or any other crop, is as man-made as a microchip, a magazine or a missile."
> —Tom Standage, *An Edible History of Humanity*

As humans killed off and supplanted predators, they took up herding. As they started to grow and tend their own crops, it became convenient to keep some of the animals confined to one's home base rather than follow their natural movements—in other words, to enslave them. As humans learned to engineer plant foods, they learned also to engineer animals to serve ever more human needs. They learned to make animals docile and obedient, subjecting them to mutilations; perpetual confinement; loss of relationships with offspring, other family members, and friends; and early death. Some animals were bred for rapid growth, some for larger size, some smaller, some to guard other enslaved animals, some to track or kill those designated as enemies. Human settlements attracted free-living animals to easy plant and animal pickings. To protect human children, enslaved animals, crops, and stored food supplies, humans extended to "pests" the enemy designation they had long applied to predators. Gone was humans' original experience of other animals living harmoniously as coequal persons in great variety and abundance, composing Earth's original symphony of color, sound, and motion.

Despite the inferiority of original agriculturists' diet to the far more nutritious original plant diet,[14] agriculturists overpopulated each area they "settled" as women gave birth more often, not constantly having to carry their children about the landscape.[15] "Settler" seems an innocuous term, but each time a human community seeks "greener pastures," its members perpetrate a holocaust against nonhuman animals in the new area. Destroying trees and other vegetation to establish agriculture drives countless animals from their homes, kills baby birds and other nesting animals, and wreaks havoc on nature. The hunt is always on for predators, other dangerous animals, and rats, mice, and others labeled as "vermin" who live especially well amid civilization, making use of crops, stored foods, and human waste. The cumulative impact is what I call the **biocaust** as three plant or animal species go extinct per hour according to the preeminent biologist Edward O. Wilson,[16] and no animal is safe despite *Homo complexus'* innate biophilia. Even as human-rights ideology took hold in England and spread to North America, slaughtering and breeding nonhuman animals (complementary components of the ongoing eliminationist endeavor) remained the first orders of business. And just as humanism paradoxically had designated some human groups less than human at demagogues' convenience through the ages, Europeans set to work on the human beings who had inhabited the Americas for many thousands of years, as recently as 1879, arguing in court that an American

Indian was not a "person" under the law.[17] Finding it especially useful to put human slaves, who would resist malaria, to the miserable task of draining Southern swamplands and tending to the personal and economic needs of high-status Southern whites (the Mason-Dixon Line approximates the historic northern limit of malaria in North America), the weaponed class subjected millions of Africans and their descendants to one of humans' most shameful institutions. Such institutionalized atrocities as the American Holocaust and human slavery derive from the logic inherent in humanism that any kind of animal, including human animals, can be less than human.[18]

Humans' various holocausts against nonhuman animals, including the eliminationism inherent in breeding out of them their natural traits and ways of life (this debasement makes them especial objects of both human affection and cruelty), brought limitless disaster upon human beings, who until relatively recently were ignorant of organisms invisible to the naked eye. Hundreds of infectious diseases that chickens, pigs, cows, rabbits, camels, sheep, goats, horses, dogs, and others had adapted to over millions of years wreaked havoc on humans who assumed they could enslave other animals with impunity. Supernatural explanations arose for smallpox, bubonic plague, influenza, and other scourges that in actuality were zoonotic. Though it is well documented, few people yet realize that today's AIDS disaster originates in animal abuse and poor human nutrition in Cameroon, possibly also in Europeans' enslaving human beings there to assist them in killing trees for the timber and rubber industries (institutionalized animal abuse) in the late 19th or beginning of the 20th century.[19] Poor food rations drove slaves to butcher forest animals, including chimpanzees, from whom the virus entered at least one open human wound, over time causing the pandemic. Lyme disease and many others come from supplanting enough forest with human habitation to transfer to humans parasites who otherwise would have remained harmless in acclimated nonhuman animals.[20] Nor were the origins of "diseases of affluence"—non-communicable afflictions linked to the meat, dairy, fish, and egg industries—known until recent times. How sadly ironic that, even with the connection established, the ruling classes persist in promoting such pseudo-foods among human populations emerging from poverty—only to find themselves going from dirt-floor hut to factory town to hospital.

War, human slavery, and poverty arise from the unnatural way of life that grew out of animal abuse and humanism. Possessing land rather than just living on it, enslaving nonhuman animals and owning their genetic lines, manufacturing devices for controlling nonhuman animals and forcing them to labor for humans, and developing irrigation canals that required constant dredging moved dominant humans to force some members of their species to do the most undesirable tasks. The enslavement of horses and camels made warriors far more powerful and capable of driving vast herds of cattle long distances. Kurgan people from the Russian steppes crushed non-warlike agrarian societies in central Europe some 6,000 years ago[21]—a process perpetually repeated, eventually extending to the American West, where supplanting native bison helped exterminate plains Indians and make the world safe for transcontinental railroads. Humans' original way of life might have involved drought, but that did not constitute poverty of some vis à vis wealth of others. It took *Homo complexus'* culturally evolving practice of seizing more than an ape's share of Earth's wealth to institute poverty and a rationalizing ideology that blames the poor. Thus, animal abuse is a root cause even of human miseries that do not appear linked to it at first glance. Nor do we have to touch animals to abuse them: we just have to cut down trees; protect our crops; construct roads, buildings, and parking lots; make dishes, furniture, carpets, appliances, musical instruments, paper, televisions, computers, and snack foods; and operate ships, railroads, automobiles, and airplanes.[22] No wonder the industry-government-university-media complex backlash against environmental and animal advocacy has been so determined and thorough!

III. Advocating for a Humane and Just Future

"Who gonna take away his license to kill?"
—Bob Dylan, "License To Kill"

Because animal abuse is civilization's predominant policy and a root cause of the big human problems, animal advocates should be able to dominate public discourse and policymaking. For the most part, they labor at the margins, emphasizing anticruelty measures as a "starting point" without articulating an "end point," and urging people to eliminate meat, dairy, fish, and eggs from their diet even though long experience and research show that (1) very few people change their diet based on facts, and (2) mind management, propaganda, and policy determine diet, not the other way around.[23] I spent much of my first quarter-century of full-time animal advocacy addressing superficial symptoms while neglecting root causes. It was frustrating, exhausting, and demoralizing, like working to extinguish a massive fire by blowing out flames rather than dousing the underlying white-hot embers fueling the biocaust. Now, I work each day to supplant the *Homo sapiens*/ "killer ape" narrative and humanist ideology with the *Homo complexus*/ tyrannized peaceable ape narrative and new-animalist ideology.

Hundreds of thousands of years after the first spear, the weaponed class is still sticking it to the majority. The industry-government-university-media complex maintains civilization's animal abuse infrastructure, not because of cruelty or a lack of compassion, but because animal abuse, eliminationism, and human overpopulation make our species dependent on animal abuse. Like disease or crime, ending animal abuse overnight would crash the global human economy, disrupting the semi-orderly perpetual holocaust against enslaved animals, and chaotically setting billions of humans upon the last remaining free-living animals and each other. Animal advocates must reckon with the embers, not the flames—not because it is never possible to rescue a nonhuman animal from terrible suffering, punish someone for cruelty to animals, get someone to "go vegan," or eliminate a particular corporate assault on nonhuman animals, but because absent fundamental policy change reversing the radical change set in motion by the original hunting cabal, improvements can only occur at the margins, never helping a net number of animals. The needed change demands that we serve as Thomas Paines, Elizabeth Cady Stantons, and Martin

Luther Kings, not as Florence Nightingales, Jonas Salks, or Mother Teresas, great as the latters' gifts to humanity stand in their own right.

Unlike the dawn of terror culture, the present moment finds humans inhabiting a desolate world, stripped of most life. The powdery beaches where people love to vacation were covered with living beings just a couple of centuries ago, their oceans teeming with so many fish that you could not see the bottom. Lacking original humans' infinitely rich daily experience of an animal-saturated world (with no expectation of perpetual safety, buildings, climate control, rapid transportation, mass societies, mass media, or constant amusements and "lifestyle" considerations), humans today do not see the animal abuse at the heart of their misery. They are not heartbroken because they are not paying attention, and the industry-government-university-media complex works daily to keep it that way. Surely moral apes, who can imagine something so relatively paltry as their own enhanced status and the immediate safety of their own troop, can imagine something far greater: a living world that is not in the process of dying; a living world that they are not personally complicit in destroying; a living world that will not consist only of human beings and human-engineered animals dodging floods, droughts, blizzards, bombs, toxic chemicals and gases, epidemics, and parasites. The effort to be popular, raise funds, and avoid persecution and ostracism prevents many organizers, spokespersons, and other advocates from promoting radical ideas and policy. But nothing less can create the needed change; we must stop piddling while Earth burns.

Whereas humanist dictionaries define "animalism" as the doctrine that man is a mere animal with no soul or spiritual quality, the new animalism presumes that all animals, as persons (bodies) have the meaningful experiences humans call "spirit"; that "mere" does not accurately describe any animal or any other component of the infinite web of life; that humans are not inherently entitled to perpetual safety against nature or to more than an ape's natural share of Earth's wealth; that all animals' wellbeing and fulfillment should be humans' top priority. Civilization affords no meaningful protection to anyone lacking equal guaranteed autonomy, ecology, and dignity rights. Human beings have made considerable progress toward establishing such rights for themselves, but their humanist ideology obscures the reality that rights of humans without rights of the other animals intensifies the paradoxical dynamic we now comprehend: what "we" do to "them," "we" do to "us."

The move from humanism to the new animalism, from animal abuse to rights of all animals as the basis of governance, is a struggle against injustice, so we will do well to elicit the moral indignation humans naturally experience at animal abuse rather than emphasize compassion, which positively affects those in our presence, not policy. Belittled as "anger" by the industry-government-university-media complex, moral indignation is the human trait most likely to instigate radical policy change. The Constitution refers to establishing justice, not promoting compassion. Moral indignation fueled the abolition movement to eliminate human chattel slavery, the women's suffrage movement, the Nuremberg Trials, and much more. When people view a film like *Earthlings*, showing many of humans' worst atrocities against nonhuman animals, they experience moral indignation. Invoking compassion rather than moral indignation might hamper the needed political engagement: How do I compassionately set on the course of ultimate extinction practices that today constitute millions of human beings' livelihoods as well as human-engineered animals many people love?

Many of those who directly harm nonhuman animals today in the vast and ever-growing animal abuse industries would rather work in a school, a store, a bank, a restaurant, or a nonprofit organization if they could (except maybe the experimenters), where their contribution to animal abuse would be indirect rather than direct. As long as animal abuse remains civilization's overarching policy, demonizing people based on their work will accomplish little. Demanding that all of our institutions tell the truth and that policy be based on morality, not rationalization, can phase out the worst suffering as atrocities become recognized as such rather than retain acceptability as services to humans.

The advocacy method I have been implementing on behalf of Responsible Policies for Animals acknowledges both the necessity and the difficulty of creating radical change. Variously attributed to John and Samuel Adams is this colorful version of a political truism: "It does not take a majority to prevail, but rather an irate, tireless minority keen to set brush fires in people's minds." For years, RPA has been demanding that our colleges of agriculture tell the truth about humans and the other animals, and stop providing training, research, sales, collusion, and promotions for the meat, dairy, fish, and egg industries; that state and US officials compel the colleges do that and in other ways shift policy away from animal abuse; that public radio and other news venues stop calling humans "predators" and feigning surprise at nonhuman animals' complex intelligence; and, more recently, that colleges implement a Beyond Humanism program due to humanism's enormously harmful substantive and dynamic flaws. Caught up in work, rattled by financial concerns and mental and physical illness, seized by infinite mass-media distractions and amusements, and given to travel, a significant part of the biocaust, to "get away from it all," most humans will not dedicate themselves to any political activity, let alone a radical endeavor with many risks and few short-term rewards. My personal experience confirms the value of the advice that the great civil-rights organizer Bayard Rustin received from his grandmother: "Do what is right."[24] I hope this brief narrative of our species and its biocaust will persuade readers to take up the only struggle likely to create the much-needed change: justice for all animals. All of Earth's beating hearts are genetically interrelated, and nature does not create inferior and superior beings, only beings. ✑

Notes

[1] Matthew Cartmill, *A View to a Death in the Morning: Hunting and Nature through History* (Cambridge: Harvard University Press, 1993).

[2] Richard Leakey, *The Origin of Humankind* (New York: Basic Books, 1994).

[3] Milton R. Mills, "The Comparative Anatomy of Eating," Responsible Policies for Animals, Inc, accessed August 28, 2014, http://www.RPAforAll.org/mills.html.

[4] Rene J. Cappon, *The Associated Press Guide to News Writing*, 3rd ed. (Lawrenceville, NJ: Peterson's, 1999).

[5] Donna Hart and Robert W. Sussman, *Man the Hunted: Primates, Predators, and Human Evolution*, expanded ed. (New York: Westview, 2009); David Quammen, *Monster of God: The Man-Eating Predator in the Jungles of History and the Mind* (New York: Norton, 2003).

[6] Thorstein Veblen, *The Theory of the Leisure Class* (New York: Macmillan, 1899); Dorothy L. Cheney and Robert M. Seyfarth, *Baboon Metaphysics: The Evolution of a Social Mind* (Chicago: University of Chicago Press, 2007); Dale Peterson, *The Moral Lives of Animals* (New York: Bloomsbury, 2011); Frans De Waal, *Good Natured: The Origins of Right and Wrong in Humans and Other Animals* (Cambridge: Harvard University Press, 1996).

[7] Stephen Post and Jill Newmark, *Why Good Things Happen to Good People* (New York: Broadway, 2006); Dacher Keltner, *Born To Be Good: The Science of a Meaningful Life* (New York: Norton, 2009).

[8] Stephen R. Kellert and Edward O. Wilson, ed., *The Biophilia Hypothesis* (Washington, D.C.: Island Press, 1993).

[9] Elisabeth Tova Bailey, *The Sound of a Snail Eating* (Chapel Hill: Algonquin, 2010).

[10] Sam Harris, *The Moral Landscape: How Science Can Determine Human Values* (New York: Free Press, 2010).

[11] Daniel Jonah Goldhagen, *Worse Than War: Genocide, Eliminationism, and the Ongoing Assault on Humanity* (New York: Public Affairs, 2009); Charles Patterson, *Eternal Treblinka: Our Treatment of Animals and the Holocaust* (New York: Lantern, 2002); David Livingstone Smith, *Less than Human* (New York: St. Martin's, 2011).

[12] Paul R. Ehrlich and Anne H. Ehrlich, *The Population Explosion: From Global Warming to Rain Forest Destruction, Famine, and Air and Water Pollution— Why Overpopulation Is Our #1 Environmental Problem* (New York: Simon and Schuster, 1990); Clive Ponting, *A Green History of the World: The Environment and the Collapse of Great Civilizations* (New York: Penguin, 1993).

[13] John W. Dean, *Conservatives without Conscience*, 2nd ed., (New York: Penguin, 2007); Ian S. Lustick, *Trapped in the War on Terror* (Philadelphia: University of Pennsylvania Press, 2006); Andrew J. Bacevich, *The Limits of Power: The End of American Exceptionalism* (New York: Holt, 2009).

[14] Charles B. Heiser Jr., *Seed to Civilization: The Story of Food*, 2nd ed. (San Francisco: W.H. Freeman, 1980); Tom Standage, *An Edible History of Humanity* (New York: Walker & Company, 2009).

[15] Ehrlich and Ehrlich, *Population Explosion*; Standage, *Edible History*.

[16] "Human Population Growth and Extinction," Center for Biological Diversity, accessed August 23, 2014, http://www.biologicaldiversity.org/programs/population_and_sustainability/extinction/index.html.

[17] Bill Kent, "A Jew Adopted by Indians in the West," review of *Magic Words* by Gerald Kolpan, *Philadelphia Inquirer*, July 1, 2012.

[18] David E. Stannard, *American Holocaust: The Conquest of the New World* (New York: Oxford University Press, 1992); Marjorie Spiegel, *The Dreaded Comparison: Human and Animal Slavery*, 2nd ed. (New York: Mirror Books, 1989).

[19] David Quammen, *Spillover: Animal Infections and the Next Human Pandemic* (New York: Norton, 2012); Craig Timberg and Daniel Halperin, *Tinderbox: How the West Sparked the AIDS Epidemic and How the World Can Finally Overcome It* (New York: Penguin, 2012).

[20] Arno Karlen, *Man and Microbes: Disease and Plagues in History and Modern Times* (New York: Touchstone, 1996); Richard S. Ostfeld and Clive G. Jones, "Peril in the Understory," *Audubon,* July/August, 1999; Alicia Chang, "Study: Risk of Lyme Disease Increases as Forests Shrink," Associated Press, February 23, 2003.

[21] Jeremy Rifkin, *Beyond Beef: The Rise and Fall of the Cattle Culture* (New York: Dutton, 1992).

[22] Responsible Policies for Animals (RPA), *Animal Abuse: The Whole Story* (Glenside, PA: RPA), accessed August 2014, http://www.rpaforall.org/animalabuse-thewhole-story.pdf.

[23] Joshua Frank, "Meat as a Bad Habit: A Case for Positive Feedback in Consumption Preferences Leading to Lock-In," *Review of Social Economy* 65, no. 3 (2007): 319-348; Harvey Levenstein, *Paradox of Plenty: A Social History of Eating in Modern America* (New York: Oxford University Press, 1993); Jeff Blyskal and Marie Blyskal, *PR: How the Public Relations Industry Writes the News* (New York: Morrow, 1985); Edward Bernays, *Propaganda* (Brooklyn: Ig, 2005. Originally published New York: Liveright, 1928); Stuart Ewen, *PR! A Social History of Spin* (New York: Basic Books, 1996); George Lakoff, *The Political Mind: Why You Can't Understand 21st-Century American Politics with an 18th-Century Brain* (New York: Viking, 2008).

[24] Nancy Kates and Bennett Singer, *Brother Outsider: The Life of Bayard Rustin*, 2002, DVD.

No Innocent Bystanders

by Angel Flinn

Every year in New York City, thousands gather for a widely publicized event called "Meatopia," which is described as "a Texas-sized two day weekend of meat, mirth, and the celebration of animals and the way great chefs prepare them."[1] Founded and hosted by *TIME* magazine food columnist Josh Ozersky, Meatopia has been called, "a meat-lover's paradise" (*New York Magazine*), "spectacular" (*Esquire*), a "bacchanal of pork, beef, lamb, chicken, duck, turkey and quail" (*New York Times*), and "a glorious city of meat" (*Huffington Post*).

Known as "the crown jewel" of this event, a butchery contest sponsored by Whole Foods draws an excited crowd, hollering and cheering as animal carcasses are slashed and sliced by Whole Foods workers competing for the Best Butcher Trophy. As described by Ozersky, "The crowd felt it, too. They moved right up to the tables, close enough to get hit by flying bits of fat and gristle. They didn't care. And neither did I. I just wanted a part of that butchering magic."[2]

Two thousand years ago, the gladiator fights of ancient Rome were highly anticipated occasions that put the whole population of the city in a mood of celebration. During these events, men, women and children would gather by the thousands, cheering as enslaved individuals (many of them prisoners of war) were forced to fight to the death for the enjoyment of the crowd. Far from an underground activity carried out in secret by disreputable individuals, the gladiator fights were attended by everyone, from emperors and politicians to parents and their children. The Vestal Virgins, women dedicated to lives of religious service, were given preferential seats. In *Rome's Vestal Virgins*, Robin Lorsch Wildfang describes the following:

> At the time, only Seneca protested the carnage of the arena; most other Roman authors were silent or approving. Gladiatorial games…continued, in one form or another, until AD 404, when Honorius finally abolished [them] altogether, prompted by the death of a monk who had entered the arena, endeavoring to stop the fight, and was stoned to death by the indignant crowd.[3]

In the United States, between 1882 and 1930, almost 2,500 African Americans were documented as being killed by lynch mobs.[4] According to these numbers, there was a person of color lynched every single week, for nearly 50 years. Lynchings often drew large crowds due to the fact that they were advertised in the local papers. Photos were taken of the victims, with white spectators posing alongside them, and these images were published in newspapers and used for postcards. Spectators took home body parts as memorabilia, including fingers, noses, ears and even genitalia, which were often laid out on display for onlookers. Many of those lynched had participated in minor crimes, such as petty theft, but most of them had done nothing more than simply associate with, or even look at, a white woman.[5]

There are 150 documented cases where lynching victims were female. At least four were known to have been pregnant. In 1914, so the story goes, 17-year-old Marie Scott was sexually assaulted in her own home after two drunken white men broke in and found her getting dressed. Her brother heard her screaming, kicked down the door and killed one of her attackers. When he fled the scene, an angry mob took out their anger on Marie, and hanged her from a telephone pole.[6]

It was 1971 in Australia when indigenous Australians were first included in the National Census. Prior to that, the legal status of these individuals was equivalent to that of "flora and fauna."[7] Since the British settlement in 1788, the Aboriginal people had been forced to abandon their traditional homes, had had their children stolen by the state, and were hunted like wild animals. According to a 1999 report,

> The first white settlers came to Tasmania in 1803, and by 1806 the serious killing began. ...They were systematically disposed of in ones, twos and threes, or in dozens, rather than in one massacre. ...In 1824, settlers were authorised to shoot Aborigines. ...Vigilante groups avenged Aboriginal retaliation by wholesale slaughter of men, women and children. ...Considered "wild animals", "vermin", "scarcely human", "hideous to humanity", "loathsome" and a "nuisance", they were fair game for white "sportsmen."[8]

In 1997, a government appointed inquiry into this treatment of the Aboriginal people concluded that it was genocide.[9] There are no official numbers available, but estimates put the Aboriginal population somewhere between 250,000 and 750,000 at the time of the European invasion in 1788. That number was down to 31,000 in 1911.[10] So called "Nigger Hunts" continued well into the 1960s.[11]

Like the crowd throwing stones at the monk stepping into the gladiators' arena, the spectators salivating over "a duck stuffed inside a chicken stuffed inside a turkey"[12] are as proud of and devoted to our 21st century wrongs as the citizens of ancient Rome were to theirs.

Civilization is not a state of rest. Our society's values and ethics are an evolving phenomenon, and the refinement of our culture is an ongoing process of learning to discern right from wrong and justice from injustice.

We must be willing to examine the biases and bigotries of the present, and see them with the same critical eyes we use to view humanity's heinous crimes of the past. Until we do, we will remain trapped by our ignorance and prejudice, locked, by our own hands, in an age that is much darker than the one we just may be on the brink of stepping into.

What will humanity be in another 150 years, or 50, or even 5 for that matter, when you consider how urgently we need to change? What will our values be that will help us look back at who we are now and shudder at the wrongs we used to condone? Legally sanctioned violence against the innocent...Living beings bought and sold like inanimate objects...The fundamental rights of some sacrificed for the gratification of others...Whoever the victims are, these actions remain the marks of a yet-to-be civilized society, and they taint ours today just as they did every era of the past.

Today, when we stop and give a thought to the men and women dragged to their deaths with the taunts of an angry mob ringing in their ears, we might wonder how our fellow humans, of any time and place, could possibly have enjoyed such a spectacle. If we allow this to move in on us, we might try to conceive of what it must have been like for someone whose path, for some reason, had led him or her to the end of the noose, rather than to being one of the faces in the crowd. We might try to imagine the anger pulsing in their veins, the fear showing in their faces, and the sorrow they must have felt knowing that they were completely defenseless against a heartless horde.

And if we really allow this to move in on us, we might even breathe a word of thanks to that mysterious power we call "goodness" that by some miracle we have been delivered from the way we were then, and more than anything, that the same power of goodness might yet be working still to deliver us from the way we are now. ✆

Notes

1. "Meatopia," Pearl Brewery, accessed August 23, 2014. http://www.atpearl.com/calendar/meatopia.

2. Josh Ozersky, "The Butcher Mystique," *Eat Like a Man* (blog), *Esquire*, July 24, 2012, http://www.esquire.com/blogs/food-for-men/whole-foods-butcher-contest-10984149.

3. Robin Lorsch Wildfang, *Rome's Vestal Virgins: A Study of Rome's Vestal Priestesses in the Late Republic and Early Empire* (New York: Routledge, 2006), 32.

4. Stewart E. Tolnay and E.M. Beck, *A Festival of Violence: An Analysis of Southern Lynchings, 1882-1930* (Urbana: University of Illinois Press, 1995).

5. "People and Events: Lynching in America," *The Murder of Emmett Till*, American Experience, PBS, accessed August 23, 2014, http://www.pbs.org/wgbh/amex/till/peopleevents/e_lynch.html.

6. Henrietta Vinton Davis, "Black Women Who Were Lynched in America," *Henrietta Vinton Davis's Weblog* (blog), August 1, 2008, http://henriettavintondavis.wordpress.com/2008/08/01/black-women-who-were-lynched-in-america/.

7. "About the 1967 Referendum," Victorian Curriculum and Assessment Authority (VCAA), *AusVELS Sample Unit: 1967 Referendum*, teacher resource, VCAA 2012, accessed August 23, 2014, http://www.vcaa.vic.edu.au/Documents/auscurric/sampleunit/1967referendum/aboutreferendum.pdf.

8. Colin Tatz, *Genocide in Australia*, AIATSIS Research Discussion Papers no. 8 (Canberra: Australian Institute of Aboriginal and Torres Strait Islander Studies, 1999), 14-15, http://www.aiatsis.gov.au/_files/research/dp/DP08.pdf.

9. "Report Calls Australian Aboriginal Policy 'Genocide,'" *CNN/Reuters*, May 20, 1997, http://www.cnn.com/WORLD/9705/20/briefs/aborigines/.

10. Brett Stone, "Report Details Crimes Against Aborigines," *World Socialist Web Site*, September 7, 1999, http://www.wsws.org/en/articles/1999/09/geno-s07.html.

11. John Pilger, "How the Murdoch Press Keeps Australia's Dirty Secret," *New Statesman*, May 12, 2011, http://www.newstatesman.com/australasia/2011/05/pilger-australia-rights.

12. Josh, "Looking Back at the Best Butcher Contest," Meatopia, September 13, 2012, http://meatopia.org/looking-back-at-the-best-butcher-contest/.

Why Compassion is Essential to Social Justice

by Katrina Fox

Growing Up with Racism, Sexism, and Homophobia

"You're a filthy little Arab who should go back to where you came from." So said my adoptive mother for the first time when I was age 6, after I'd spilled crumbs on the floor from a biscuit I was eating. "No wonder your real mother didn't want you." The impact of this cruel remark was instant and lasted for decades. As humans are wont to do, I made it mean that I was unlovable and would never be good enough.

Factual inaccuracies aside (my birth father was Persian, not an Arab), it was—unbeknownst to me at the time—my first experience with racism. The idea that anyone who wasn't a white English person was inferior was further solidified by my dad's constant referencing of "bloody wogs" to describe black people. I quickly learned to deny my ethnic heritage right into my 20s—if anyone asked, I said I was part Spanish or Italian. I even went so far as to have a nose job in 1993, partly to remove a small bump, but I can't deny I was pleased the adjustment made me look less obviously half Iranian.

Around the age of 10, in 1976, I became obsessed with the women in the hit TV show *Charlie's Angels*. I started a scrapbook, and asked my classmates to save any newspaper or magazine clippings featuring the trio of glamorous female detectives. In addition, my best friend Susan and I told everyone we loved each other. It was an innocent enough comment, but a boy in our class said he thought we were lesbians. It was the first time I'd heard the word, and when he explained what it meant, without any judgment, I was happy to take it on. But when I told the teacher I was a lesbian, she was horrified and told me not to say that word again or I'd be sent to the headmaster to be punished. This was my first experience with homophobia. And, in his typical uncreative manner, good old dad confirmed my suspicions that same-sex love and affection was bad by yelling "bloody poofs" at the TV screen whenever footballers hugged each other after one of their teammates scored a goal. Cue more disempowerment.

My first experience with sexism happened around a similar time, when I asked to play football and rugby and was told by both the boys and the teachers that I couldn't because I was a girl.

So, before I'd even hit puberty, I'd learned that if you weren't white, straight, and male, there was something wrong with you and you didn't deserve to participate in life on an equal footing. Essentially, you were "lesser than" privileged others, although I didn't have the fancy language for it back then.

By age 11, I'd learned that animals had it even tougher. My jaw literally dropped open when I learned that the beef burger on my plate had once been part of a beautiful, living cow. While I was brought up on a council estate just outside of south London in the UK, I'd visit my cousin in the country occasionally where I'd climb over fences into farmers' fields to stroke the cows and give them apples, with no clue that they would be trucked off to an abattoir and killed. Learning that I'd been ingesting the dead bodies of these gentle creatures made me feel sick, and I became—without knowing the word at the time—vegetarian immediately.

Although I embraced feminism, queer rights and animal advocacy in my early 20s, and found a plethora of examples of culturally entrenched sexism, racism, homophobia, and speciesism, I didn't make the connections between these forms of oppression until much later—almost a decade, in fact, when I was introduced to veganism by a schoolteacher on an anti-vivisection demo. It was finding out about the cruelty involved in the dairy industry in particular that made the light bulbs in my head start to go off.

I learned that in order to produce milk, a cow must be kept pregnant and lactating, a process carried out by restraining her in a head stall and artificially inseminating her; that shortly after birth, calves are torn away from their mothers, who bellow for several weeks with grief; that dairy cows are hooked up to milking machines—after suffering the agonizing ordeal of having their horns and, on occasion, excess teats cut off with scissors solely for aesthetic reasons; that mastitis—the inflammation of the mammary glands—is the most common affliction affecting dairy cows around the world and causes them severe pain; that this relentless cycle of forced endless pregnancy, birthing, and lactation puts so much pressure on the reproductive systems of cows that they become spent—verging on dead at around four to five years of age, whereas naturally they would live for a couple of decades.

It was this moment that the connections between feminism and animal rights became obvious: how could I call for my own reproductive autonomy while actively supporting the assault on female nonhuman animals' reproductive systems through the consumption of dairy? As Shy Buba wrote on *The Vegan Woman* blog, "It's contrary to feminism to defend one type of female body while using and abusing another."

Fighting Back or Fighting Ourselves?

Over the years, I've been involved with both mainstream gay, lesbian, bisexual and sex and/or gender diverse communities, as well as alternative queer groups. Within both communities, there are passionate individuals and groups campaigning against one or more forms of oppression while perpetuating other forms. For example, the rise of "black face" and other modes of appropriation of native cultures by white performers in queer feminist circles; sexism, racism, and misogyny within the animal rights movement; and speciesism in the majority of campaigns for human rights.

It both breaks my heart and frustrates me when my queer, feminist friends and colleagues speak out so passionately about homophobia, sexism or racism in one breath, while updating their Facebook statuses describing the sentient being they ate for lunch or serving the dead bodies or secretions of tortured farmed animals at events to celebrate equality or advancement for women or queer folk. And when the issue of animal oppression is raised (in the same way that they attempt to gain support for their particular cause), reactions generally fall into two camps: "I know, but I don't care enough to change my lifestyle to give up my gustatory delights," or "I don't want to know because I don't want to give up my power and privilege. Besides, (insert type of creature here) tastes so good."

Some are often accompanied by a patronizing smile and a comment along the lines of, "Aw, your love of animals and vegan lifestyle is so sweet." Imagine the reaction if you said that about their anti-racism work.

Unsurprisingly, such disagreements result in an interminable amount of infighting—in which I admit I've contributed my share. Activist movements are full of people who have experienced cruelty, oppression, discrimination, and often physical violence. We've been told that we're "broken," "wrong," "not good enough,"—not only by individual people, but through the perpetuation of overt as well as the insidious reinforcement of what is considered culturally acceptable or unacceptable.

Depending on the educational or emotional resources we have access to at any given time, many of us will live in a state of unconsciousness about our own or others' oppression, reacting with anger each time we are triggered by others' comments. Many of us are fuelled by a deep-seated rage, which can on one hand be a motivator to take action against injustice, yet unchecked on the other hand destroys not only our own sense of peace but very often any power or leverage we may get to achieve our goals of liberation. While we're busy putting all our energy into fighting each other and our potential allies, it seems oppressors are finding new ways to hold onto and extend their privileges.

Integrating the Shadow Self and Embracing Compassion for All
In July 2011, my personal life was a mess. Despite being in a relationship

of 18 years with a woman who loved me very much and living in an apartment that I co-owned, I was deeply unhappy and dissatisfied with my life. My career as a freelance writer and editor wasn't bringing me the joy it used to; I felt like I'd lost my writing mojo and felt resentful and trapped. Up until that time, I believed that life *happened* to me, that my feelings ran the show and I was at the mercy of external circumstances—in other words, despite my obvious privileges, I was a victim.

Fortunately, a close friend offered a different perspective on my situation, one which suggested that I had a choice in how I acted, reacted, and behaved. At the age of 46, I was finally ready to hear the pearl of wisdom that personal development gurus had been spouting for decades. I felt not just a light bulb but a whole panorama of bright stadium lights switch on in my mind. The following 12 months saw me devour books, audio recordings, and DVDs, and attend workshops and seminars, all of which taught me that the past only defines you if you let it; it is possible to consciously choose to move beyond it and decide who you want to become.

Now, I realize this may be all very well for a white-skinned, middle-class lesbian with certain privileges, and I'm not suggesting it's easy (I still struggle with negative self-talk, but it's lessening as I equip myself with the tools of self-awareness), but I have come to believe that compassion for self and others is the key to making a difference in the world. As I allowed myself to be open to new possibilities, I found myself exposed to individuals who had figured out the importance of integrating our shadow parts into our lives, instead of running away from them.

Our "shadow side" is anything we dislike about ourselves that we'd rather others did not know about us. It can range from a sense of entitlement and righteousness to feeling incompetent, like a failure or a fake.

In 2012, I met and conducted an interview with author Andrew Harvey who coined the term "sacred activism," a mixture of radical action/activism and spirituality. What I like about Harvey's philosophy is his acknowledgement of the need to do intense work around the personal and cultural shadow (our own private wounding as well the shadow cast by a society that is "narcissistic, self-absorbed and utterly suicidal in its pursuit of domination of nature").

Harvey believes that positive social change will not be achieved by activists fuelled solely by anger or by "bliss bunnies" who meditate and do little else. In addition to personal and group shadow work, one of the more confronting aspects of sacred activism is learning to love and forgive the perpetrators of oppression, cruelty, and horrendous injustices. This is a challenging one, and I am not sure I am quite ready to embrace this, yet intuitively it rings true.

"It doesn't mean you don't act against their policies," Harvey told me. "Gandhi didn't hate the British, but acted systematically to unseat them. Martin Luther King, Jr. didn't hate white Americans, but fought with sacred power to bring in civil rights. Not hating people, and instead forgiving them, doesn't mean you let the policies or actions continue, but it does mean your whole action is not action against; it's *for* a vision that includes [the perpetrators] and their healing. Gandhi believed the British were killing themselves by gunning down the Indians, so his action was on behalf of both. King understood that white Americans pretending to love Jesus while dishonoring their black brothers and sisters were destroying a part of their soul, so his actions were on behalf of White Americans and black people."

It is a tough one. Attempting to love and forgive those who carry out the most heinous atrocities on people, animals, and the environment is not a place I have reached yet, but I am teetering on the edge of compassion, with the awareness that the perpetrators of violence, cruelty and destruction are acting from a place of fear, self-loathing, and unconsciousness. When I was around nine, I deliberately killed a centipede. For no particular reason other than I could. I suppose I felt powerless, and this was a way I could feel powerful over another being. I felt guilty and ashamed for many years afterwards. I have also been reactive, unkind, and harsh to various people throughout my life—as most of us have.

We all seek love, significance, and belonging. In that search we may hurt others. It is because we do not love ourselves that our ego needs power over others, rather than empowerment. As social change makers, we owe it to ourselves, and to humanity, animals, and the planet, to take action that comes from a place of compassion: for others and ourselves. ☙

A Woman, a Cat, and a Realization

by Beatrice Friedlander

I work in animal advocacy and devote the better part of my time to thinking about animals. I have taken on the difficult task of trying to change society's attitudes and behavior toward animals, with the goal of ensuring that they are valued and respected as individuals.

Most of us who work to improve the lives of the powerless realize that there is a connection among various forms of oppression. "Linked oppressions" sounds very dry and intellectual. While it is not necessary to experience first-hand domestic violence, animal abuse, sexism, racism, homophobia, or ageism in order to understand them, one must come to grips with these phenomena on a personal, even visceral, level in order to be an effective advocate, and to compellingly communicate the enormity of the problem and affect change.

My understanding of these issues came gradually. I was one of those "Muddlers" to whom Tom Regan dedicated his book *Empty Cages* to be distinguished from those who, in Regan's typology, either were born Animal Rights Advocates (DiVincians), or had one life-altering experience (Damascans) to set them on the path.[1] Instead, I am one of those who gradually developed—muddled into, as it were—a consciousness of how we treat animals, and a commitment to devote my energies to improving their lot.

A few moments do, however, stand out in my journey. One of those came in 1990, when I had a "connecting the dots" experience.

I had always liked animals, but never gave them much thought until the mid-1980s when I began to consider their place in the world, to think about our conflicted and complex relationships with them, and to seek out ways to help them. I began volunteering at the Humane Society, but these issues and this work had no connection with my "day job" as an attorney.

That changed one day when I read a notice in the Michigan Bar Journal that said, "Attorneys interested in animal law contact Wanda Nash." That was the first time that I realized that my occupation and my avocation (and increasingly, my passion) could be connected.

Fast-forward about 15 years: by then I had quit my "day job" and was increasingly involved in animal issues. I continued my volunteer "hands-on" work at shelters, rescues, and sanctuaries. That call to "attorneys interested in animal law" had resulted in the creation of the Animal Law Section of the State Bar of Michigan, the first such statewide organization of attorneys. I was a founding member (and continue my involvement to this day). I was serving on the board of several groups, and was a member of various committees working on ways to improve the lives of animals. Although not practicing law, I was using my legal knowledge in these efforts.

In 2007, I began working at the Animals and Society Institute, where I serve as its Acting Executive Director. One of the organization's major programs addresses the cycle between animal abuse and other violence, so I work with these concepts as part of my job.

That being said, I only truly (and viscerally) came to understand the reality of the connection between domestic abuse and animal abuse about two years ago.

I had been invited to lecture at the University of Michigan Law School student animal law group on the intersection between animal abuse and other violence, a presentation that I had given many times before.

In preparation for this, I'd added material that emphasized the legal and legislative responses to the cycle of violence. This included information on the increasing number of states that made some forms of animal abuse a felony; laws allowing judges to order psychological counseling for those convicted of animal abuse; legislation permitting family animals to be included in personal protection orders; creation of registries, similar to those for sex offenders, that would keep track of animal abusers; and the admissibility of evidence of animal abuse in domestic violence prosecutions.

The presentation also addressed the co-occurrence of animal abuse and domestic violence. I cited some of the many studies which document the prevalence of animal abuse in homes where there was domestic violence, primarily among Caucasian women;[2] another extending this finding to Latina victims of domestic violence;[3] and a third confirming the findings among women in the Republic of Ireland.[4]

I noted the effects on children, with research demonstrating that children exposed to domestic violence are more likely to have abused animals than those who have not been so exposed.[5]

Particularly gripping were the studies showing that up to 48% of women factor their companion animals' welfare into the decision of leaving or staying with an abusive partner, and the timing of seeking shelter.[6]

Shortly before I left the office to drive to campus for the talk, I got a telephone call from Barb, a woman who works at the cat shelter where I volunteer. "I don't know what to do. A social worker just called here. She needs help for a woman who is in an abusive home," Barb said. "The police are telling this woman that she must leave today, before her husband returns from work. The social worker says that there is a place for her in a domestic violence shelter. However, the woman has a cat and she refuses to leave home without her cat. The DV shelter won't accept animals." I knew that our shelter, a limited admission facility operated by a private foundation, did not provide temporary housing and certainly was not equipped to provide assistance in these circumstances.

What to do? I recalled that a friend who volunteered at the local Humane Society had mentioned a program there that provides temporary housing to animal victims of domestic violence. Several phone calls later, the social worker was put in touch with staff at the Humane Society to arrange shelter for the cat.

Other than finding out that the Humane Society was able to take the cat that day, I don't know the ending to the story. I often think of them and their fate. I can only hope that the woman and her cat were soon reunited, able to begin a new life together free from violence, and able to begin healing from the wounds inflicted by their abuser.

What I do know is that the woman and her cat have come to personify for me the cycle of violence. Their experience has made the statistics and studies, the laws and the rules of evidence, come alive.

I am not suggesting that animal advocates use emotional arguments. Intellectual discourse and careful reasoning, the use of statistics and studies to make one's point, and a professional demeanor are necessary tools to enable us in the movement to accomplish our long-term goals. But having a deep investment in one's work is also necessary. The plight of this woman and this cat provided that connection for me.

I like to believe that now, when I speak of the interconnectedness of animal abuse and human violence, I provide the information and knowledge necessary to make the case, while being an empathic storyteller who encourages others to not only understand, but also to care about the problem. I want them to connect the dots for themselves. ❧

Notes

[1] Tom Regan, *Empty Cages: Facing the Challenge of Animal Rights* (Lanham, MD: Rowman & Littlefield, 2004).

[2] F.R. Ascione, "Emerging Research on Animal Abuse as a Risk Factor for Intimate Partner Violence," edited by K. Kendall-Tackett and S. Giacomoni, *Intimate Partner Violence* (Kingston, NJ: Civic Research Institute, 2007): 3.1-3.17; E.B. Strand and C. A. Faver, "Battered Women's Concern for Pets: A Closer Look," *Journal of Family Social Work* 9, no. 4 (2005): 39-58.

[3] C.A. Faver and A.M. Cavazos, "Animal Abuse and Domestic Violence: A View from the Border," *Journal of Emotional Abuse* 7, no. 3 (2007): 59-81.

[4] M. Allen, B. Gallagher, and B. Jones, "Domestic Violence and the Abuse of Pets: Researching the Link and Its Implications in Ireland," *Practice* 18, no. 3 (2006): 167-181.

[5] F.R. Ascione, C.V. Weber. T.M. Thompson, J. Heath, M. Maruyama, and K. Hayashi, "Battered Pets and Domestic Violence Animal Abuse Reported by Women Experience Intimate Violence and by Nonabused Women," *Violence Against Women* 13, no. 4 (2007): 354-373; C.L. Currie, "Animal Cruelty by Children Exposed to Domestic Violence," *Child Abuse and Neglect* 30 (2006): 425-435; A. Duncan, J.C. Thomas, and C. Miller, "Significance of Family Risk Factors in Development of Childhood Animal Cruelty in Adolescent Boys with Conduct Problems," *Journal of Family Violence* 20 (2005): 235-239.

[6] See note 2 above, first reference; P. Carlisle-Frank, J.M. Frank, and L. Nielsen, "Selective Battering of the Family Pet," *Anthrozoös* 17 (2004): 26-42; C.A. Faver and E. B. Strand, "To Leave or to Stay? Battered Women's Concern for Vulnerable Pets," *Journal of Interpersonal Violence* 18, no. 12 (2003): 1367-1377.

In the Doing and the Being

by Lori B. Girshick

There are many beautiful aspects of life—breathtaking vistas, magnificent animals, blossoming flowers, and acts of generosity and kindness—but at the same time, there are disturbing aspects like chronic hunger and intentional behaviors such as torture, factory farming, and sexual objectification. I have long been acutely aware of these contradictions, which has motivated me to find ways to work for social justice. One of the keys I've discovered in this is the importance of developing an analysis of a particular situation and acting on that analysis. Doing nothing would involve complicity in a system I oppose, while acting within my ability is a way to contribute to social healing and progress. What matters most is that, in my actions and being, I attempt to reflect the world I would like to see. Working for social change is both an inner as well as outer effort, and both have given meaning to my life.

To live a life with intention is of great importance to me. I feel my life has purpose, and this purpose is to help increase justice in our world. As time goes on, however, I sometimes wonder what the connection is between my efforts to make change within myself and my outer work for the social change I yearn for and feel is necessary. I refuse to believe that steps toward micro-level integrity are possible, but that macro-level change is impossible. Growing up, I never thought that this would become one of my primary issues. The world has not changed in as many positive directions as I expected it would.

I consider myself fortunate because I developed a political consciousness at an early age. I had brothers who were conscientious objectors during the Vietnam War. I grew up at a time when there was *de jure* and *de facto* racial segregation, and as a youngster, I remember seeing a billboard reading "The Ku Klux Klan Welcomes You" when my family was vacationing in the South. The events of the 1960s through 1980s significantly influenced my developing political awareness. Resistance to the Vietnam War and support of the Civil Rights movement framed my understanding of my responsibility to others.

My first political analyses were around nuclear weapons, war, racism, and poverty. The understanding of oppression, power, and privilege that I formed was primarily focused on white privilege and social class. But because the analysis of each "ism" reflects the same hierarchical arrangement of privileges, with structures to enforce them, it was an easy step for me to see the interconnections of these "isms" and to see the need to deal with them simultaneously. We cannot end racism without confronting classism, sexism, speciesism, heterosexism, and so on. Any existing oppression tends to support the others because the framework of privilege operates through them all. Some people believe that individuals are inherently competitive and that those at the top deserve to have more—more money and power, more influence and access. But structures of power reinforce how some groups are consistently advantaged while others are consistently disadvantaged and can rarely achieve this "more." The established narrative blames the individual, and distracts awareness away from the inequities built into the system. These ideologies must be recognized and also undermined so that the concept of equality includes not only equality of opportunity and access, but also equality of result.

My work in the domestic and sexual violence fields has allowed me to articulate this interconnection of structure and ideology in my public speaking and writing. I began to work directly in these fields in 1990 when I was hired as a community educator and volunteer coordinator for a domestic violence agency in California. When people watch a video of abused women or hear abused women and men speak about the beatings, rapes, and dominations experienced at the hands of partners and ex-partners, these people are clearly moved with compassion for their plight. However, feeling compassion for these individual survivors is very different from understanding that there is a social system that influences and condones this violence, a legal system that inadequately addresses it, a media system that encourages power-over, and a sexist belief system inherent in the religious teachings, gender roles, and traditions that form the context in which we all operate.

It is easy for someone to believe that if a particular person simply changed his or her behavior, or left his or her abuser, that the abuse would stop (which, by the way, is not true, since stalking frequently occurs, and more murders happen at this time than when people stay with their abusers). I've found it helpful to remember that these abusive social institutions have been created by people, and so we as people also have the power to remake them. People created this social system in the first place and we are the ones who will have to remake it. It will take some time, but the alternative to change is the continuation of domestic violence in millions of relationships, the molestation of children by their "loving" parents and relatives, and the rape of countless women and men daily. To understand the complexity of the system more, we are not only talking about abusive power in personal relationships, but within the churches, the military, the sports industry, and many work environments. There is rampant sexual victimization in all these institutions, in spite of their clinging to the absurd claims of "zero tolerance."

Once I started to teach women's studies in the 1990s, I resonated most with the label of "eco-feminist." To me, this means I understand the interconnection of people, animals and the Earth, and that my primary concern is for non-exploitation and justice. I had already been active in animal rights work since the early 1980s, becoming a vegan in 1982. At the same time, I became involved in the nonviolent direct action movement, both in committing civil disobedience (CD) and as a trainer in nonviolent theory and practice for those engaging in CD. My CD actions were primarily anti-nuclear, but also included anti-intervention in Central America. Eco-feminism brings together all my core values: veganism, nonviolence, non-exploitation of people and animals, and living lightly on the Earth. Other essential keys for me are engagement, direct action, healthy body and mind, Buddhist meditation, and gratitude. I have moved steadily towards consuming less, reusing, recycling, and buying products that last longer, harm the environment less, are not made in sweatshops, and are not tested on animals.

Being a vegan is the complete expression of my core values; I believe using animals and animal byproducts is exploitive and symbolizes the extent to which people are numbed to the consequences of their actions. People are separated from nature because they abuse and kill animals, rationalizing it as necessary, normal, and of no consequence to the animals. Our society is founded upon animal consumption and use, and people are blinded to the horror of this. Packaging meat in a way that does not look like an animal separates the consumer from the fact the product contains what was once a living creature with feelings, family, and a community. This encourages a mental and emotional disconnect, and creates enormous alienation both from the self and from nature. I cannot fathom the extent to which a person working in a slaughterhouse, a technician or doctor in a vivisection lab, or an employee at a factory farm has dulled his or her sense of kindness and distanced himself or herself from the natural world. Choosing to be a vegan allows me to live ethically and in harmony with nature. In fact, because we eat food every day, throughout the day, food choices make a continuous difference, so changing them can be revolutionary.

The objectification and commodification of animals is a process that also happens to women. Nevertheless, some women wear the fur or leather coats that animals need for themselves, some women bring their children to zoos to see animals behind bars, and some women view circuses as entertainment for their families. I have found it hard to understand why women doing animal rescue work still eat meat. When I remind myself that we are disconnected from the suffering of nonhuman animals and that we are conditioned to adopt an attitude of speciesism, I can understand how this happens. Women are subjected daily to media depictions that reinforce their own degradation. Worse still, girls and women are sexually assaulted regularly, and are abused, beaten, and murdered. It is so common (like meat-eating and animal testing) that it is a ho-hum fact of life. Oh, you experienced incest as a girl? So did I. Next. It is so common that there is no social outrage, though we might be raging privately, of course. Still, on the social level we see the slaughter of nonhuman animals by humans because animals are here for us; we see the murder and the rape of women by men because women are here for men. And how could we not have internalized these cultural messages? The mindset of oppression is thoroughly ingrained in our individualistic, competitive, and binary culture. You are "deserving," or you are not. It's your own "fault," or you would have succeeded.

It is disturbing to me that mass movements have changed to the point that today it's rare to have an anti-war protest that seems to have much influence. This is not to discount internet actions, local organizations fighting in decentralized ways, blogs, sitting in at representatives' offices, and the Occupy actions. But how effective can it be when march permits are flat-out denied, or permits are issued for zones within barricades that are far from the people we are trying to reach? Or when police beat or pepper spray protesters and force us to bear physical risks in exercising our constitutional rights as citizens to speak out? After 9/11, those of us who had engaged in civil disobedience often had to stop. What had been a political statement with a short jail stay or a fine after arrest was now six months in federal prison (for example, at protests at the School of the Americas at Fort Benning, Georgia, or at the Y-12 nuclear facility in Oak Ridge, Tennessee—both sites at which I have committed civil disobedience). Many of us had to engage in other forms of protest because we could not risk losing our jobs and being away from our families for so long. The acts of civil disobedience committed by Martin Luther King, Jr. and thousands of others during the civil rights movement would be responded to by law enforcement today as "domestic terrorism." We would not have gained the benefits of the extension of political rights to minorities and the dignity of interpersonal relationships between people of different races. What a loss that would have been, and by extension, what a loss it is today. Injustice grows due to marginalizing the voices for stopping wars in Iraq, Afghanistan, and other countries, for holding Wall Street bankers and investors accountable, or for stopping Monsanto and GMO foods. The Keystone pipeline protest actions are inspiring, but it seems clear where the actual power to make decisions lies—and I fret that it is not with the people who suffer and bear the costs, but with those who reap the financial profits and control the media and governance.

I have felt for a long time that silence is complicity. So my commitment has been to not shut up, though I appreciate reminders, support, and encouragement. One year when I was in between sixth and seventh grade, my family went on a camping trip to Washington, DC. We arrived at our campground in the evening, setting up our tent in the dark. In the morning we read the camp rules, and discovered the campground did "not allow blacks." We promptly packed up and left. Even at this young age, I knew this policy was wrong. The war in Vietnam certainly affected me, and I stood every Sunday at the town hall in the hour-long silent vigil for peace. In high school, my parents and I drove to DC for the last massive demonstration against the war. I will never forget the sight of tanks in the streets—to protect whom exactly? Today with the militarization of local police, officers have Kevlar vests, padded turtle suits, wooden and rubber bullets, pepper spray, sound canons, tasers, helicopters, and, yes, even tanks. Yet it is nonviolent protestors who are public enemy number one.

As a sociologist, my work has been to help give voice to those who have less access to be heard. My writings have been based on interviews with people in prison, survivors of lesbian rape, and transidentified people—all marginalized people facing societal views that stigmatize them, laws that harm them or exclude them, and policies that do not address their needs. In the classroom, I teach from a social justice perspective. My goal is for students to realize how social issues affect them. We do many experiential exercises, watch videos that engage, but still, many young people are so shut down or indoctrinated by an ethic of individualism that it is difficult to break through their indifference. I try to have a loving presence, and I hope to be a positive role model. Most of the students have never thought in in-depth ways about the topics we cover in our classes, and I hope they see there is another way of thinking about poverty, fossil fuels, eating animals, gender roles, and consumerism.

We must challenge disconnection. Without acknowledgement of our emotional connection—some might call it a spiritual connection—to each other and nature, people are reduced to isolated individuals without responsibilities to larger communities, ceding their power to those at the top. Humans are essentially social beings, and interactions are what make us human. Speech, physical motor skills, and moral codes develop within social interactions. We are not autonomous objects going through social life, but social beings in community. The cost of denying this has been huge—wars, exploitation, and tremendous suffering have resulted. We need to heal our disconnect, and embrace our wholeness. We are never truly individual in the social and political sense, though we certainly have unique personalities. But our psychology is not the same thing as our social being. There is no choice we make that is without social impact—whether it is the relationships we form, the jobs we hold, the items we consume and eat, or the way we vote. Our social choices affect the well-being of people we know, as well as those far away in both space and time.

Today my politics continue to be progressive. In many ways, I am more radical today because of globalization and its consequent increase of factory farms, pollution, environmental destruction, and worker exploitation. Much of my work focuses on individuals. I try to encourage people to see how they fit into the bigger context—to enlarge the scope of compassion people have for other humans, animals, and the Earth. For the past several years, I have been volunteering with animal rescue organizations, and have found caring for and loving animals hugely rewarding. It doesn't change the system that produces abused and neglected animals or the need to spay and neuter, but it does at least show care to these particular victims of an abusive system, and it is immediate in its impact.

But my vision is bigger than this. Everyone has a role in social change. Not everyone wants to be in the streets; some people want to water the plants and feed the cat so others can be in the streets. I'm afraid that my vision of a just society will not come until we are forced to change, perhaps after a major environmental disaster or other crisis that forces worldwide change and cooperation. There are too many knee-jerk reactions saying, "That would never work." So it might be due to climate change and dramatic impacts due to flooding or drought conditions; it might be due to the end of cheap oil and the loss of petrochemicals for fertilizers, thus reducing the grain production that feeds livestock; it might be due to a catastrophic release of nuclear radiation. Eventually, whatever supports the unsustainable path we are on—where corporate greed has ravaged the earth and created lust for short-term profits—there will be a fundamental social, political, and economic collapse. I don't feel this is a fantastical doomsday forecast, but the realistic outcome of corporate greed.

That is my fear: that it will take a calamity, and the rebuilding will be done differently out of necessity. But my hope is different—that we can change before we are forced to. I have the same vision, but we need everyone to alter the way we treat one another. We need to insist on a shift to sustainable energy and to develop sustainable transportation and agriculture systems. We need to tax corporations to raise money for housing, education, and health-care needs. We must end wars and redirect conflict-resolution to peaceful means. We need a vision for spaceship Earth where we are not competitors but a collective where every person, without state borders, has a decent standard of living for health and happiness. I really believe, based on my eco-feminist vision, that all people can embrace cooperative, compassionate values if needs are met and fears diminished.

Unfortunately, power has become increasingly concentrated. A relatively few wealthy individuals have wrested control away from an otherwise democratic government and altered the course of history (i.e., war, torture, and loss of civil liberties after 9/11). Global financial leaders convene surreptitiously to undercut demands and eviscerate our voices. Non-elected corporate heads make binding trade agreements that hold more power than votes by elected bodies. Citizens have become consumers and have been dumbed-down (or outright lied to) by the mainstream media so they do not have the critical tools they need to understand what is going on. I believe people today feel less able to voice their views than ever. Yes, it's frustrating, all these blocks to the voices of change. We must see our common humanity and act in ways that reflect our common interests. We must stop being complicit in the framework of pitting one group's interests against those of another group. There is only one community, the global community. "Act locally, think globally" becomes ever more pertinent. Every choice I make, every consuming "vote," every manner in which I treat someone is speaking truth to power.

Engagement is important because I make better choices when I am informed. I do not want "holidays" from the news, or to ignore horrible events or facts. I prefer to do something about them in some way, large or small. I do, and will, act in a way that reflects what I yearn to see. There is nothing more worth working toward than a just society where people live without suffering, and animals and the Earth are respected. When there is no exploitation, there is no fear.

Gratitude is essential because it keeps me open and able to engage. Without gratitude, I feel I would be overwhelmed with despair. I choose not to despair. Along with disturbing events, there is also much beauty in the world. I don't ever want to overlook the beauty. I speak out to counter the injustice and to affirm the beauty. I struggle with my search for a meaningful life. Apparently, social justice is something that must be kept alive in the mind and heart, and in our dreams, and with sustenance by the wonders of daily living—a hike in the forest or desert, playing with a cat, sharing an organic vegan meal with a friend—these and other everyday graces keep us going.

Joy? Sadness? Healing? Frustration? Some satisfaction, and a heck of a lot of struggle. ❦

Social Responsibility, Reflexivity, and Chasing Rainbows

by Rachel Alicia Griffin

"We are now faced with the fact that tomorrow is today. We are confronted with the fierce urgency of now. In this unfolding conundrum of life and history there is such a thing as being too late."

—Martin Luther King, Jr.,
Beyond Vietnam: A Time to Break Silence, 1967

As a critical intercultural scholar activist, I have often found myself awake late at night, pondering whether or not optimism is feasible in a world plagued by so much systemically orchestrated devastation. Thus at any given moment—and really *every* moment—someone somewhere is hurting not by their own doing, but rather because they do not have access to enough power to protect themselves from the imposition of domination. Coupling this reality with the embrace of self-reflexivity as a means to turn my critical eyes inward,[1] I move through the world both reproducing and resisting systemic oppression as a heterosexual, able-bodied, US American biracial woman of color who, by way of a PhD, has become part of the middle class after growing up in the lower working class.

Extending beyond my intersectional comfort zone of marking privilege and marginalization in the lives of people, only recently have I begun the work of connecting human, animal, and environmental devastation. Having learned not to "expect perfection in an imperfect world,"[2] what follows are my reflections on how I began to connect the dots in my own life and activist efforts. I share my journey here in the hopes that doing so will foster similar connections for others.

In US American society, we have a number of cultural clichés such as "time will tell" and "in good time" that invite passivity while discouraging civic engagement. From my standpoint, the time for reflection, accountability, and fierce advocacy against injustice is now. Since there is "such a thing as being too late,"[3] I want to acknowledge that much of what has been destroyed—lives and resources—cannot be recovered and that perhaps we have simply gone too far in our "profoundly unjust and fundamentally unsustainable"[4] world. Yet excusing ourselves from bearing witness to anguish, desperation, and loss represents, in my mind, a dangerous sham that even the most privileged will be able to preserve for only a limited amount of time. Therefore, I move forward with the belief that connecting the dots can deepen our commitment to the socially just understanding that the world, as it is in this moment, simply is not the best that it can be. Embracing possibilities, I process through three lessons drawn from my experiences that have fostered my ability to see the interdependence between various forms of cultural devastation. These lessons have also helped me imagine the world differently through a shift from a single reality to multiple realities, and from an "either/or" to a "both/and" outlook.

Lesson One: On Broken Binaries and Enduring Contradiction

Looking back to my childhood, my first conscious encounter with the imposition of domination and the need for an opposing outlook came early. Born in 1980 to a teenage white woman in Detroit, Michigan, I attended school in the predominantly white suburbs. One of my earliest memories is of me sitting on a bench with my feet dangling off the edge while my mother was filling out my elementary school forms in the main office. I overheard the school secretary's tone and, with my 5-year-old mind, took it to mean she was yelling at my mom. She was upset because my mom had checked the "Caucasian" box *and* the "African-American" box even though she was only supposed to check one or use the "Other" box. I was enthralled, and listened closely because my mom was in trouble; of course, at the time I did not understand the politics surrounding why this "mean" woman was "yelling" at my mom. However, I did understand that the boxes were worth getting upset over because I recognized the tone in my mom's voice as no-nonsense—as in, her way was the *only* way. Watching her stand at that counter and insist that I was not an "Other" and that she would not be checking only one box was powerful enough to leave a strong impression.

Sitting on that bench was the first of countless moments when I would learn that my biracial body did not fit into what I now understand as the Western binary of "black" or "white," which also functions to secure, for example, "right" or "wrong"; "good" or "bad"; "civil" or "uncivil"; and "us" or "them." From my perspective, my lifelong navigation of and refusal to abide by the racial binary created an avenue for me to understand our world as fluid as opposed to fixed, and as both/and as opposed to either/or. Welcomed by some and annoying to others, starting at a young age, I replaced definitive periods with inquisitive question marks. It consciously began with my insistence (modeled by my mother) on identifying as biracial even though I am often asked to be black *period*—as in, too dark to be white and less complicated/difficult/taboo. The practice of naming my own identities eventually, with time and increased self-confidence, morphed into a damning of the boxes that I never seemed to fit into, and caused me to ask questions like, "What if everyone is in between?" and "What if I am double instead of half-and-half?" These racialized struggles, written on and expressed through my own body, opened me up to the complexity of both/and in multiple contexts and helped me become more comfortable with the discomfort of contradiction.

Since my very existence is in opposition to dominant racial norms (e.g., "black *and* white" as opposed to "black *or* white"), to speak for myself and survive as I am, I have come to peace with the discomfort that feeling contradiction or being marked as contradictory can bring.

Extending my lived experiences beyond the context of racial binaries, I am working toward acknowledging all of the ways that contradiction, informed by privilege and marginalization, encompasses my life. For example, I purchase name-brand "professional" clothing that can undeniably be linked to inhumane sweatshop labor and shipping practices that leave carbon footprints throughout the world, and yet I wear my "professional" clothes to bolster my credibility as a female faculty member of color at a traditionally and predominantly white institution. Another example, of which there are many, I understand the toxicity of technology and yet I am typing this essay, which advocates for social justice, on my computer with my cell phone, printer, and microwave close by. Paying close attention to these moments of contradiction, to consciously mark both resistance and complicity, is the first lesson that has helped me get better at connecting the dots. While I do not believe that each individual person can productively work against every form of injustice, I do find great meaning in transparency and accountability with regard to our choices.

Lesson Two: On Knowing Versus Understanding

As a survivor of domestic violence and sexual assault, I have spoken all over the country for 10 years advocating against gender violence in general and men's violence against women in particular. Speaking nationally has taught me how to draw strong connections between various acts of violent injustice to create multiple possibilities for audience members to situate gender violence as an issue of vast importance. To be frank, I approach audiences with the assumption that most people, myself included, are self-interested (in that we are not readily willing to listen unless we understand what any given issue has to do with our daily lives). Exemplary of my approach, I position date rape, for example, as equally as important as robbery and murder. This is not to imply that date rape is more important or more painful than other forms of violence, but rather to highlight the value of exploring one form of violence at a time to make our societal need for change more manageable and less overwhelming. My approach has been expanded to new heights via the Green Dot Strategy that philosophically highlights the broad spectrum of power-based violence in our culture, and our communal responsibility to mobilize against such acts.[5]

Power-based violence can be understood as any form of violence that entails force, threat, or intimidation.[6] Quite valuable to the labor of connecting the dots is the emphasis on how power and domination function similarly to fuel multiple forms of violence, such as mass shootings, police brutality, human trafficking, widespread cruelty to animals for food and other uses, mass incarceration, hate crimes, bullying, murder, and gender violence. By fusing several violent acts together with the consideration of power, the understanding that violent acts do harm, destroy, spread terror, erode safety, and severely undermine the potential of life on a global scale becomes more tangible and, importantly, more urgent to address. With urgency at heart, we can begin to bridge the gap between knowing and understanding. Helping us map the difference between the two in *Echoes from the Holocaust: Philosophical Reflections on a Dark Time*, Rosenberg says:

> *Knowing*…refers to factual information or the process by which it is gathered. *Understanding*…refers to systematically grasping the significance of an event in such a way that it becomes integrated into one's moral and intellectual life… One can know a great deal about the Holocaust without understanding it. Facts can be absorbed without their having any impact on the way we understand ourselves or the world we live in.[7]

The important shift from knowing to understanding is commonly (but not always) accompanied by emotion and compassion—both of which are necessary to connect the dots. Through speaking and teaching, I have become convinced that oftentimes (but not always) people are apathetic toward issues of social justice because they are simply unaware of and/or cannot plausibly imagine the extent of harm, suffering, and loss that pervasive injustice breeds. For example, asking myself the following questions has helped me shift closer from knowing toward understanding how the dots are connected between human, animal, and environmental devastation in the context of gender violence:

- What do sex trafficking, puppy mills, and *The Bachelor* have in common?
- What are the links between the garbage patch in the Pacific Ocean, strip mining, and treating women like trash?
- Where do racism, deforestation, and rape ideologically converge?
- How do I (as opposed to "do I"), in my everyday life, intentionally and unintentionally support sex trafficking, puppy mills, *The Bachelor*, the mass of garbage in the Pacific Ocean, strip mining, treating women like trash, racism, deforestation, and rape?

Lesson Three: On Listening, Humility, and Vulnerability
Through embarrassment, shame, and guilt in relation to my privilege, I have come to understand listening, humility, and vulnerability as essential if I want to productively work toward social justice. I have to listen—even when what I hear breaks my heart and hands me my privileged ass, I have to listen. I also have to listen when I want to run, cry, scream, and distance myself from the pain that my privilege imparts. Listening is also indispensable to grasping the reality that there are aspects of oppression that I cannot fully understand because they cannot be found in words or pictures but, rather, are lived through bodies. For example, when I talk about men's violence against women to groups of men, I ask them to realize that their male privilege in our patriarchal world protects them from having to reckon with the extreme likelihood of being sexually violated in their lifetime. I also tell them that they can read thousands of books and listen to thousands of female survivors' stories and still never understand what it is like from an embodied standpoint to live in a rape culture. Hence, there are things that women understand from within our female bodies that men simply cannot fully understand. In response, I have

encountered men from coast to coast who contest this by pointing to what they know as an indication of their understanding, and although I stand firm, I can relate to their impassioned desire to claim full understanding of a lived experience even when it is not their own. Looking closely at my own life, it is easy for me to slip into the reasoning that as an academic, I can understand anything if I read and listen enough. Yet the reality is that I cannot fully grasp what it means, for example, to endure oppression as a queer woman, starving child, or formally uneducated adult.

This is where both humility and vulnerability come to fruition. Drawing from lesson two, if we work to shift from knowing toward understanding, we must do so cognizant of our privilege and what Moraga and Anzaldúa[8] deem "theories of the flesh," which reflect "distinctive interpretations of the world…carved out of the embodied, historical, and material reality of a group's life experiences."[9] In this vein, particularly in relation to our privilege, we must trust that people who are hurting know more about their pain from the inside than we can from the outside.

Therefore, our activism, ability to create a more just world, and for some, our desire to be a "good" person becomes dependent upon and guided by those who are hurting, as opposed to our desire to help. Embracing the vulnerability of this approach has been difficult for me to do intentionally as a woman of color in a world that has yet to fully recognize my humanity. For example, being held accountable to my heterosexual privilege by a queer white woman renders me vulnerable to her white privilege much in the way that I imagine her being accountable to her white privilege renders her vulnerable to my heterosexual privilege. While vulnerability has brought the chill of fear to my skin and tears to my eyes, I do not believe that I (or we) can afford to allow fear or pain to absolve our social responsibility to reckon with the interconnected nature of injustices—both those we see/know/understand/feel and those that have yet to enter our consciousness. The moments when I have understood this the most are when I have been asked hard questions that, despite all of my education, I have had to admit with transparent shame that I cannot answer:

- Whose land do I live on?
- Who picks the produce that I eat?
- Where does my trash go?
- What does my cell phone do to our world?
- Where have my shoes been?

Perhaps most importantly:

- What has been done in the name of my privilege?
- What has been done in the name of my comfort?

To even begin to respond to the depths of despair and damage that such questions, when answered transparently, will likely reveal, I rely deeply on listening, humility, and vulnerability. Even when doing so hurts more than I ever would have imagined.

Chasing Rainbows

Returning to where this essay began, I enjoy reading the speeches of Martin Luther King, Jr. as a source of encouraging inspiration, not because he embodied civil rights activism and leadership with fault-less inclusion,[10] but rather because he paid close attention to love and to what I interpret as chasing rainbows (i.e., the journey toward a more socially just world).[11] For example, in his speech entitled "A Time to Break Silence," quoting Arnold Toynbee, he says "Love is the ultimate force that makes for the saving choice of life and good against the damning choice of death and evil. Therefore, the first hope in our inventory must be the hope that love is going to have the last word."[12] When I revisit this passage, I momentarily let my desire to critique the binaries offered subside to allow the significance of love to take root. Also voicing the importance of love is bell hooks, who says, "Love heals. We recover ourselves in the act and art of loving."[13] Through the embodiment of "critical love,"[14] I see/feel/

imagine the power and possibilities of chasing rainbows.

Like Shange,[15] I invoke the colorful imagery of rainbows to signify the importance of both individual beauty and joint interdependence. Whenever I see a rainbow, I marvel at the spectacular mixture of water and sunlight and then laugh out loud at my little girl self who believed that she could chase and find the end of a rainbow. I remember running toward rainbows on the playground and being puzzled by the trickery—when I moved, the rainbow moved too! Eventually embracing defeat, I would watch it for as long as I could, and then hope for another chance to chase the possibility. As an adult socialized to accept impossibility as definitive, I have shifted from decrying rainbow trickery, to regarding rainbows as delicate and beautifully elusive. Yet recently I have found myself wondering about the chase. For me, chasing rainbows offers a metaphorical means to connect the dots through a sense of virtuous hope that has the potential to birth a genuine culture of engagement, as opposed to a culture of divisive/disconnected/indifference. Chasing rainbows represents chasing the ideal essence of interdependence, equality, social responsibility, compassion, and reflexivity even when it is unlikely that we will find perfect harmony in our disharmonious world. What if the magic can be found in the chase? What if the very moment that we think we find/capture/seize the rainbow only to be met with raw disappointment, is the very same moment that we turn toward faith and possibility? What if our journey toward the imagined but always elusive socially just ideal is what really matters? It matters to me. Does it matter to you? ✇

Notes

1 H. Lloyd Goodall, *Writing the New Ethnography* (Oxford: AltaMira Press, 2000); D. Soyini Madison. *Critical Ethnography* (Thousand Oaks, CA: Sage Publications, 2005); Ronald J. Pelias, "The Critical Life," *Communication Education* 49 (2000): 220-28.

2 Rachel Alicia Griffin, "'Yes We Can,' 'Yes We Did,' but No We Haven't: Marking a Moment While Remembering Reality," *Reflections: Narratives of Professional Helping* 16 no. 1 (2010): 10.

3 James M. Washington, ed., *A Testament of Hope: The Essential Writings and Speeches of Martin Luther King, Jr.* (New York: HarperCollins, 1986), 243.

4 Robert Jensen, "Beyond multiculturalism: Taking power and privilege seriously in teaching diversity," keynote delivered at The Pedagogy of Privilege: Teaching, Learning, and Praxis Conference, Denver, CO, June 2009.

5 "Ending Violence: One Green Dot at a Time," *Green Dot. Etcetera*, 2010, http://www.livethegreendot.com/.

6 Ibid.

7 Alan Rosenberg, "The Crisis in Knowing and Understanding the Holocaust," edited by A. Rosenberg and G. E. Meyers, *Echoes from the Holocaust: Philosophical Reflections On a Dark Time*. (Philadelphia: Temple University Press, 1988), 382.

8 Cherrie Moraga and Gloria Anzaldúa, *This Bridge Called My Back: Writings by Radical Women of Color* (New York: Kitchen Table, Women of Color Press, 1983).

9 D. Soyini Madison, "That Was My Occupation: Oral Narrative, Performance, and Black Feminist Thought," *Text and Performance Quarterly* 13, no. 3 (1993): 229.

10 I make this point not to disrespectfully defame his memory but rather to highlight how the Civil Rights Movement and its visible leadership fell quite short of taking an intersectional approach to social justice. This is not to say that we cannot focus on one issue or identity group at a time but it is to mark how our efforts against one form of oppression (e.g., racism) can simultaneously strengthen another form of oppression (e.g., sexism). For example, Ms. Rosa Parks is often positioned as secondary to Dr. King when in reality she, alongside many other black women, were advocating for civil rights long before Dr. King became a celebrated leader. More pointedly, when Ms. Parks was helping to lay the foundation for the Civil Rights Movement, Dr. King was still in high school. (Danielle L. McGuire, *At the Dark End of the Street: Black Women, Rape, and Resistance—A New History of the Civil Rights Movement from Rosa Parks to the Rise of Black Power* [New York: Knopf, 2010].)

11 Martin Luther King, Jr., *Strength to Love* (Philadelphia: Fortress Press, 1981).

12 See note 3 above.

13 bell hooks, "Living to Love," edited by G. Kirk & M. Okazawa-Rey, *Women's Lives: Multicultural Perspectives*, 5th ed. (New York: McGraw-Hill, 2010), 250.

[14] Rachel Alicia Griffin, "Navigating the Politics of Identity/Identities and Exploring the Promise of Critical Love," edited by Nilanjana Bardhan and M. Orbe, *Identity Research and Intercultural Communication: Reflections and Future Directions* (Lanham, MD: Lexington Books, 2012), 207-221.

[15] Ntozake Shange, *For Colored Girls Who Have Considered Suicide When the Rainbow is Enuf* (New York: MacMillan, 1975).

Eating Animals and the
Illusion of Personal Choice

by Robert Grillo

Of all the rationalizations we make for eating animal products in an age when we now know this is unnecessary for our health or survival, the *personal choice defense* is one of the most popular. It is stated either as a simple affirmation such as, "Eating meat is a personal choice," or it is merely implied in the casual way animal and plant food choices are discussed, as if the two sets of options are somehow morally equivalent, interchangeable and equally innocuous.

This deliberate blurring of distinctions between animals and plants has become in itself a popular way to neutralize the ethics behind our food choices. Ironically, it has been adopted by those who consider themselves conscious omnivores. In a recent Intelligence Squared debate, Joel Salatin glibly remarked that even a potato has a face. In an article in *The New Yorker*, Michael Pollan elevates claims behind plant sentience and intelligence, while in other interviews and articles Pollan ridicules the minds of chickens and a steer, fueling the belief that they exist only for the purposes we've designated for them. Even many secular thinkers still seem to embrace an unquestioned and outmoded belief in dominion.

Dominion is about disempowering animals. Disempowering victims—whether human or nonhuman—means stripping them of their identity or reducing their identity down to just one vice or menial purpose that conveniently serves the interests of their oppressors.

This disfigured identity is aggressively promoted, and eventually becomes assimilated into society as *fact*, becoming the justification for treating victims as *others*. Thus, women are paid less than men for the same position. Child slave laborers *don't exist*, concealed as invisible resources of production that the public never hears about or sees. Africans were defined by pro-slavery politicians as limited to functioning as slaves rather than as individual members of a free Caucasian society. The 40% of Ethiopia's poor population *don't exist* to that same country's livestock industry[1]—one of the world's largest —which pillages the country's scarce natural resources to cater to lucrative meat export markets, rather than feeding its poor through sustainable, plant-based agriculture. Jews in Nazi Germany were identified as *vermin* who didn't deserve to live in an Aryan world. Tutsis in the Rwandan genocide were named and killed as *cockroaches*. Animals are *here for us* with no intrinsic value of their own. They are *the ghosts in our machine* who either don't exist, or matter so little that even our momentary taste sensations rank above the value of their very lives.

People who invoke the personal choice defense typically feel compelled to go beyond just affirming this belief to expressing their *open-mindedness* about their vegan and vegetarian friends, acknowledging that they too are making personal choices that are *right* for *them*. Yet, upon closer examination, the choice to eat animals, whether it is never, once a week or every day, is not strictly a *personal* choice. Eating animal products is indeed exercising a choice, but then so is the choice to injure, defame, rape, or murder another human being. I argue that because *personalizing* the consumption of animal products categorically excludes animals from the domain of public discourse and social justice, the solution is to *de-personalize* animal food choices as a necessary step in assimilating nonhuman animals into our moral community.

Eating Animals is Made "Personal" Only Upon Public Scrutiny

The ethics of food choices had never been discussed at the dinner table, much less defined as *personal*, until a growing number of vegans and vegetarians—by their very presence at the table—questioned the legitimacy of eating animals. A person who tells you that eating animal products is a personal choice, is experiencing a state of cognitive dissonance. Deeply entrenched beliefs are being challenged, and that challenge causes them to defend their established beliefs. In other words, **they have made this issue *personal* precisely in response to vegans making it public.** Making the issue *personal* is a nice way of saying, "I don't want to be judged or held accountable for my actions that harm animals." So this is not so much an attempt to defend eating animals as it is a defense intended to block any further discussion or evaluation. Moreover, personalization removes animals from public discourse and keeps them tucked away in our closet of denial and silence.

There is No Free Choice Without Awareness

The irony is that while non-vegans defend their choice to eat animal products as a *personal* one, they will nonetheless go to great lengths to defend it publicly when confronted with a vegan. Like some apologetic white liberals who defend themselves by defiantly exclaiming to a new black acquaintance "But I have black friends, too!," some will painstakingly explain how intimately they understand the vegan lifestyle. After all, they will assure you, they have already heard and evaluated vegan friends' reasons for going vegan, and they deeply respect them for it.

They've carefully considered being vegan themselves, they will tell you, but have concluded that *it's just not for them*. In this conclusion, they are essentially declaring that caring about animals is "optional," a morally relative option. When pressed further, instead of arriving at some novel new argument for eating animal products in an age that presents them with an increasing number of alternatives, they simply revert back to the traditional arguments that are all pretty much centered around what social psychologist Melanie Joy calls the Three Ns of justification: *eating animal products is normal, natural and necessary.*[2]

But their reasoning reveals the fact that they have sorely misunderstood even the most fundamental tenets of veganism. By simply reaffirming the supremacy of personal choice, they simultaneously reaffirm the belief that even trivial palate pleasures can be made more important than life and death itself. This reaffirmation requires a suspension of moral reasoning. One forgettable meal = an entire lifetime cut drastically and violently short.

Mere "Personal" Choices Don't Have Victims

Let's take a look at the issue from the animal victim's perspective, which has been completely denied by the non-vegan's unexamined assumption that animals have no interest or understanding of the value of their individual lives. In essence, nonhuman animals are denied victimhood because they are viewed as objects, rather than animals who actually have lives that matter to them, full of rich experiences and interests. The notion that *conscious omnivores* think they have done their due diligence by examining the pros and cons of eating animals means nothing for the animals who value their lives as we do. Without a doubt, the animals we raise for meat, dairy, and eggs are sentient in the same manner we are, with at least as much of an interest in staying alive, avoiding pain and suffering, and seeking pleasurable experiences as our companion animals.

As Canadian activist Twyla Francois so aptly puts it:

> All animals have the same capacity for suffering, but how we see them differs and that determines what we'll tolerate happening to them. In the Western world, we feel it wrong to torture and eat cats and dogs, but perfectly acceptable to do the same to animals equally as sentient and capable of suffering. No being who prides himself on rationality can continue to support such behavior.[3]

Justice Informs Our Choices

Choice requires free will and a basic understanding of the options and their consequences. In the spirit of justice, we live in a society where our actions and choices are governed by what society deems acceptable.

If we choose to maim, rape, enslave, or kill someone, our actions have consequences and are punishable by law. In a democratic society, we generally understand on principle and in practice that we are free to do what we want as long as it doesn't harm, exploit, or infringe upon the same rights and freedoms of others.

Yet, for the non-vegan, the choice of eating animals is divorced from the standards of justice we uphold for ourselves, since justice, according to this specious worldview, does not apply to nonhuman species. Therefore, there are no visibly negative consequences to eating animals. The victims have already been transformed into products, and therefore remain conveniently absent, both physically and psychologically, from those who cause their suffering and death. This absence is the basis of the denial inherent in the claim that we are making a personal choice to eat animal products. Framed from this fictional perspective, these choices then become perceived as *harmless*—as harmless as eating an apple that has fallen from the tree. Moreover, this belief is reinforced by a variety of cultural norms, such as the consumer's routine experience of viewing these products, which are sanitized, pristinely packaged, and elegantly assembled on store shelves.

The Negation of Choice
In reality, the choice to eat other animals paradoxically annihilates choice and free will for others who were designed by nature as free agents like us. This choice necessitates the domination and violation of animals against their will, as well as their murder and dismemberment by no choice of their own.

In the words of author Carol Adams:

Objectification permits the oppressor to view another being as an object. The oppressor then violates this being with object-like treatment, e.g., the rape of women that denies women freedom to say no, or the butchering of animals that converts animals from living breathing beings to dead objects. This process allows fragmentation, brutal dismemberment and finally consumption. [...] Consumption is the fulfillment of oppression, the annihilation of will, of separate identity.[4]

Moreover, the artificial breeding, exploitation, enslavement, killing, and profiteering from the slaughtered corpses of some 60 billion land animals and another 60 billion to 1 trillion marine animals every year worldwide is certainly not a personal matter for individual consumers, no more than is any other form of oppression that exploits some for the benefit of others. On the contrary, the animal industrial complex depends on a system of laws, standards, political power structures, institutionalized violence, economies of scale, and vast and complex distribution networks. In sheer scale and degree of suffering, the ongoing atrocity against farmed animals dwarfs all human atrocities combined. The most shocking and contemptible aspect of this system is that it is unnecessary. Plant-based alternatives to animal products are growing in number and availability. The nutritional science on the health benefits and advantages of a vegan diet is overwhelming and this understanding continues to permeate mainstream culture. For the vast majority of us who have other options, the only question left to answer is an ethical one: *If we can live healthy lives without harming anyone, why wouldn't we?*

Notes

1 Richard Oppenlander, *Food Choice and Sustainability: Why Buying Local, Eating Less Meat, and Taking Baby Steps Won't Work* (Minneapolis: Langdon Street Press, 2013).

2 Melanie Joy, *Why We Love Dogs, Eat Pigs, and Wear Cows: An Introduction to Carnism* (San Francisco: Conari Press, 2010).

3 Twyla Francois, "Photo Gallery: The People and Quotes That Inspire Us," Free From Harm, http://www.freefromharm.com.

4 Carol J. Adams, *The Sexual Politics of Meat: A Feminist-Vegetarian Critical Theory* (New York: Continuum International Publishing Group, 1990).

Carnism: Why Eating Animals is a Social Justice Issue

by Melanie Joy

1968: The year of revolutions, the year of social transformation. Martin Luther King, Jr. delivers his prophetic "Mountaintop" speech; a day later, King is assassinated. Massive student and worker demonstrations in the streets of Paris radicalize the country and catalyze a fundamental shift in French cultural and political values. *Star Trek* features the first scripted interracial kiss on a United States television network. The anti-nuclear power crusade evolves into a global environmental movement. The year 1968 was a watershed year for cultural change—a year of civil rights, sexual liberation, and social transformation. And it was the year I met someone who was to become the catalyst for my life's work for social justice. It was the year I met my dog, Fritz.

When we adopted Fritz, I was just two years old, and he was just two months old. Fritz was my first dog, but he was also my first friend; we did everything together. We played together, napped together, got scolded together when my mother would find me sneaking him my food under the kitchen table. And Fritz was also my first heartbreak, when he died at the age of 13 from liver cancer.

It was my experience of having such a close connection with another being, of learning to compartmentalize that sense of connection (to reserve my compassion for dogs and cats and horses while I continued to eat pigs and chickens and cows), and of later reconnecting with myself and nonhuman animals that ultimately led me to the social justice efforts that mark my life's work. In other words, despite my experience of having such a meaningful relationship with a nonhuman being, I learned to deny my connection with other animals and with myself, a denial that enabled me to unwittingly participate in an atrocity that I would never otherwise have supported. And it was, essentially, my relationship with my dog that informed my understanding that animals have intrinsic worth, that our connections with other beings are genuine and tremendously valuable, and that the most frequent and intimate way in which most of us relate to nonhuman animals—through eating their bodies—requires a profound disconnection and causes a profound injustice. It was my relationship with my dog that led me to recognize that eating animals is a social justice issue.

The essay below is reprinted with permission from One Green Planet, www.onegreenplanet.com.

I don't eat lamb...You feel guilty. It just feels kind of like...they are very gentle. Well, cows are [gentle, too, but] we eat them. I don't know how to describe it...It seems like everybody eats cow. It's affordable and there are so many of them but lambs are just different...Seems like it's okay to eat a cow but it's not okay to eat a lamb...the difference is weird.
Interview subject: 43-year-old meat eater

I don't [think of animals raised for meat as individuals]. I wouldn't be able to do my job if I got that personal with them. When you say "individuals," you mean as a unique person, as a unique thing with its own name and its own characteristics, its own little games it plays? Yeah? Yeah, I'd really rather not know that. I'm sure it has it, but I'd rather not know it.
Interview subject: 31-year-old meat cutter

Consider the above statements. A meat cutter wouldn't be able to carry on with his work if he thought about what he was doing. A meat eater is affectionate toward one species but eats another and has no idea why. Before being asked to reflect on their behaviors, neither of these individuals thought there was anything odd about the way they relate to the animals that become their food, and after such reflection their awareness quickly "wore off." So the meat cutter kept the unpleasant reality of his job at bay and continued to process animals, while the meat eater suppressed his mental paradox and continued to eat them.

What is perhaps most extraordinary about the sentiments above is that to most of us—including those of us who are committed to critically examining our beliefs and behaviors, and the impact of our choices on others—they are *not* extraordinary. All of us who are born into a dominant, meat-eating culture have inherited this paradoxical mentality: we know the animals we eat are individuals, yet we'd rather not know it. We'd feel guilty eating certain animals, yet we take pleasure consuming others. We cringe when faced with images of animals suffering, yet we dine on their bodies multiple times a day. We love dogs and eat pigs and yet we don't know why.

Widespread ambivalent, illogical attitudes toward a group of others are almost always a hallmark of an oppressive ideology. Oppressive ideologies require rational, humane people to participate in irrational, inhumane practices and to remain unaware of such contradictions. And they frame the choices of those who refuse to participate in the ideology as "personal preferences" rather than conscientious objections.

It is essential that those of us who espouse progressive values and thus support social justice initiatives recognize the paradoxical mentality of meat. Because although this mentality is pervasive, it is not inherent in our species—it is the product of an oppressive ideology so entrenched that it is invisible, its tenets appearing to be universal truths rather than ideologically driven assumptions. This ideology shapes and is shaped by the same type of mentality that enables other oppressions, and it is therefore essential to address if we hope to create a more just social order. Eating animals is not simply a matter of personal ethics; it is the inevitable end result of a deeply entrenched, oppressive *ism*. Eating animals is a social justice issue.

Carnism: The Ideology of Meat

Carnism is the invisible belief system, or ideology, that conditions us to eat certain animals. Carnism is the opposite of veganism; we tend to think it is only vegans (and vegetarians) who bring their beliefs to the dinner table. But when eating animals is not a necessity for survival, as is the case in much of the world today, it is a choice—and choices always stem from beliefs. Most of us, for instance, eat pigs but not dogs because we don't have a belief system when it comes to eating animals.

Yet most of us have no idea that when we eat animals we are in fact making a choice. When we are growing up, forming our identity and values, nobody asks us whether we want to eat animals, how we feel about eating animals, whether we believe in eating animals. We are never asked to reflect upon this daily practice that has such profound ethical dimensions and personal implications. Eating animals is just a given; it's just the way things are. Because carnism operates outside of our awareness, it robs us of our ability to make our choices freely—because without awareness, there is no free choice.

Carnism, like other oppressive, or violent, ideologies whose tenets run counter to core human values, must use a set of social and psychological defense mechanisms that disconnect us, psychologically and emotionally, from the truth of our experience. In so doing, carnism enables us to support unnecessary violence toward others without the moral discomfort we would otherwise feel. In short, because we naturally feel empathy toward animals and don't want them to suffer, and yet we nonetheless eat animals, carnism must provide us with a set of tools to override our conscience so that we support an oppressive system that we would likely otherwise oppose.

Denial: See No Evil, Hear No Evil, Speak No Evil

The primary defense of carnism is denial: if we deny there is a problem in the first place, then we don't have to do anything about it. And denial is expressed through invisibility; carnism remains invisible by remaining unnamed so that eating animals is seen as a given rather than a choice, an impartial act rather than an ideological practice. Moreover, the victims of the system are kept out of sight and thus conveniently out of public consciousness. *Animal victims* are, for instance, routinely and legally forcibly impregnated and castrated, and their beaks, horns, and tails are cut off—all without any pain relief. They spend their entire lives confined in windowless sheds, in crates so small they can barely move, and it is not uncommon for them to have their throats slit while conscious or to be boiled alive. The dismembered bodies of slaughtered beings are everywhere we turn, and yet we virtually never see these animals alive.

Justification: Conservatism in the Guise of Progressivism

The secondary defense of carnism is justification; when invisibility inevitably falters, we must be provided with a good reason for continuing to eat other beings. Carnism teaches us to justify eating animals by teaching us to believe that the myths of meat are the facts of meat. There is a vast mythology surrounding meat, but all myths fall in one way or another under the Three Ns of Justification: eating meat is normal, natural, and necessary. And these same myths have been used to justify violent behaviors and beliefs throughout human history, from war to slavery to all forms of bigotry against humans (misogyny, homophobia, etc.).

The Three Ns are antithetical to progressive values. Progressives by definition are those who challenge entrenched social norms, question dominant definitions of human nature and history, and seek to transform an oppressive status quo. And historically, the Ns have been used to discredit progressive movements, framing the ideologies these movements promote as abnormal, unnatural, and unnecessary. (Consider, for instance, the reaction to the suffragists: it was widely believed that if women were to vote it would defy the natural order and destroy the nation.) Yet most well intentioned progressives have unwittingly embraced the Three Ns of carnism, either by ignoring the issue of farmed animal exploitation altogether or at best by supporting the increasingly popular "humane" and "sustainable" meat movements, movements which reflect the same conservative tradition-alism that has always been used to justify ideologies which exploit a disempowered group of others.

Eating Meat is Normal: Violence in Moderation

What we call normal is simply the beliefs and behaviors of the domi-nant culture. It is the carnistic norm. And carnism as a social norm is so entrenched that it blinds us to the fact that "humane meat" is a contradiction in terms. Most of us would, for instance, never condone killing a perfectly healthy six-month-old golden retriever who "had a good life" simply because we like the way her thighs taste, and yet carnism prevents us from seeing the immorality of doing the exact same thing to cows, pigs, chickens, and other farmed animals. Any moral difference between animal species that carnistic culture teaches us to believe in is a pure rationalization.

Eating Meat is Natural: Violence as a Tradition

What we call natural is simply the dominant culture's interpretation of history. It reflects not human history, but carnistic history; it refer-ences not our fruit-eating ancestors but their flesh-eating descendants. And more importantly, infanticide, murder, and rape are at least as longstanding as eating animals and are therefore arguably as natural—yet we don't invoke the longevity of these practices as a justification for them. In the words of author Colleen Patrick-Goudreau, do we really want to use the behavior of the Neanderthals as the yardstick by which to measure our current moral choices?

The argument that eating meat is natural is a key premise of the sus-tainability movement. Many proponents of this movement claim that the reason we buy our meat from grocery stores rather than hunt and kill animals ourselves is because modern food production methods have removed us from the (natural) process of killing so that we have become overly sensitized to harming animals. Such an argument is reminiscent of the portrayal of slavery abolitionists as "sentimental." The "sustainable meat" argument is founded on a traditionalist worldview which frames the progressive values of empathy, compassion, and reciprocity (doing unto others) as qualities to be transcended rather than cultivated.

"But They Eat _____ in _____!": Cultural Carnism

Carnism is a global phenomenon. In meat-eating cultures around the world, people tend to feel comfortable eating only those species they learned to classify as edible; all the rest they perceive as inedible and often as disgusting (e.g., pigs in the Middle East) or even unethical (e.g., dogs and cats in the US, cattle in India) to consume. And all cultures tend to see their own classification of edible animals as rational and judge the classifications of other cultures as disgusting and/or offensive. So, while the type of species consumed changes from culture to culture, people's experience eating animals remains remarkably consistent.

Most people assume that because eating animals is universal, it is not ideological. The wide variation of species consumed across cultures — rather than being seen as evidence of carnism — often leads to the assumption that eating animals is a morally relative (and thus morally neutral) practice. Yet, just as, for instance, the marrying off of 12-year-old girls in Sudan is no reason for us to consider sexual relations with children morally neutral, the eating of dogs in Korea is no reason for us to consider eating pigs (or other animals) morally neutral. If the mere existence of analogous practices in other cultures ethically justified our own behaviors, we would have no reason to question the ethics of even the most heinous of crimes. While we of course should not condemn the traditions of other cultures as immoral, we can, as thoughtful observers, examine our own culture's attempts to justify eating certain animals against this broader cultural backdrop.

Eating Meat is Necessary: Violence is a Given

What we call necessary is simply what is necessary to maintain the dominant culture. Today, the evidence that a diet without animal products is nutritionally sound (and likely even healthier than a carnistic diet) is overwhelming. For those of us who are economically and geographically able to choose what we eat, eating meat is necessary only to sustain the carnistic status quo.

Framing eating animals as a biological necessity de-moralizes what is a fundamentally moral issue. In other words, if we believe that eating animals is unavoidable then we also believe that it is amoral, and we are alleviated of the responsibility of reflecting on the ethics of our choices.

Institutionalized Carnism: Systemic Oppression

The reason so many progressives have not rejected the Three Ns of carnism is because carnism is structural; it is built into the very structure of society and is therefore a form of institutionalized oppression. And when an ideology is institutionalized, it is also internalized. In other words, those of us who are progressive often don't challenge the Three Ns because we don't see them for what they are, as we have learned to look at the world through the lens of carnism.

Cognitive Distortions: Internalized Carnism

Carnism, like other violent ideologies, uses a set of cognitive defenses that distort our perceptions of those on the receiving end of our choices. These defenses act as psychological and emotional distancing mechanisms. For instance, carnism teaches us to see certain animals as objects, so that we refer to the turkey on our Thanksgiving platter as something rather than someone. Carnism also teaches us to see animals as abstractions, as lacking in any individuality or personality and instead simply as members of an abstract group about which we've made generalized assumptions: a pig is a pig and all pigs are the same. And as with other victims of violent ideologies, we give them numbers rather than names. And carnism teaches us to place animals in rigid categories in our minds so that we can harbor very different feelings and carry out very different behaviors toward different species: dogs and cats are family and chickens and cows are food.

From Absurdities to Atrocities: The Mentality of Oppression

When we look at the world through the lens of carnism, we fail to see the absurdities of the system. So we see, for instance, an advertisement of a pig holding a butcher knife and gleefully dancing over the fire pit in which she is to be cooked ("asking" to be killed and consumed) and we take no notice, rather than take offense. Or we are told by the corporate conglomerates who profit from the bodies of those whose eggs and milk we consume that the animals in their well-concealed factories are free from harm, and we unquestioningly accept such a claim—despite the fact that it is illegal for civilians to obtain access to these buildings or even to photograph them from a distance.

As Voltaire aptly said, if we believe absurdities, we shall commit atrocities. Carnism is but one of the many atrocities, one of the many violent ideologies, that are an unfortunate part of the human legacy. And although the experience of each group of victims will always be somewhat unique, the ideologies themselves are structurally similar. The mentality that enables such violence is the same.

It is the mentality of domination and subjugation, of privilege and oppression. It is the mentality that causes us to turn someone into something, to reduce a life to a unit of production, to erase someone's being. It is the might-makes-right mentality, which makes us feel entitled to wield complete control over the lives and deaths of those with less power—just because we can. And to feel justified in our actions, because they're only...savages, women, animals. It is the mentality of meat.

Injustice Begets Injustice: Carnism as an Interlocking Ism

Many progressives appreciate Martin Luther King, Jr.'s declaration that injustice anywhere is a threat to justice everywhere, because we appreciate that oppressions are interlocking, reinforcing one another. Progressive social change thus requires not simply liberating specific groups, but challenging the foundations of oppression itself. For if we fail to pick out the common threads that are woven through all violent ideologies, we will be doomed to create atrocities in new forms, to merely trade one form of oppression for another. To create a truly humane and just society, then, we must include carnism in our analysis.

Including carnism in progressive analyses requires a paradigm shift: we must recognize the systemic nature of eating animals. We must appreciate that, just as feminists who challenge patriarchy, for instance, are not simply "imposing their personal views" on society, those who challenge carnism are not simply "imposing their personal choices" on others. Eating animals cannot be reduced to simply a matter of personal ethics any more than can the refusal to allow people of color to enter one's privately owned establishment.

Justice Begets Justice: Toward an Inclusive Social Analysis

The flipside of MLK's aforementioned quote is that justice anywhere is a threat to injustice everywhere. The oppressive-powers-that-be depend on a divide-and-conquer mentality that pits oppressed groups against one another, as though oppressions were rungs on a hierarchical ladder rather than spokes on a wheel. And while it is impossible for anyone to take on all causes, we can and should value any cause which seeks to create a more just and compassionate society. As ethicist Peter Singer muses, "I cannot help wondering what exactly it is that [people working for human welfare] are doing for human beings that compels them to continue to support the...exploitation of farm[ed] animals."

Progressive social change is not merely about changing policies, but about changing hearts and minds. Genuine and lasting change requires a paradigm shift, a transformation of the mentality that propped up the old order. We must knock out the foundations of oppression and cultivate the values that form the foundation of justice, values such as compassion, integrity, and reciprocity. And to challenge injustice everywhere, we must practice justice everywhere: on streets, in the courtroom—and on our plates.

Social Justice, Sincerity, and Sustenance

by Lisa Kemmerer

Among social justice advocates—including well-known authors on the environment (such as Lester Brown)—there is an increasing tendency to rail against corn-based biofuel. When breezing through articles on corn or world hunger, it is easy to find alarmist commentaries claiming that ethanol production is a serious threat to food distribution, stealing corn from the mouths of the hungry, and driving up food prices—exacerbating poverty and causing yet more starvation.[1] Indeed, the use of ethanol in the U.S. has "increased dramatically from about 1.7 billion gallons in 2001 to about 12.9 billion in 2012."[2] And this shift has diverted food staples, especially corn, to produce fuel, a trend that is encouraged by federal incentives.[3]

Nonetheless, for those genuinely concerned about diverting corn (and other grains) from the mouths of the hungry, animal agriculture ought to be the primary concern. Cattle, pigs, and poultry consume the vast majority of US grains—70% (60% in the EU) are fed to farmed animals.[4] In the US, 73 million acres (30 million hectares) are devoted to growing corn, 80% of which is fed to farmed animals at home and abroad. Seventy-three million acres are devoted to soybeans, of which not quite half are fed to farmed animals.[5] It is inefficient and nutritionally wasteful to feed corn (and soy) to farmed animals —and unethical. Consuming animal products (rather than directly eating grains) wastes 80-90% of the protein that grains hold, 90-96%

of grain's calories, and 100% of their carbohydrates and fiber.[6] If we want to feed the hungry, we need to eat grains directly, and avoid dairy, eggs, and flesh. For those who are genuinely concerned about feeding the 842 million people who suffer from hunger worldwide,[7] ethanol is not the problem. Consuming animal products is the problem.

World hunger is but one reason to rethink our taste for flesh, dairy, and eggs. There are at least four other serious concerns associated with the consumption of animal products, including environmental degradation. Animal agriculture uses much more fresh water, petroleum, and land than does a plant-based diet, and contributes significantly to climate change, freshwater depletion, deforestation, and the Earth's ever-expanding dead zones. When we buy "beef," for example, we are buying the destruction of rainforests in order to graze cattle and to grow crops to feed cattle and chickens and turkeys and pigs. We are supporting an industry that has become one of the leading contributors to greenhouse gases, and the primary cause of the Earth's water areas that are devoid of oxygen and therefore cannot support life.[8] Fishing methods are indiscriminate, so those who eat fish also destroy ecosystems and wildlife, and pay for bycatch—incidental deaths such as those of endangered sea turtles and playful dolphins who are drowned in nets of pulled from the water along with target species. Those consuming fish and other sea life pay for the silent collapse of fish populations as well as the destruction of their underwater ecosystems under the weight of trawls.

Human health and healthcare costs provide a third reason to rethink omnivorous inclinations. According to the Centers for Disease Control and Prevention (CDC), the two leading causes of death are heart disease and cancers, both linked to a diet rich in animal products. The third is chronic lower respiratory disease, also linked to diet because animal agriculture releases such things as dust, ammonia, hydrogen sulfide, and smoke into the air, not to mention the burning of fossil fuels and release of methane. The fourth is stroke, also a health problem known to be linked with a diet rich in animal products.[9] The seventh cause of death is diabetes; obesity is increasingly prevalent in nations with diets rooted in animal products. We are suffering and dying prematurely (along with the turkeys, pigs, cows, and fishes) because of our tendency to eat dairy, eggs, and flesh—and the animals we are eating are suffering and dying as well. Those who wish to take care of their health, reduce healthcare costs, optimize chances for a full life, and minimize misery, are better off choosing a well-balanced plant-based diet.

Those concerned about racism, heterosexism, ableism, ageism, or sexism provide the fourth reason to follow the vegan path, in this case as a matter of consistency and solidarity.[10] For example, cows, hens, and sows suffer the longest and the most severely on factory farms *because* they are females. Cows are repeatedly and forcibly impregnated to produce milk for human mouths. Sows are repeatedly, forcibly impregnated to produce piglets, and are then kept in extreme confinement while pregnant and nursing. Hens exploited for eggs are also kept in extreme confinement, and are not allowed so much as the freedom to spread their wings. These females suffer *because* of their female biology—they are exploited for their reproductive capacities. They suffer not only from physical violation and confinement, but also psychologically and emotionally when their young are stolen from under their watchful eye. Hens exploited for fertile egg production never even glimpse their young. Female animals are imprisoned in battery cages (hens) and gestation crates (hogs), and tormented in rape racks (largely cows, but also other animals) and farrowing pens (hogs), in order to produce reproductive eggs, nursing milk, and young—in order to produce products and profits for their oppressors, including those who consume animal products.

Fifth, and most obviously, a diet rooted in flesh, eggs, and milk causes suffering and premature death for chickens, fish, turkeys, pigs, cattle, and other farmed animals. While females in the dairy and egg industries suffer the most, all farmed animals suffer: Their lives are controlled by human beings from forced pregnancy to premature death. Bovines killed for flesh live less than one year, while those who make their way to sanctuaries can live upwards of twenty years.

Hogs not used for reproduction are killed after just 6 months, though pigs could easily live 15 years. Chickens raised for flesh reach market weight just 45 days after they hatch, though they might otherwise live for fifteen years.[1] Given the horrific conditions in which many farmed animals live, it is perhaps a blessing that they are killed at such tender ages, though this is little consolation—those killed are quickly replaced in order to satisfy consumers who purchase animal products.

Finally, teachings from every major religion encourage us to take care of our health, and to choose a life of compassion and service rather than exploit and oppress those who are vulnerable.[12] Animal products are an extravagance: we can live quite well without flesh, dairy, and eggs—in fact, we are likely to be considerably healthier. Consuming animal products wastes precious grains that could otherwise preserve the lives of those who are desperate for food, causes severe environmental degradation, and harms and destroys living beings prematurely. For all of these reasons—for all of the above reasons—the spiritual life requires conscientious consumers to reject animal products. Religious teachings require that we take into account the sufferings and needs of others, that we be more conscious of how we might help or harm others, and that we make the necessary changes, whenever possible, to do so.

These are the five most compelling reasons to rethink consumption of animal products. I remember the five reasons with the Italian word for "love," AMORE. "A" represents animal suffering. "M" stands for medical reasons. "O" is for oppression—oppression of those who are vulnerable, for example females of all species, those who suffer from hunger, and those who are poor and must work all day slaughtering animals, among others. "R" represents religious teachings that universally encourage compassion, self-sacrifice, and service for the vulnerable. "E" reminds us of environmental degradation linked with animal agriculture.

It is perhaps reasonable to continue eating animal products if vegan foods are simply not an option (availability, cost, or due to the power of others). If you are reading this book, you almost surely do not qualify. For those of us who can buy bulk grains and frozen, fresh, or canned greens, the vegan option is the only moral option. If we care about those who are starving, if we are concerned about the planet and ecosystems, if we want to protect our health or reduce the costs of health care, if we wish to reduce oppressions of other people and the sufferings of farmed and fished animals, or if we have spiritual inclinations or a commitment to religious teachings, we must turn to a plant-based diet. Blaming ethanol for taking a bite out of the corn supply while consuming flesh, eggs, or dairy, is hypocritical. The best way to fight world hunger is to go vegan. Those who are sincere in their commitment to social justice, protecting the environment, human health, and animals, must shift to a plant-based diet—or admit that they really don't care about these particular issues after all. ☙

Notes

1. Timothy Wise, "US Corn Ethanol Fuels Food Crisis in Developing Countries," *Al Jazeera*, October 10, 2012, http://www.aljazeera.com/indepth/opinion/2012/10/201210993632838545.html; Kay McDonald, "Paying more for Food? Blame the Ethanol Mandate," *CNN*, August 20, 2012, http://www.cnn.com/2012/08/20/opinion/mcdonald-corn-ethanol/.

2. "Ethanol," U.S. Department of Energy, accessed August 30, 2014, http://www.fueleconomy.gov/feg/ethanol.shtml.

3. "Federal Laws and Incentives for Ethanol," U.S. Department of Energy, "Alternative Fuels Data Center," last updated July 1, 2014, http://www.afdc.energy.gov/fuels/laws/ETH/US.

4. Richard A. Oppenlander, *Comfortably Unaware: Global Depletion and Food Responsibility… What You Choose to Eat is Killing our Planet* (Minneapolis: Langdon Street Press, 2011), 12; Henning Steinfeld, Pierre Gerber, Tom Wassenaar, Vincent Castel, Mauricio Rosales, and Cees de Haan, *Livestock's Long Shadow: Environmental Issues and Options* (Rome: FAO, 2006), 272.

5. "Major Crops Grown in the United States," EPA's Ag Center, last updated April 11, 2013, http://www.epa.gov/agriculture/ag101/cropmajor.html.

6. Stephen R. Kaufman and Nathan Braun, *Good News for All Creation: Vegetarianism as Christian Stewardship* (Cleveland: Vegetarian Advocates Press, 2004), 18.

7. "Hunger Statistics," World Food Programme, accessed August 16, 2014, http://www.wfp.org/hunger/stats.

8. Lisa Kemmerer, *Eating Earth: Dietary Choice and Planetary Health* (Oxford: Oxford University Press, 2014).

9. "Leading Causes of Death," Centers for Disease Control and Prevention (CDC), last updated July 14, 2014, http://www.cdc.gov/nchs/fastats/leading-causes-of-death.htm.

10. Lisa Kemmerer, ed., "Appendix," *Sister Species: Women, Animals, and Social Justice* (Urbana-Champaign: University of Illinois Press, 2011).

11. Ibid.

12. Lisa Kemmerer, *Animals and World Religions*, (Oxford: Oxford University Press, 2012).

Mother Corn, Father Pumpkin, Sister Bean...

by Rita Laws

It was 1994 and I had plenty of assignments, but the research I was doing had nothing to do with them. I was trying to answer a question that had been gnawing away at me for some time. I had been a vegetarian since my early twenties and, as a member of the Oklahoma Choctaw Nation, had always wondered how important of a role meat played in the diet of my people before the onset of European influences. Research had shown me that a vegetarian or vegan diet was certainly natural for the human body. From our teeth to our gut, we are designed for a plant-based diet, just like most of our distant primate relatives. Was such a diet part of the history and culture of my father's people?

It wasn't just curiosity that drove me; it was my health. Like so many American Indians, I was battling obesity. Some studies have shown that when people of any race identify the plant-based foods that have traditionally been central to the diet of their ancestors, and then add them back into their diet, it helps to control weight. I knew that corn, pumpkin, and beans were the mainstay of the Choctaw diet, made into a daily stew and eaten with bread made from corn or acorn flour. But what about meat?

What I learned surprised me. Meat was rarely consumed among my people before 1492. Just as tobacco was smoked briefly only during ceremonies, meat was eaten infrequently. It isn't easy to kill a rabbit with a bow and arrow. And it wasn't necessary. The native peoples of the Americas have been described as the greatest farmers in the history of the planet. Nearly half of the plant foods grown worldwide today were cultivated first by New World Indians, including sweet and white potatoes, many kinds of beans, nuts, berries, and fruits. Three of the most popular flavors in the world, chocolate, vanilla and strawberry, are all gifts from America's first farmers.

They concentrated their genius on agriculture in part because they did not have domesticated animals to eat. The only domesticated animal in North America was the dog. A few tribes had domesticated the turkey, but that was primarily for their beautiful feathers. They also did not have horses to ride or iron-making technology to make heavy-duty cutting weapons. And they had no gun powder, guns or rifles to take down large prey. Hunting large or fast animals and processing them is difficult without these inventions.

After 1492, meat slowly crept into the menu of all tribes because it was suddenly easy to catch and kill all kinds of animals. Further, the introduction of domesticated animals like sheep, goats, cows, chickens, and pigs made meat and animal products accessible without hunting, and metal axes and blades made killing them and using their hides much easier.

When the Spaniards noted that the Aztecs, Mayan and Zapotec people enjoyed life spans twice as long as theirs, they did not attribute this to the diet of these tribes. But the native healers knew about the link between food and health. The children ate only plant-based foods for the first decade of life and when illness struck, were advised to return to the arms of Mother Corn to encourage wellness.

Sadly, wisdom seems to have failed us as a people when we embraced the new flesh-filled diet of the West. But consider that imported diseases like smallpox, bubonic plague, measles, whooping cough and influenza killed 80% of the people in the New World after Columbus landed, and then it is easier to understand. We'll never know exactly how many people were here in the late 15th century and what the total death count was, but modern day estimates from the most knowledgeable sources consistently put the Native American death toll at 80 to 90% in the first century after the Europeans landed.

That means that 80% of the elders and the healers and the wise ones died, too. It was a devastated group of nations trying to survive the loss of their people, their land, and sometimes, trying to survive war, that chose to adapt to the new ways and adopt many of them, instead of resisting.

These diseases and others common in Europe but not as deadly for Europeans raced ahead of settlers and settlements wiping out millions of people before non-Indians ever saw the native communities or learned of their culture. Native villages weakened by one disease were easily wiped out by a second or third that swept through the surviving populace. It was the remnants of once-great cultures that settlers saw, and they didn't even realize it.

Had this holocaust not occurred, or had the native people been able to record their histories in books and libraries before the plagues struck, we might know a great deal more about how and what various tribes ate on a daily basis and during special celebrations. We might know, for example, if there were tribes that could have used more animal products but chose not to. But instead what we have are some oral histories and observations from non-Indians, mere bits and pieces of information.

Thankfully, there was enough information to make a case that at least some Indian nations ate little to no meat on a daily basis 500 years ago. So in 1994, I gathered up what I could find and put all of this research into an article entitled "Returning to the Corn" and it was published in *Vegetarian Journal* that same year.

Almost immediately, reprint requests began arriving, and then requests by local and statewide vegetarian organizations for me to come and speak on the same topic. Online, the article has appeared on dozens of different non-profit sites. To this day, I continue to receive reprint requests and "fan mail." None of my articles or books has had an impact that comes close to that article. Apparently many other people had also wondered about how the diet of the Old World changed America.

The New World was not a vegan utopia prior to 1492. However, in hindsight, it is clear that certain activities and inventions sent the Old World in one direction and the New World in another. The lack of domesticated food animals, horses, guns and iron-making technology steered the New World toward agricultural development and away from meat-eating. The daily intake of most people was primarily plant-based, and meat in the form of fish or small game was typically, depending on the tribe of course, infrequent. Life spans were longer and the number and diversity of food crops was amazing when compared to the Old World. Some Europeans thought they'd landed in the Garden of Eden; for example, the Indians had carefully cultivated 47 different varieties of berries over the millennia.

American Indian nations have worked hard to maintain their individual cultural identities. Many have classes where the native language is taught. There are gatherings where the ancestral dress is observed and the old dances and songs are repeated. Books are written with the old folk tales and the tribal histories. But there are areas where many native people continue to blindly follow the European way and the daily diet is one of those. Many of us do not even know the name of our own ancestral core crop.

No one can change North America back to the healthier and more animal-friendly place it was five centuries ago but each of us can look for ways to help animals and ourselves, and to minimize the negative things that happen to them, and to encourage peaceful behavior. You don't even have to be a vegetarian or a vegan to do that. First, investigate your own background and the core crops of your ancestors. Try to incorporate them into your diet at least a few times per week and see how that makes you feel.

Then look around and see how you can help the animals who live nearby. You can volunteer at an animal shelter, foster a dog, adopt a cat, plant something to encourage wild birds, bell the neighborhood cat, put up a birdhouse or a bat house, donate to a wildlife fund, or simply go online and type in the name of your city or state after the question: "How can I help animals in..." You will pull up a whole list of non-profits eager to avail themselves of your time, energy or donation. We may not be able to change the entire world, but we can change the little piece of it where we live—for the better.

The article below originally appeared in *Vegetarian Journal*, September/October 1994, and is reprinted with permission.

Returning to the Corn
Rita Laws

How well we know the stereotype of the rugged Plains Indian: killer of buffalo, dressed in quill-decorated buckskin, elaborately feathered headdress, and leather moccasins, living in an animal-skin teepee, master of the dog and horse, and stranger to vegetables. But this lifestyle, once limited almost exclusively to the Apaches,[1] flourished no more than a couple hundred years. It is not representative of most Native Americans of today or yesterday. Indeed, the "buffalo-as-lifestyle" phenomenon is a direct result of European influence, as we shall see.

Among my own people, the Choctaw Indians of Mississippi and Oklahoma, vegetables are the traditional diet mainstay. A French manuscript of the eighteenth century describes the Choctaws' vegetarian leanings in shelter and food.[2] The homes were constructed not of skins, but of wood, mud, bark, and cane. The principal food, eaten daily from earthen pots, was a vegetarian stew containing corn, pumpkin, and beans. The bread was made from corn and acorns. Other common favorites were roasted corn and corn porridge. (Meat in the form of small game was an infrequent repast.) The ancient Choctaws were, first and foremost, farmers. Even the clothing was plant-based: artistically embroidered dresses for the women and cotton breeches for the men. Choctaws have never adorned their hair with feathers.

The rich lands of the Choctaws in present-day Mississippi were so greatly coveted by nineteenth-century Americans that most of the tribe was forcibly removed to what is now called Oklahoma. Oklahoma was chosen both because it was largely uninhabited and because several explorations of the territory had deemed the land barren and useless for any purpose. The truth, however, was that Oklahoma was so fertile a land that it was an Indian breadbasket. That is, it was used by Indians on all sides as an agricultural resource. Although many Choctaws suffered and died during removal on the infamous Trail of Tears, those that survived built anew and successfully in Oklahoma, their agricultural genius intact.

George Catlin, the famous nineteenth-century Indian historian, described the Choctaw lands of southern Oklahoma in the 1840s this way:

> [T]he ground was almost literally covered with vines, producing the greatest profusion of delicious grapes...and hanging in such endless clusters...our progress was oftentimes completely arrested by hundreds of acres of small plum trees... every bush that was in sight was so loaded with the weight of its...fruit, that they were in many instances literally without leaves on their branches, and quite bent to the ground...and beds of wild currants, gooseberries, and (edible) prickly pear.[3]

(Many of the "wild" foods Anglo explorers encountered on their journeys were actually carefully cultivated by Indians.)

Many of the Choctaw foods cooked at celebrations even today are vegetarian. Corn is so important to us it is considered divine. Our corn legend says that is was a gift from Hashtali, the Great Spirit. Corn was given in gratitude because Choctaws had fed the daughter of the Great Spirit when she was hungry. (Hashtali is literally "Noon Day Sun." Choctaws believe the Great Spirit resides within the sun, for it is the sun that allows the corn to grow!) Another Choctaw story describes the afterlife as a giant playground where all but murderers are allowed. What do Choctaws eat in "heaven?" Their sweetest treat, of course: melons, a never-ending supply.

More than one tribe has creation legends that describe people as vegetarian, living in a kind of Garden of Eden. A Cherokee legend describes humans, plants, and animals as having lived in the beginning in "equality and mutual helpfulness."[4] The needs of all were met without killing one another. When man became aggressive and ate some of the animals, the animals invented diseases to keep human population in check. The plants remained friendly, however, and offered themselves not only as food to man, but also as medicine, to combat the new diseases.

More tribes were like the Choctaws than were different. Aztec, Mayan, and Zapotec children in olden times ate 100% vegetarian diets until at least the age of ten years old. The primary food was cereal, especially varieties of corn.[5] Such a diet was believed to make the child strong and disease resistant. (The Spaniards were amazed to discover that these Indians had twice the life span they did.) A totally vegetarian diet also ensured that the children would retain a lifelong love of grains, and thus live a healthier life. Even today, the Indian healers of those tribes are likely to advise the sick to "return to the arms of Mother Corn" to get well. Such a return might include eating a lot of atole. (The easiest way to make atole is to simmer commercially produced masa harina corn flour with water. Then flavor it with chocolate or cinnamon, and sweeten to taste.) Atole is considered a sacred food.

It is ironic that Indians are strongly associated with hunting and fishing when, in fact, "nearly half of all the plant foods grown in the world today were first cultivated by the American Indians, and were unknown elsewhere until the discovery of the Americas."[6] Can you imagine Italian food without tomato paste, Ireland without white potatoes, or Hungarian goulash without paprika?[7] All these foods have Indian origins.

An incomplete list of other Indian foods given to the world includes bell peppers, red peppers, peanuts, cashews, sweet potatoes, avocados, passion fruit, zucchini, green beans, kidney beans, maple syrup, lima beans, cranberries, pecans, okra, chocolate, vanilla, sunflower seeds, pumpkin, cassava, walnuts, 47 varieties of berries, pineapple, and, of course, corn and popcorn.

Many history textbooks tell the story of Squanto, a Pawtuxent

Indian who lived in the early 1600s. Squanto is famous for having saved the Pilgrims from starvation. He showed them how to gather wilderness foods and how to plant corn.

There have been thousands of Squantos since, even though their names are not so well-known. In fact, modern agriculture owes its heart and soul to Indian-taught methods of seed development, hybridization, planting, growing, irrigating, storing, utilizing, and cooking.[8] And the spirit of Squanto survives to this day. One example is a Peruvian government research station tucked away in a remote Amazon Indian village called Genaro Herrera. University-trained botanists, agronomists, and foresters work there, scientifically studying all the ways the local Indians grow and prepare food. They are also learning how to utilize forests without destroying them, and how to combat pests without chemicals. The trend that moved some North American Indian tribes away from plant-food-based diets can be traced to Coronado, a sixteenth-century Spanish explorer. Prior to his time, hunting was a hobby among most Indians, not a vocation. The Apaches were one of the few tribes that relied heavily on animal killing for survival.[9]

But all that changed as Coronado and his army traversed the West and Midwest from Mexico. Some of his horses got away and quickly multiplied on the grassy plains. Indians re-tamed this new denizen, and the Age of Buffalo began.

Horses replaced dogs as beasts of burden and offered excellent transportation. This was as important an innovation to the Plains Indians as the automobile would be to Anglos later on. Life on the Plains became much easier very quickly.

From the east came another powerful influence: guns. The first American settlers brought their firearms with them. Because of the Indian "threat," they were soon immersed in weapons development and succeeded in making more accurate and powerful weapons.[10] But they also supplied weapons to Indians who allied themselves with colonial causes. Because it was so much easier to kill an animal with a rifle than with a bow and arrow, guns spread quickly among the Indians.

Between the horse and the rifle, buffalo killing was now much simpler.

The Apaches were joined by other tribes, such as the Sioux, Cheyenne, Arapahos, Comanches, and Kiowas. These tribes "lost the corn," gave up agriculture, and started living nomadic existences for the first time. It was not long before their food, clothing, and shelter were entirely dependent on one animal, the buffalo.

George Catlin lamented this fact as early as 1830.[11] He predicted the extinction of the buffalo (which very nearly happened) and the danger of not being diversified. Catlin pointed out that, were the Plains Indians only killing a buffalo for their own use, the situation might not be so grave. But because the great beasts were being slaughtered for profit, they were destined to be wiped out.

It was the white man who profited. There was an insatiable Eastern market for buffalo tongue and buffalo robes. In 1832, Catlin described a wholesale buffalo slaughter carried out by 600 Sioux on horseback. These men killed 1400 animals, and then took only their tongues. These were traded to whites for a few gallons of whiskey. The whiskey, no doubt, helped to dull the Indian talent to make maximum use of an animal. Among the tribes that did not trade with whites, each animal was completely used, down to the hooves. No part went to waste. And buffalo were not killed in the winter, for the Indians lived on autumn-dried meat during that time.

But now buffalo were killed in the winter most of all. It was in cold weather that their magnificent coats grew long and luxuriant. Catlin estimated that 200,000 buffalo were killed each year to make coats for people back east. The average hide netted the Indian hunter one pint of whiskey.

Had the Indians understood the concept of animal extinction, they may have ceased the slaughter. But to the Indians, the buffalo was a gift from the Great Spirit, a gift that would always keep coming. Decades after the disappearance of huge herds, Plains Indians still believed their return was imminent. They danced the Ghost Dance, designed to bring back the buffalo, and prayed for this miracle as late as 1890.

Despite the ease of and financial incentives for killing buffalo, some tribes did not abandon the old ways of the plains. In addition to the farming tribes of the Southeast, tribes in the Midwest, Southwest, and Northwest stuck to agriculture. For example, the Osage, Pawnee, Arikaras, Mandans, Wichitas, and Caddoans remained in permanent farming settlements. Even surrounded by buffalo, they built their homes of timber and earth. And among some of the Indians of the Southwest, cotton, basketry, and pottery were preferred over animal-based substitutes such as leather pouches.

Catlin was eerily accurate when he predicted dire consequences for the buffalo-dependent tribes. To this day, it is these Indians who have fared the worst from assimilation with other races. The Sioux of South Dakota,[12] for one, have the worst poverty and one of the highest alcoholism rates in the country. Conversely, the tribes that depended little or not at all on animal exploitation for their survival, like the Cherokee, Choctaw, Creek, and Chickasaw, are thriving and growing, having assimilated without surrendering their culture.

In the past, and in more than a few tribes, meat-eating was a rare activity, certainly not a daily event. Since the introduction of European meat-eating customs, the introduction of the horse and the gun, and the proliferation of alcoholic beverages and white traders, a lot has changed. Relatively few Indians can claim to be vegetarians today.

But it was not always so. For most Native Americans of old, meat was not only not the food of choice, its consumption was not revered (as in modern times when Americans eat turkey on Thanksgiving as if it were a religious duty). There was nothing ceremonial about meat. It was a plant, tobacco, that was used most extensively during ceremonies and rites, and then only in moderation. Big celebrations such as Fall Festivals centered around the harvest, especially the gathering of the corn. The Choctaws are not the only ones who continue to dance the Corn Dance.

What would this country be like today if the ancient ways were still observed? I believe it is fair to say that the Indian respect for non-human life forms would have had a greater impact on American society. Corn, not turkey meat, might be the celebrated Thanksgiving Day dish. Fewer species would have become extinct, the environment would be healthier, and Indian and non-Indian Americans alike would be living longer and healthier lives. There might also be less sexism and racism, for many people believe that, as you treat your animals (the most defenseless), so you will treat your children, your women, and your minorities.

Without realizing it, the Indian warriors and hunters of ages past played right into the hands of the white men who coveted their lands and their buffalo. When the lands were taken from them, and the buffalo herds decimated, there was nothing to fall back on. But the Indians who chose the peaceful path and relied on diversity and the abundance of plants for their survival were able to save their lifestyles. Even after being moved to new lands they could hang on, replant, and go forward.

Now we, their descendants, must recapture the spirit of the ancient traditions for the benefit of all people. We must move away from the European influences that did away with a healthier style of living. We must again embrace our brothers and sisters, the animals, and "return to the corn" once and for all.

Notes

1   Angie Debo, *A History of the Indians of the United States* (Norman, OK: University of Oklahoma Press, 1970), 15.

2   Oklahoma Choctaw Council Inc, *Choctaw Social and Ceremonial Life* (Oklahoma City, OK: Oklahoma Choctaw Council, 1983), 37-38.

3   George Catlin, *Letters and Notes on the Manners, Customs, and Conditions of North American Indians, Volume II* (New York: Dover Publications, 1973), 46.

4   J. Ed Sharpe and Thomas B. Underwood, *American Indian Cooking and Herb Lore* (Cherokee, NC: Cherokee Publications, 1973), 4.

5   Gene Matlock, "Good Health and the Traditional Diet," *AMERIKKUA!* 8, no. 4 (Fall 1990/Winter 1991): 5.

6   Raven Hail, *Native American Foods Coloring Book* (Scottsdale, AZ: Raven Hail Books, 1979), 3.

7   Jack Weatherford, "The Culinary Revolution," *Indian Givers* (NY: Crown Publishers, 1988).

8   Ibid., Chapter 5, "Indian Agricultural Technology."

9   Debo, *A History of the Indians*, 16-17.

10   John D. Billingsley, "Small Arms," *Encyclopedia Americana*, vol. 25 (1972): 103.

11   Catlin, *Letters and Notes*, 253-263.

12   Michael Dorris, *The Broken Cord* (New York: Harper & Row, 1989), 80.

Until Every Belly is Full

by Keith McHenry

Food is essential to understanding the connections between humans, animals, and the environment. This has become increasingly evident on my journey with Food Not Bombs, where I have had the privilege to join the global struggle to protect our ecosystems while helping bring peace and compassion to all who share the Earth.

This journey has taken me to Africa, the Middle East, the Americas, Europe, and Asia. My experience in the Philippines reinforced my understanding of how we all rely on the natural world. Millions of people in a mega city like Metro Manila depend on the health of the sea and soil to survive. My first introduction to the circle of compassion in Southeast Asia started north of central Manila. I met the young Food Not Bombs volunteers at the city square in Baliwag, Bulacan, Philippines, on a sunny February day in 2013. After greeting one another, we walked through the "traditional market" asking each vender for one or two items from their stall to use in our free vegan meal. Being poor themselves, they were honored to share—a garlic bulb at the first stand, a baggy of shaved coconut at another, five carrots at the next stall. Many of those we sought food from had grown or harvested their crops themselves, relying on the ecosystem to provide the water and nutrition required to cultivate their crops. In 30 minutes, we had gathered enough that we could prepare a tasty vegan lunch on a fire outside a volunteer's home. Shredded coconut was warmed and squeezed through a cloth to become broth for Ginataang Bilo-bilo.

Once our meal for roughly a hundred people was complete, we caravanned by tricycle back to the center of town holding our food and equipment on our laps. Not long after setting out the food under the banner "Food Not Bombs—We won't stop until every belly is full," a line of hungry people assembled to eat and talk. Plastic bags slipped over plastic bowls made it possible to safely provide meals to nearly 100 people with just 30 bowls. Some of the hungry even brought their own plastic bag to reduce waste and expense. Orphaned street children were eager to eat and tease us about our banners and flyers. The adults who joined us worked in the local markets, picked through garbage, and in some cases lived under bridges. Many had labored in the fields outside of Manila, or fished the bays before leaving for the city. I witnessed extreme hunger in Sapang Palay, Bulacan; Dasmarinas, Cavite; Sucat, Muntinlupa; Taguig, Makati; Cubao, Quezon City; and Davao City. Although there is an abundance of food in the Philippines, millions are going hungry. The International Food Policy Research Institute reports that from 2010 to 2012, undernourished Filipinos accounted for nearly 17 percent of the total population of 92.34 million.[1]

Hunger has profound global impact, and it is not limited to those affected by drought and war in places like Africa. Every being needs to eat, from the simple amoeba and single-cell bacteria to the grey whales and elephants, to the largest redwoods, to millions of humans. While access to nutritious food should be a universal right, economic and political conditions make it nearly impossible for many to find life-sustaining nourishment. I am saddened by the steady increase of Americans who tell me they have not eaten in nearly a week.

Food is so important that many experts believe it was the increased cost of food that sparked the Arab Spring.[2] Millions could relate to Tunisian produce vendor Mohamed Bouazizi, of Sidi Bouzid, when he torched himself out of frustration in December 2010. That crisis started three years before, when a confluence of events made access to food difficult for hundreds of millions of people.

Climate change, commodity speculation, and corporate claims to intellectual property rights united to cause a dramatic increase in the cost of food. The price of staples nearly doubled in 2007.[3] Droughts, floods and other extreme weather events reduced harvests and made cultivation difficult. This is a trend that continues to impact food production. Droughts decimated the harvest of grains and produce in many areas of the world. One of the world's largest wheat exporters, Russia, banned the export of wheat in 2010. Governments often subsidize flour, as in the case of Egypt, in order to reduce popular dissent. Many were forced to increase their prices so dramatically that many of the world's poorest people found themselves paying half their income just to eat.[4] Floods destroyed rice cultivation in Asia, driving up the cost of another staple for billions of people.[5]

Another further issue impacting the price of food was the housing crisis in the United States. When the US housing market crashed, speculators started to invest in the one thing everyone needs—food— at the same time US government policies encouraged an increase in the use of corn ethanol in gasoline. Authors Marco Lagi, Yavni Bar-Yam, Karla Z. Bertrand, and Yaneer Bar-Yam of the New England Complex Systems Institute in Cambridge, Massachusetts, studied the impact of speculation on increased food prices. In their 2011 study called "The Food Crises: A Quantitative Model of Food Prices Including Speculators and Ethanol Conversion," they reported:

> Claims that speculators cannot influence grain prices are shown to be invalid by direct analysis of price setting practices of granaries. Both causes of price increase, speculative investment and ethanol conversion, are promoted by recent regulatory changes—deregulation of the commodity markets, and policies promoting the conversion of corn to ethanol.[6]

Forbes columnist Jesse Colombo noted, "While the late-2008 Global Financial Crisis resulted in a 48% plunge in commodities prices, they staged a quick and powerful recovery, rising 112% from the depths of the crisis to a mid-2011 peak that surpassed the prior 2008 peak by over 10%." For example, corn increased by 348%, wheat by 275%, and oats by 300% from 2001 to 2011, with the sharpest increases following the collapse of the US housing market in 2007 and 2008.[7]

Corporate control of food production is adding to the crisis. Agro-giant Monsanto made the bold move to nearly double the price of some of its key seed and chemical combinations. Other seed companies followed their example. Monsanto states, "Without the ability to patent and profit from our efforts, there would be little incentive to develop the technology that thousands of farmers use today." Monsanto executive Robert Fraley was quoted in *Farm Journal*, "What you're seeing is not just a consolidation of seed companies, it's really a consolidation of the entire food chain."[8]

Philip H. Howard from Michigan State University has written:

> Since the commercialization of transgenic crops in the mid-1990s, the sale of seeds has become dominated globally by Monsanto, DuPont and Syngenta. In addition, the largest firms are increasingly networked through agreements to cross-license transgenic seed traits.[9]

Sadly, instead of helping to end hunger, the food industry is driving farmers off their land. Contracts that force farmers to buy seeds and chemicals every season have forced many into bankruptcy, often causing these proud stewards of the land to kill themselves. I watched one such suicide on September 10, 2003, during a protest against the World Trade Organization. I stood a few yards away from 55-year-old Lee Kyang Hae, the president of South Korea's Federation of Farmers and Fishermen, when he climbed the chain link fence protecting the delegates and stabbed himself to death. Song Nan Sou, president of the Farmers Management Association spoke out, saying, "His death is not a personal accident, but reflects the desperate fighting of 3.5 million Korean farmers."[10]

A March 19, 2014 Associated Press (AP) report claimed that

"More than 100,000 farmers commit suicide in India every year while under insurmountable debts."[11] In 2008, Prince Charles spoke at a Delhi conference, claiming that the issue of genetically modified crops (GM) had become a "global moral question," and denouncing the biotech industry, noting, "the truly appalling and tragic rate of small farmer suicides in India, stemming [...] from the failure of many GM crop varieties."[12]

Andrew Malone wrote about Indian farmers and their struggle to pay for genetically modified (GM) seeds and chemicals in a November 2, 2008 *Daily Mail* article:

> Official figures from the Indian Ministry of Agriculture do indeed confirm that in a huge humanitarian crisis, more than 1,000 farmers kill themselves here each month. Simple, rural people, they are dying slow, agonizing deaths. Most swallow insecticide—a pricey substance they were promised they would not need when they were coerced into growing expensive GM crops.[13]

Ending world hunger is possible. According to the Food and Agriculture Organization, 72% of the food that people eat comes from small farms and gardens.[14] Activists like Vandana Shiva, Raj Patel, and Ronnie Cummins, as well as groups like La Via Campesina, Food Not Lawns, The Cornucopia Institute, Food First!, and the Organic Consumers Association are organizing to increase the percentage of food cultivated by women and independent farmers.

While the focus is mainly on human suffering, all beings may face hunger. Nothing may highlight how circles of compassion are required to sustain our ecosystem more than the universal need for food—from the smallest phytoplankton to the largest whale. Trees need nutrients from soil, and light from the sun. Bacteria need a nutritious host. Livestock can't survive without fresh water, grasses, and grains. You and I also need foods like fruit, vegetables, and grains to survive. A study by scientists at Dalhousie University in Nova

Scotia first published in the July 29, 2010 issue of *Nature,* reported that the global population of phytoplankton has fallen about 40% since 1950.[15] Phytoplankton are at the base of the global food chain, take in carbon dioxide, and produce half the world's oxygen. Along with providing as much oxygen as all the terrestrial plants and trees, phytoplankton feed many animals in our oceans, including whales, small fish, shrimp, zooplankton, and jellyfish who, in turn, provide food for other marine animals. The research suggests that rising sea temperatures are responsible for the steady decline in phytoplankton populations. The US National Oceanic and Atmospheric Administration (NOAA) reports that the oceans are warming. Jay Lawrimore, chief of climate analysis at NOAA's National Climatic Data Center told *Scientific American*, "The global temperature has increased more than 1 degree Fahrenheit [0.7 degree C] since 1900 and the rate of warming since the late 1970s has been about three times greater than the century-scale trend."[16]

Hunger and poverty in Asia and Africa have contributed to the extinction and near extinction of many larger animals. I often saw wild animals for sale on the roads of Nigeria as "bushmeat." Transnational corporations and free-trade policies have encouraged timber harvesting and mining in many wilderness areas, but these wealthy companies often fail to provide adequate income to their workers or local communities, causing people to poach increasing numbers of endangered species. Greater hunger in urban areas has also provided an expanded market for bushmeat, increasing pressure on wildlife. Mining and logging have also destroyed native habitats. One solution suggested by experts with the Bushmeat Crisis Task Force to slow the killing of endangered wildlife is to introduce cattle and other livestock. But this also contributes to deforestation, reducing the natural habitats needed to support native animals. Primatologist Dr. Jane Goodall has spent decades working with apes in Africa. She says, "The bushmeat crisis is the most significant and immediate threat to wildlife populations in Africa today."

The Jane Goodall Institute of Canada reports that over 5 million tons of bushmeat are shipped from the Congo Basin every year.[17] Nearly 300 chimpanzees were slaughtered for bushmeat in The Republic of Congo alone in 2003. The total value of the bushmeat trade around the world is estimated to be worth $1 billion annually.

At the same time that wildlife in the bush is being devastated in West Africa, the fisheries off the coast are also in danger. The United Nations Food and Agriculture Organization notes that all West African fisheries are now over-exploited. Coastal fisheries have declined 50% in the past 30 years, mostly due to over-fishing by industrial fleets based in the European Union, using equipment where each ship is able to net tens of thousands of pounds of fish each day.[18]

Industrial fishing is also driving marine species to extinction. The crisis is not limited to Africa. The British Broadcasting Corporation reported that "Around 85% of global fish stocks are over-exploited, depleted, fully exploited or in recovery from exploitation." Over 400 million people, many living in extreme poverty, depend on fish to survive. Scientists believe fish stocks in tropical seas could be reduced by another 40% by 2050, when millions of more people may be depending on fish for food.[19]

Ironically, human decisions can force animal and plant species to face their own famines, and this, in turn, can cause human populations to face starvation. Rainer H. Brocke, of SUNY College of Environmental Science and Forestry at Syracuse, studied the history of human impacts on wildlife in New York State. His studies showed the impact of public policy on increased deer populations when hunters were paid $20 for each cougar and wolf killed.[20] When the natural predators of the local deer were eliminated, their numbers increased. Local natural resource managers reported that the overpopulation of deer caused over-grazing, and new government policies encouraging the hunting of deer caused their population to crash again. Native people relying on deer for food, clothing, and spiritual well-being saw their sacred animal threatened and, in turn, their economy and faith threatened.

When humans face starvation, wildlife can be threatened with extinction. The Rwandan Civil War caused many to flee their farms and jobs in 1993, causing millions of people to seek food, shelter, and firewood in Virunga National Park in the Democratic Republic of Congo, which was known as Zaire at the time. The deforestation and reliance on wildlife for food threatened many endangered species. Many animals also faced extinction in Akagera National Park in Rwanda, when the Tutsi used the park in their campaign to take over the government. Tutsi leaders implemented a policy of predator eradication to protect their 650,000 to 2 million heads of Ankole cattle.[21]

The history of food austerity is tragic. One of the first recorded human famines started in 408 BC when Alaric I, King of the Visigoths, first blockaded Rome, stopping grain shipments to the city. Widespread famine throughout Europe eventually resulted due to the collapse of the Roman Empire. Political and economic policies are often the root causes of these famines. Drought, floods, and pests would not have caused so much hunger if it were not for decisions made that favored the elite classes. While some famines can be caused by natural events such as volcanoes, droughts, and floods, most of the time people are forced to go hungry because of political or economic policies and calculations.[22]

Africa is the "poster child" of famine, so I have made a point of traveling to the continent to offer assistance with local Food Not Bombs groups. Hunger in Africa is caused by policies that favor corporate profits over democracy and peoples' needs. While descending toward Addis Ababa Bole International Airport, I could see dozens of modern greenhouses on the slopes of Mount Entoto. I soon learned from local human rights activists in Addis Ababa that Dutch Tulip exporters owned many of these greenhouses, and were using Ethiopia's scarce fresh water to grow flowers to sell to Europeans. Local Food Not Bombs volunteers took me to visit the market, as well as the B-class markets to recover produce. They pointed out that the best quality food was exported to the Middle East, China, and Europe. Ethiopians could buy the discarded produce deemed unfit to export. It wasn't long before I saw container loads of Ethiopian vegetables, fruit, grains, meat, and dairy passing through Addis Ababa on its way to cargo jets at the Bole Airport as hungry Ethiopians watched their food pass them on the way to more profitable markets.

On August 17, 2011, World Bank economist Wolfgang Fengler declared, "This [famine] crisis [in Ethiopia] is manmade. Droughts have occurred over and again, but you need bad policymaking for that to lead to a famine."[23] Professor Alemayehu G. Mariam has studied the food crisis in Ethiopia, warning of another famine starting in 2013. In his article on the "Summit on The New Alliance for Food Security and Nutrition" in Chicago where President Barack Obama gave the keynote address, Mariam states:

> The tragic irony is that as millions of Ethiopians starve, Saudi Arabian, Indian agribusinesses commercially farm Ethiopia's most fertile lands to export food to their countries and China stealthily implements its plans for the penetration of Ethiopia's agricultural sector. What a doggone crying shame! So much for 'double digit growth', 'doubling the economy', 'surplus production' and 'three meals a day'![24]

Obama announced on May 18, 2012, at the summit of African leaders from Ghana, Tanzania, Benin, and Ethiopia:

> The New Alliance for Food Security and Nutrition is a shared commitment to achieve sustained and inclusive agricultural growth and raise fifty million people out of poverty over the next ten years by aligning the commitments of Africa's leadership to drive effective country plans and policies for food security; the commitments of private sector partners to increase investments where the conditions are right; and the commitments of the G-8 to expand Africa's potential for rapid and sustainable agricultural growth.[25]

Professor Mariam goes on to say:

To implement the "New Alliance" and spark a Green Revolution in Africa, dozens of global food companies, including multinational giants Cargill, Dupont, Monsanto, Kraft, Unilever, Syngenta AG, have signed a 'Private Sector Declaration of Support for African Agricultural Development.'[26]

His statement echoes the news I heard the day I left Ethiopia. Obama announced that Bill Gates would donate millions of dollars of GMO seeds and chemicals to Ethiopia through the New Alliance for Food Security and Nutrition, coordinated by the Alliance for a Green Revolution in Africa.[27] South African author Raffaella Delle Donne reports:

> The Alliance for a Green Revolution in Africa falls under the Gates Foundation's Global Development Program, whose senior program officer is Dr. Robert Horsch—an employee of biotech giant Monsanto for 25 years and part of a team that developed Roundup Ready GM crops.[28]

One of the most well-documented human famines devastated Ireland, sending tens of thousands to the United States and other former British colonies. The Great Famine is a classic example of a country exporting its food for profit while its people starve. Author Thomas Gallagher notes in his 1982 book, *Paddy's Lament: Ireland 1846-1847—Prelude to Hatred*, that during the first winter of the Irish potato famine in 1846–47, invoices and ships' manifests indicated that landlords exported 17 million pounds sterling worth of grain, cattle, pigs, flour, eggs, and poultry, while as many as 400 thousand Irish peasants starved to death. Gallagher points out a common feature of most famines that "there was an abundance of food produced in Ireland, yet the landlords exported it to markets abroad."[29]

The Great Famine in Ireland had a significant impact for people living in the United States. Millions of Irish moved to the New World, fleeing the famine. Over a million people starved to death from 1845 to 1852. Irish economist Cormac Ó Gráda points out, "Although the potato crop failed, the country was still producing and exporting more than enough grain crops to feed the population. But that was a 'money crop' and not a 'food crop' and could not be interfered with." [30] Lord John Russell came to power proclaiming that the free market would provide food for the Irish. Legislative policies also contributed to the famine. The February 13, 1847 issue of *Illustrated London New* wrote of the landlords, "There was no law it would not pass at their request, and no abuse it would not defend for them." The Acts of Union passed in 1800 set the legal course depriving the Irish of their rights to land. This set in motion a legal structure forcing the poor to work the land for export crops. In 1846, journalist John Mitchel reported that the Irish people were "expecting famine day by day" caused not by "the rule of heaven as to the greedy and cruel policy of England." [31] He also noted that the Irish people "believe that the seasons as they roll are but ministers of England's rapacity; that their starving children cannot sit down to their scanty meal but they see the harpy claw of England in their dish." The people, Mitchel wrote, watched as their "food melting in rottenness off the face of the earth," all the while, watching "heavy-laden ships, freighted with the yellow corn their own hands have sown and reaped, spreading all sail for England." [32] Ireland was but one of many Commonwealth territories to face hunger because England imposed—by law and economic policy—a pattern that continues to this day. We call them "Free Trade Agreements."

Similar to the case leading up to The Great Famine, the United States has now introduced its own "Acts of Union" type laws that are being used all across the country against its own homeless and poor citizens. Laws against sitting in commercial districts, or standing near automatic teller machines and other places of money exchange, criminalize the poor.

A new trend of regulating, and even banning the sharing of free meals in public, is also sweeping the United States with a coordinated nationwide effort to block the return of the Occupy Movement and the growing resistance to corporate exploitation and environmental destruction. Authorities may be worried about the public response to cuts in food stamps, WIC, and unemployment payments. Bans and limits on the sharing of food in public have increased in the past couple of years.

On August 15, 1988, riot police arrested nine Food Not Bombs volunteers for a park infraction that was not related directly to providing free food for the hungry. San Francisco police made over a thousand arrests for sharing meals with the hungry, ending the overt campaign to stop Food Not Bombs in 1997. Since the first arrests in San Francisco, other municipalities have made arrests on occasion. It was not until 2006, when the city of Orlando passed its Large Group Feeding Permit Law Section 18A.09-2, that American cities started to control and ban the sharing of meals with the hungry in earnest. After winning an appeal in the Eleventh Circuit Court of Appeals, the city of Orlando started arresting people for sharing vegan meals with the hungry. Many other cities watched to see if they could successfully implement their own Large Group Feeding laws, but the arrests in Orlando inspired public outrage, and the hacking of tourism and government websites by the hacktivist group "Anonymous."

Unfortunately, with the news that Los Angeles was planning to introduce its version of the law, it became clear that restricting the sharing of meals in public was becoming a nationwide trend. The US Justice Department, with its Community Oriented Policing Program, is one of several national agencies coordinating this campaign to ban feeding hungry people in public. I had learned of the Justice Department's interest in developing policies against "quality-of-life crimes" as far back as 1986 when the Boston Police officials spoke about the "Broken Window" theory at the monthly Kenmore Square Business Association meeting. They stated that retail business was harmed by the presence of homeless people who were ruining the quality of life for the shopping public. The association announced a campaign to drive the homeless and poor out of Kenmore Square so they would not be visible during the American League Play Off games at Fenway Park. The association published a newsletter encouraging merchants to take photos of those appearing unsightly while calling the police to have them removed. Dumpsters were also to be locked so no one could eat out of the trash. A March 1982 article in the *Atlantic Monthly* by social psychologists George L. Kelling of the School of Criminal Justice at Rutgers University and James Q. Wilson at Harvard introduced the idea of zero tolerance for even the smallest possible infractions.[33] On September 18, 2013, Los Angeles City Council members Tom LaBonge and Mitch O'Farrell introduced the Non-Commercial Feeding Motion Resolution 13-1238 before the Council, sending it to the Public Works and Gang Reduction Committee meeting.[34] In the summer and fall of 2013, police in one city after another tried to stop people from sharing food in public. Volunteers were ordered to stop their regular meals in Sacramento, Santa Monica, Chico, Olympia, Seattle, Taos, Boulder, Raleigh, Portland (OR), Saint Louis, Worcester, and Birmingham.

The United Nations World Food Programme (WFP) provides some dire statistics on the number of families and children that are struggling to stave off hunger and malnutrition. They note that 842 million people in the world did not have enough to eat in 2011, 2012, and 2013. They report that this is down 17% from the number of people who were suffering malnutrition in 1990.They also state that "the vast majority of hungry people (827 million) live in developing countries, where 14.3 percent of the population is undernourished." The WFP reports, "Asia has the largest number of hungry people (over 500 million) but Sub-Saharan Africa has the highest prevalence (24.8%of population)." Another shocking statistic in the WFP report says, "If women farmers had the same access to resources as men, the number of hungry in the world could be reduced by up to 150 million." Sadly they also report, "Poor nutrition causes nearly half (45%) of deaths in children under five—3.1 million children each year." Additionally, "66 million primary school-age children attend classes hungry across the developing world, with 23 million in Africa alone." Finally, they claim that only "$3.2 billion US dollars is needed per year to reach all 66 million hungry school-age children."[35]

As dire as conditions are, there are many circles of compassion. Grassroots movements are teaching organic gardening, and are farming vacant lots in cities all over the world. For example, I recently visited organic farms in Addis Ababa, and toured Integrated Biofarm Enterprise, a metropolitan composting project coordinated with the city. I also had the honor of visiting with Dr. Vandana Shiva on several occasions. We first met in Geneva in 1997 at a conference on the formation of a global campaign to stop the World Trade Organization. Dr. Shiva started Navdanya in 1984 in response to the massacres in Punjab and the Bhopal Chemical disaster. Today, it has its own seed bank and organic farm spread over an area of 45 acres in Uttrakhand, North India. Navdanya has conserved more than 5,000 crop varieties, including more than 3,000 types of rice, 150 kinds of wheat, 150 varieties of kidney bean, 15 types of millet, and several varieties of pulses, vegetables, and herbs. It also organizes conferences and protests, and has provided leadership in the effort to protect the biodiversity of the earth.[36] A further example is the Institute for Social Ecology in Vermont, which has been on the forefront of research and implementation of solutions to the ecological crisis and hunger. ISE Director Brian Tokar has written several books on the linkages between human, animal, and environmental justice, including *Toward Climate Justice: Perspectives on the Climate Crisis and Social Change* and *Agriculture and Food in Crisis: Conflict, Crisis, and Renewal*, co-edited with Fred Magdoff.

Back in the late 1990s, a young Food Not Bombs activist in Oregon named Heather Flores lived for a while on a farm near Interstate 5 in the Willamette Valley. I visited her place one rainy afternoon after sharing vegan meals with hungry people in downtown Eugene. She had a seed bank and nearly an acre of vegetables and herbs. She explained that as she was working in the garden, she often noticed trucks loaded with sod driving south toward California. She was alarmed. Oregon was trucking lawns to the desert areas of California, Nevada, and Arizona, while people in Oregon were going hungry. In 1999, Heather talked with the other volunteers of the Eugene

Food Not Bombs and hatched the idea for the first Food Not Lawns community garden. Before long, other Food Not Bombs groups were digging up lawns and vacant lots to start their own Food Not Lawns community gardens. In just a few years, Food Not Lawns activists were inviting local people, who had been depending on Food Not Bombs for meals, to join them in growing their own food. Volunteers are using Heather's book *Food Not Lawns* to help organize their own community gardens.

Urban gardening is becoming popular. In Detroit, for example, Keep Growing Detroit and the Garden Resource Program have transformed the "Auto City" into a garden city. Keep Growing Detroit's website says:

> Urban gardens and farms play an important role in the City of Detroit. They provide hundreds of thousands of pounds of fresh, nutritious fruits and vegetables for families and strengthen our communities by connecting neighbors, providing an attractive alternative to trash-strewn vacant lots, improving property values, and reducing crime.[37]

The movement to slow climate change is also growing. Aboriginal people in Canada started the Idle No More campaign seeking to stop oil and coal extraction while supporting sustainable energy and agriculture. The United Nations has even voiced support for a transition toward a plant-based diet to help reduce the impact on the climate by industrial meat and dairy production.[38]

Efforts to protect and support our animal neighbors continue to increase, as groups such as Farm Animal Rights Movement, The Jane Goodall Institute, International Primate Protection League, Mercy For Animals, A Well-Fed World, Sea Shepherd Conservation Society, Food Empowerment Project, Farm Sanctuary, and many other grassroots organizations take the lead in building a circle of compassion for the animal beings of our world, often by encouraging people to embrace a vegan diet.

The number of groups and projects seeking to end human, plant, and animal hunger is too numerous to name here, but I am sure your heart will lead you to the program that most resonates with you. There is hope. The United Nations Special Rapporteur on the right to food, Olivier De Schutter, gave a presentation on March 10, 2014, at the end of his six-year term, saying:

> The eradication of hunger and malnutrition is an achievable goal. However, it will not be enough to refine the logic of our food systems—it must instead be reversed.... The greatest deficit in the food economy is the democratic one. By harnessing people's knowledge and building their needs and preferences into the design of ambitious food policies at every level, we would arrive at food systems that are built to endure.... Food democracy must start from the bottom up, at the level of villages, regions, cities, and municipalities.[39]

After three decades of collecting, preparing, and sharing free vegan meals with the hungry, I am still moved by how many of us have empty bellies. I am shocked by the number of people that rush up to the Food Not Bombs meal worried we might have run out. It is becoming more and more common for people to say they have not eaten in days. This in the world's wealthiest country. All this suffering can be alleviated not by simply growing more food but by making fundamental changes in our society and economy. By transforming the system that places profit and power over the health of our fellow beings and the environment to one that exists in harmony with all. As overwhelming as the crisis of world hunger is, if each one of us dedicates time, energy, and passion towards making this transition, change is possible. Join your friends and family in providing vegan meals for the hungry, and cultivate vegetables, grains, and fruit for your neighbors. Talk with those you might never otherwise speak with and seek their advice. Think outside the box of convention. Focus on the projects you have passion for and consider dedicating years to seeking the change that most moves you. Persistence, dedication, creativity, and compassion will not only make your own life full but empower you and your community to bring an end to the suffering. The circle of compassion is alive and growing, and you can help by contributing your ideas, time, and enthusiasm. ⊗

Notes

[1] Food and Agriculture Organization of the United Nations (FAO), International Fund for Agricultural Development (IFAD), and World Food Programme (WFP), *The State of Food Insecurity in the World 2012: Economic Growth Is Necessary but Not Sufficient to Accelerate Reduction of Hunger and Malnutrition* (Rome: FAO, 2012), http://www.fao.org/docrep/016/i3027e/i3027e.pdf.

[2] John Vidal, "Climate Change: How a Warming World is a Threat to Our Food Supplies," *The Guardian*, "The Observer," April 13, 2013, http://www.theguardian.com/environment/2013/apr/13/climate-change-threat-food-supplies.

[3] Editorial, "The World Food Crisis," *New York Times*, April 10, 2008, http://www.nytimes.com/2008/04/10/opinion/10thu1.html.

[4] Emad Omar, "Egypt Crisis Threatens Food for Poorest: World Food Programme," *Reuters*, April 11, 2013, http://www.reuters.com/article/2013/04/11/us-egypt-food-idUSBRE93A0WM20130411.

[5] Joanna McCarthy, "Asia's Floods Destroys Harvests, Threatening Food Security," *ABC Radio Australia*, October 6, 2009, http://www.radioaustralia.net.au/international/radio/onairhighlights/asias-floods-destroys-harvests-threatening-food-security.

[6] Marco Lagi, Yavni Bar-Yam, Karla Z. Bertrand, and Yaneer Bar-Yam, "The Food Crises: A Quantitative Model of Food Prices Including Speculators and Ethanol Conversion" (Cambridge, MA: New England Complex Systems Institute, September 11, 2011), http://ssrn.com/abstract=1932247.

[7] Jesse Colombo, "The Commodities Bubble," *The Bubble Bubble*, accessed August 30, 2014, http://www.thebubblebubble.com/commodities-bubble/; Grace Wyler, "Surging Food Prices Are Sparking Riots All Around the World," *Business Insider*, January 11, 2011, http://www.businessinsider.com/food-riots-worldwide-2011-1?op=1.

[8] James Flint, "Agrocultural Industry Giants Moving Towards Genetic Monopolism," *Heise Online*, June 28, 1998, http://www.heise.de/tp/artikel/2/2385/1.html.

[9] P.H. Howard, "Visualizing Consolidation in the Global Seed Industry: 1996-2008" in "Renewable Agriculture," ed. Stephen S. Jones, special issue, *Sustainability* 1, no. 4 (2009): 1266-1287, doi:10.3390/su1041266.

[10] AFP, "Death, Protests as WTO Talks Begin," *Jamaica Observer*, September 11, 2003. http://www.jamaicaobserver.com/news/48813_Death--protests-as-WTO-talks-begin.

[11] Associated Press (AP), "Several Poor Farmers Commit Suicide in India," *Yahoo! News*, March 19, 2014, http://news.yahoo.com/several-poor-farmers-commit-suicide-india-095101966.html.

[12] Andrew Malone, "The GM Genocide: Thousands of Indian Farmers are Committing Suicide After Using Genetically Modified Crops," *Mail Online*, "News," November 2, 2008, http://www.dailymail.co.uk/news/article-1082559/The-GM-genocide-Thousands-Indian-farmers-committing-suicide-using-genetically-modified-crops.html.

[13] Ibid.

[14] Vandana Shiva, "Fortnight of Action for Seed Freedom and Food Freedom: 2nd October–16th October 2013," Seed Freedom, accessed August 30, 2014.

[15] David A. Siegal and Bryan A. Franz, "Oceanography: Century of Phytoplankton Change," *Nature* 466 (2010): 569-571.

[16] Lauren Morello and ClimateWire, "Phytoplankton Population Drops 40 Percent Since 1950," *Scientific American*, July 29, 2010, http://www.scientificamerican.com/article/phytoplankton-population/.

[17] Jane Goodall Institute of Canada, "Conservation & Threats: Bushmeat Crisis," Jane Goodall Institute of Canada, accessed August 30, 2014, http://www.janegoodall.ca/chimps-issuesbushmeat-crisis.php.

[18] Fen Montaigne, "Still Waters: The Global Fish Crisis." *National Geographic*, November 1, 2009, http://ocean.nationalgeographic.com/ocean/global-fish-crisis-article/.

[19] Gaia Vince, "How the World's Oceans Could Be Running Out of Fish," *BBC*, September 21, 2012, http://www.bbc.com/future story/20120920-are-we-running-out-of-fish.

[20] Rainer H. Brocke, *Reintroduction of the Cougar* Felis concolor *in Adirondack Park: A Problem Analysis and Recommendations* (Syracuse, NY: R.H. Brocke, 1981).

[21] T.J. Fewer, "Famines and the Environment: The Case of the Great Irish Famine," personal website, April 14, 1998, http://www.oocities.org/gregory_fewer/envfam.htm (original website on Geocities.com discontinued; mirrored on OoCities.org October 2009).

[22] Peter Garnsey, *Famine and Food Supply in the Graeco-Roman World: Responses to Risk and Crisis* (Cambridge: Cambridge University Press, 1989); Seamus Metress and Richard A. Rajner, *The Great Starvation: An Irish Holocaust* (Stony Point, NY: American Ireland Education Foundation, 1996).

[23] Alemayehu G. Mariam, "Ethiopia: An Early Warning for a Famine in 2013," *Ethiopian Review*, October 7, 2012, http://www.ethiopianreview.com/index/41911.

[24] Alemayehu G. Mariam, "A Glimpse of the Creeping Famine in Ethiopia," *Open Salon*, February 9, 2014, http://open.salon.com/blog/almariam/2014/02/07/a_glimpse_of_the_creeping_famine_in_ethiopia.

[25] Andrew Quinn, "Obama to Unveil Plan for Helping African Farmers," *TheChristian Science Monitor*, May 18, 2012, http://www.csmonitor.com/USA/Latest-News-Wires/2012/0518/Obama-to-unveil-plan-for-helping-African-farmers.

[26] Alemayehu G. Mariam, "Food for Famine and Thought!" *ECADF Ethiopian News & Opinions*, June 4, 2012, http://ecadforum.com/2012/06/04/food-for-famine-and-thought-alemayehu-g-mariam/.

[27] Alexis Baden-Mayer, "Obama Leaves Monsanto in Charge of Ending Hunger in Africa," Organic Consumers Association, May 23, 2012, http://www.organic-consumers.org/articles/article_25508.cfm.

[28] Keffyalew Gebremedhin, "Bill Gates Vows to Defeat Hunger & Diseases in Ethiopia: Could Entrenched Political Interests Allow Him? - PART IV," *Abugida Info*, May 6, 2012, http://www.abugidainfo.com/index.php/20238/.

[29] Thomas Gallagher, *Paddy's Lament: Ireland 1846-1847—Prelude to Hatred* (New York: Harcourt Brace, 1982).

[30] Cormac Ó Gráda, *Ireland Before and After the Famine: Explorations in Economic History, 1800-1925* (Manchester: Manchester University Press, 1994).

[31] Chris Morash and Richard Hayes, ed, *"Fearful Realities": New Perspectives on the Famine* (Blackrock, Co. Dublin: Irish Academic Press, 2000).

[32] John Mitchel, "English Rule," *The Nation*, March 7, 1846.

[33] George L. Kelling and James Q. Wilson, "Broken Windows," *The Atlantic*, March 1, 1982, http://www.theatlantic.com/magazine/archive/1982/03/broken-windows/304465/.

[34] Dan Bluemel, "Homeless Advocates Fear City Hall is Gunning for Food Charities Again," *L.A. Activist*, November 3, 2013, http://www.laactivist.com/2013/11/03/homeless-advocates-fear-city-hall-is-gunning-for-food-charities-again/.

[35] "Hunger Statistics," World Food Programme, accessed August 16, 2014, http://www.wfp.org/hunger/stats; FAO, IFAD, and WFP, *The State of Food Insecurity in the World 2013: The Multiple Dimensions of Food Security* (Rome: FAO, 2013), http://www.fao.org/docrep/018/i3434e/i3434e.pdf.

[36] Vandana Shiva, Ruchi Shroff, and Caroline Lockhart, comp., *Seed Freedom: A Global Citizens' Report* (New Delhi: Navdanya, 2012), http://www.groundswellinternational.org/wpcontent/uploads/Seed-Freedom-A-Global-Citizens-Report.pdf.

[37] Keep Growing Detroit, "Garden Resource Program." Cultivating a Food Sovereign Detroit, accessed August 30, 2014, http://detroitagriculture.net/garden-resource-program2/garden-resource-program/.

[38] Felicity Carus, "UN Urges Global Move to Meat and Dairy-Free Diet," *The Guardian*, June 2, 2010, http://www.theguardian.com/environment/2010/jun/02/un-report-meat-free-diet.

[39] "Democracy and Diversity Can Mend Broken Food Systems - Final Diagnosis from UN Right to Food Expert," Olivier De Schutter: UN Special Rapporteur 2008-2014, March 10, 2014, http://www.srfood.org/en/democracy-and-diversity-can-mend-broken-food-systems-final-diagnosis-from-un-right-to-food-expert.

Slavery. It's Still a Thing.

by Christopher-Sebastian McJetters

Hey, everyone. I'm a black guy! I know it's probably obvious to some of you when you look at me. But some people don't see race. So I have to make it clear. Otherwise, this fact will escape them entirely.

Very recently, I rounded up a group of people and asked them a simple question: "Why do we consume animals?" The responses were as simple and concise as the question itself:

"Because I like it."

"They're not like us."

"We're just superior."

"We have higher intelligence."

"It's perfectly natural."

"God put them here for us."

"We're more important."

"They don't feel pain the same way we do."

"It's just an animal."

"They don't reason or have complex emotions."

"Because we can."

"I NEED to."

"I was raised on a farm. Nothing wrong with it. We've done it for generations."

Okay, great! Second question then: "Why don't we reinstitute slavery in the United States?"

SLAVERY?!

I always want to have a camera to record the expressions when I ask that question. Let's think about it though. Are not all of these justifications the same ones that pre-Civil War Americans used to justify keeping African slaves?

Uh oh. Battle stations, everyone. I could almost see the mental wagons starting to circle. More than half of these people were Afro-American, and they were having none of my foolishness. Not even a little bit of it. But it wasn't just the blacks. The white people in the group were looking uncomfortable too. The expression on their faces was priceless. Hoodwinked! I'd drawn these two disparate groups into a subject that dare not speak its name.

There was so much fidgeting in the room that I could no longer tell if we were having a discussion or if we had declared an impromptu interpretive dance.

This response is not uncommon. I'm used to it; American slavery is the elephant in the room. However, constructive dialogue is the only way we can ever heal systemic injustice. Ignoring it only serves to perpetuate the oppression. But this goes deeper than American slavery. It's about the mindset that allowed American slavery to take root at all. At least everyone in the room could agree upon the fact that white folks should no longer be making black folks pick their cotton. Unfortunately, we seem to be perfectly comfortable with the captive breeding, torture, forced labor, and killing of others right now. But why?

If I were having this conversation 200 years ago with a white person about owning black people, I would be met with the same level of skepticism. Actually, no...this conversation would not have happened at all 200 years ago because I would be far too busy singing negro spirituals and shucking corn to articulate a position. But you get the picture. Why does one form of slavery get a pass, while we recognize the obvious violation of the other? And why do we get so doggone angry and uncomfortable when we identify these parallels?

Let's take a moment to unpack some of our prejudices against others. Let's look at some of the common visceral reactions experienced by people of color when discussing oppression. Let's push past our current perceptions, and put ourselves in the place of the victims rather than the established system that advantages us.

How dare you compare black people and animals? Those two groups are nothing alike!

Allow me to make a point of clarification. Humans *are* animals. Whether or not you believe that we are conceived from a common ancestor with bonobos, we don't exist *outside* of the animal kingdom. So it's important to deconstruct the narrative that pits "us" against "them." Also, let's listen to the correct part of the conversation. This is not a comparison of human animals to nonhuman animals. This is a comparison of like systems of oppression. Whether talking about white humans and brown ones or horses and pigs, slavery is an abuse of power. That's what we're here to examine.

I wish you would stop saying slavery. It's not the same thing.

Language is important. The very definition of slavery is the treatment of one group as property to be bought, sold, and forced into work by another group. If nonhuman animals are not slaves, are they then free? There are not many animals I know of that exist within human society who voluntarily engaged in this system. Cows do not clock in and clock out. They don't go home to their families. They don't have conversations in the lunchroom. And the only retirement package available to them at the end of their painful lives is a violent death when their usefulness to us has run out.

Of course, coming to terms with the sobering reality of slavery is probably the most difficult mental hurdle to overcome when having these discussions. Because if we are forced to acknowledge that slavery is wrong and that nonhumans are slaves, then we have a moral obligation to talk about abolition. The repercussions for our economic structure and, indeed, our way of life could be devastating. But I imagine it wasn't easy for pre-Civil War Americans either.

I'm not a bad person. Are you calling me a slave owner?
In America's historic narrative, it's easy to paint slave owners as villains, and abolitionists as heroes. But slave owners were not all bad people. Likewise, racists are not all bad people. Racism and slavery are constructs that make otherwise good people engage in really bad behavior. Unfortunately, we were all born into this construct that privileges some of us over others. The key is to *unlearn* the conditioning that teaches us that any form of oppression is okay.

But comparing black ancestors to pigs is insulting and degrading, and it trivializes the oppression they went through.
Say it with me now—*a comparison between like systems of oppression is not a comparison between two species of animal.* But even if we were comparing marginalized groups of humans and nonhumans, why do we find that offensive? At the root, most of us are insulted because we feel like we're better than another group based on physical distinctions. This is discrimination. When one group of humans does it to another group of humans, we call it racism. When humans do it to nonhumans, this is called speciesism.

Any criteria we use to establish dominance over or to except another group is discriminatory. See, the yardstick used to measure differences between "us and them" is always going to start "us" off at one-and-a-half inches. And a house built with false measurements is destined to fall down. The very act of seeking to point out our differences in a society is a rigged system designed by its very nature to determine who is better. Throughout American history, blacks have always found themselves the victims of a hierarchy that inherently favors whites. To that end, nonhumans throughout the *whole* of history have suffered the same fate, and still do today with no end in sight.

Well, what black people have suffered is far worse.

This is all a matter of perspective, isn't it? From the standpoint of the victim, one could argue that what is happening to nonhumans is actually much worse. During the 18th and 19th centuries, approximately 12.5 million Africans were shipped to the New World. Nearly 10 *billion* land animals alone are killed each year to produce meat, dairy, and eggs. And that's just in the United States. That number increases to 65 billion globally (or 6 million every hour).[1] So strictly by numbers, nonhumans have Africans beat. It could also be argued that since this exploitation existed prior to the African slave trade and still exists now, it's an aggression that deserves strong consideration.

But where is the value in tallying up who has suffered the greater injustice? Why should we choose to take on the narrative that one group has been more deeply aggrieved than another? Establishing a hierarchy of oppression only serves to help the oppressor. The better narrative—the stronger narrative—is in choosing to seek freedom for everyone. Otherwise, we're only fighting for the right to oppress someone else. Solidarity is the key to establishing equality. Division only perpetuates more tyranny.

This is all well and good, but consuming animals is a personal choice. You're forcing your beliefs on me.

Again, this is a matter of perspective. We should take a sober look at the kind of aggressions that are being perpetrated against nonhumans. Their exploitation is so complete that it's nearly invisible. Yes, they are our food. But they are also our wool sweaters, our leather shoes, our shampoo, our streets, our electronics, and even our home décor. Can we honestly say that it is our personal choice to take away the agency and sovereignty of someone else while simultaneously saying that American slavery was wrong? If holding up a mirror to expose our complicity in structural inequality toward nonhumans is forcing beliefs, then so too did abolitionists force their beliefs on Americans to end the exploitation of black people.

I'm scared.

So am I. It takes a lot of work to unlearn a lifetime of conditioning that privileges certain groups. It's equally scary when black people have discussions with white people involving race. But even though it makes us uncomfortable, it's necessary. When we can adequately understand the space occupied by both those who benefit from privilege and those who are oppressed by it, we build a bridge that can liberate us from such inequality altogether. That's why slavery matters to *all* of us. Regardless of our racial background, everyone is complicit in this system of persecution against nonhuman animals. And until we are truly present to the impact of harming the most vulnerable among us, we won't be able to deconstruct how to stop doing harm to one another.

So how did this exchange end with all these nervous people desperate to distance themselves from their participation in slavery? Same as it always does. We got angry. We got sad. We placed blame. And then something amazing happened. We took responsibility. Did all of these people walk away choosing instantly to let go of their speciesism? No. But every one of them is now more aware. And raising awareness is where it all begins.

Racism hasn't entirely been eradicated either. Fortunately, far fewer people exercise that choice. So we have these conversations. And we don't give up. ☙

Notes

[1] "Animal Death Statistics 2011," Farm Animal Rights Movement, accessed July 28, 2014, http://farmusa.org/statistics11.html.

Hunger, Meat, and the Banality of Evil

by Dawn Moncrief

Introduction — Making the Connection

Global hunger and the use of animals for food are distinct yet inter-connected forms of institutionalized injustice at the root of some of the world's most severe and persistent suffering. They are also related in tangible, sometimes counterintuitive, ways in that the vast and increasing worldwide consumption of animal-derived foods adversely impacts broader hunger alleviation and food security efforts.

For years, influential think tanks such as the International Food Policy Research Institute (IFPRI) have widely acknowledged the dangers of the world's growing appetite for animal-derived foods. In 1999, they coined the term "Livestock Revolution" in their report "Livestock to 2020: The Next Food Revolution" to describe the causes and consequences of the unprecedented increases in global meat[1] consumption, specifically increases stemming from lower- and middle-income countries.[2]

Unfortunately, as is too often the case, IFPRI did not include reducing meat consumption as part of their recommendations. Despite their research implicating the "livestock sector" as a major driver of food insecurity and natural resource depletion, they discounted efforts to reverse the trend because meat consumption was deemed to be a "demand-driven" cultural given. They contended, "It is unwise to think that the Livestock Revolution will somehow go away in response to moral suasion by well-meaning development partners. It is a structural phenomenon that is here to stay."[3]

I credit the *Livestock to 2020* report—and subsequent reports from other leading authorities that are dire in their predictions about the high costs of animal agriculture, but exclude meat reductionist measures in their recommendations—with inspiring my work to connect the dots, thereby reducing both hunger and animal consumption. I am also particularly interested in counterbalancing the disproportionate focus on the *aggregate growth totals* of meat consumption in "developing" countries, to the neglect of the much greater *existing per capita* meat consumption in "developed" countries. This unbalanced focus limits success and does not appropriately challenge the attitudes and behaviors of powerful, high-consuming individuals and countries—most notably, those making the policy recommendations.

While endorsements for reducing global meat consumption are gaining favor in some circles, the push to readily meet the rising demand for animal products is still pervasive. My goal is to increase awareness about the benefits of minimizing animal consumption so that it becomes a priority on the agendas of social justice advocates, formal and informal policymakers, thought leaders, and conscience-driven individuals with the privilege and ability to be agents of change in their own spheres.

To this end, I founded A Well-Fed World, a Washington, DC-based nonprofit organization with the dual mission to feed people and save animals. In addition to our advocacy efforts, A Well-Fed World partners with and financially strengthens plant-based food and farming programs, especially in low-income countries. We also provide support to farm animal care and rescue groups. These hands-on projects provide immediate assistance to people and animals in need, as a complement to our broader work for long-term, structural change.

This essay builds on that program base and more than 15 years of research to provide a glimpse into some of the ways in which meat exacerbates hunger by redistributing food away from the poorest of the poor. It also exposes the horrific standard "farming" practices used to produce meat, dairy, and eggs. Finally, it connects hunger and meat as systems of oppression that normalize atrocities, thereby desensitizing people and bolstering other forms of systemic violence and injustice.

Immense Suffering—Counting Victims

For sheer scale of global suffering, few things rival the immense, unnecessary, and unconscionable suffering of people hungry from lack of food, or of animals used and abused for food. Yet despite their severity and pervasiveness, efforts to alleviate global hunger lack sufficient urgency and priority, while the tragic plight of animals used for food barely registers on global agendas.

Of the world's more than seven billion people, more than 840 million are *counted* as suffering from chronic hunger. [4] While shockingly high, this is actually a conservative estimate based on strict criteria that assumes a "sedentary" lifestyle combined with prolonged caloric deficiency lasting more than a year. The number of people officially counted as hungry can more than double when "normal" and "intense" levels of activity are intermixed with the calculations. [5] The numbers of undernourished, food-insecure people increases further still when intermittent food shortages and nutritional intake are considered.

Children suffer the most severe consequences of our broken food system, with more than 6,000 dying every day of malnutrition and hunger-related causes. [6] With more than 250 children dying *every hour*, why is it so rare that global hunger makes the nightly news? In part, it's because such extreme and widespread hunger and death are the norm. In part, it's not on the news because it's not "new."

For animals, the numbers are even more mind-numbing. Between 65 and 70 billion land animals are raised and killed for food annually. [7] That's a staggering increase from the year 2000 when the death toll was 50 billion, and these numbers are expected to fully double from 50 billion to 100 billion by 2050. [8] These figures do not include aquatic animals killed in food production, whose numbers are counted in the trillions. [9] Also excluded are the millions of wildlife who are exterminated because they are considered predators or pests to agribusiness operations.

For perspective, 65 billion animals a year means more than 178 million land animals (mostly chickens, turkeys, pigs, and cows) who die in our global food production system every day. That's more than 7.4 million (7,400,000) animals every hour...more than 123,000 every minute...more than 2,000 every second. As some of the world's top per capita meat consumers, Americans are responsible for the deaths of more than 9 billion farmed animals a year.[10] That's more than 24 million food-related animal deaths every day in the US alone...more than 1 million every hour...more than 16,500 every minute...more than 275 every second.

The Injustice of Hunger — The Suffering of People

With respect to the billions of people and animals suffering as a direct result of our food production system, it is human action, intention, and lack of necessity that solidify these tragedies as injustice. Suffering in itself is not injustice. Similarly, harm is not necessarily violence. Accidents happen. Natural disasters and diseases happen. It is the choice to participate in systems that inflict unnecessary harm that constitutes violence and injustice.

Gandhi brought widespread attention to conceptualizing hunger and poverty as forms of violence. While less obvious than physical acts of violence, hunger is not merely the result of bad fortune and inadequate assistance. Hunger is also the consequence of an unjust, often corrupt, food system that allows profits to trump need, and rewards the powerful for exploiting the vulnerable.

To better understand hunger as violence, consider that the pain imposed by hunger is constant and unrelenting—physically, mentally, and emotionally. Imagine the incessant, gnawing ache of never having enough food. Imagine the need to ration those small amounts of food that do become available, then having to decide who in your family receives a particular share. Perhaps most heartbreaking—and something few of us could even begin to imagine—is the despair of watching helplessly as our children wither away because we can't feed them enough food or the right kinds of food.

Hunger is also a form of structural violence that tears through societies, destroying lives and debilitating countries. Undernourished adults and children suffer poor health, low energy levels, and a reduced ability to concentrate. This makes it all the more difficult to work the arduous hours that are often required for mere survival. For children fortunate enough to attend school, their learning is severely impaired. As food and social justice author Frances Moore Lappé explains, hunger does not even need to be chronic to have devastating generational consequences. She notes, "even short-term nutritional deficits, particularly if occurring in the first 1,000 days of life, can negatively affect health, learning, and income over one's lifetime, and even affect one's offspring."[11]

The Injustice of Meat—The Suffering of Animals

In 1963, social and political philosopher Hannah Arendt famously theorized "the banality of evil."[12] She surmised that the greatest atrocities in history are perpetrated not by monsters, but by ordinary citizens who passively accept the status quo, even when the attitudes, practices, and policies are unspeakably heinous. These atrocities persist when everyday people participate in them because "that's just the way things are done."

For contemporary examples of what Arendt termed "normalized atrocities" and "routinized violence," it would be difficult to find a category of suffering either more extreme or more commonplace than that endured by animals used in the production of meat, dairy, and eggs. As feminist and animal advocate Carol Adams explains, "Whereas women may feel like pieces of meat, and be treated like pieces of meat—emotionally butchered and physically battered—animals actually are made into pieces of meat."[13]

The cruelty becomes even more stark when juxtaposed against the peaceful nature of farmed animals. Nineteenth century essayist Thomas DeQuincey eloquently observed that "cows are amongst the gentlest of breathing creatures; none show more passionate tenderness to their young when deprived of them." Yet cows and other farmed animals endure a nonstop cycle of forced pregnancy and birth, followed by the harsh, unnatural loss of their offspring. Indeed, the exploitation of motherhood is fundamental to animal agriculture.

A dairy cow, like any mother, doesn't just spontaneously produce milk. She produces milk for her newborn calf. So to continuously produce milk for human consumption, she must be repeatedly impregnated, usually once a year for about five years. Like humans, a cow's gestation period is nine months. After a long pregnancy and a painful birth, her calf is permanently taken from her, usually within 24 hours. If the calf is female, she is doomed to the same fate as her mother. Or if not needed on the dairy, she is slaughtered for veal or cheap beef like the male calves.[14] This is the suffering in a glass of milk.

A breeding pig is likely to spend most of her life in metal crates so small that she literally cannot turn around. While gestation crates (at only 2 feet wide and 7 feet long) are now illegal in four states, they are still the most common "housing" method. A pig's gestation period is just under four months. After giving birth, she is locked immobile in a farrowing crate for three to four weeks. Her piglets are deprived of maternal comfort as they nurse through metal bars. After three or four years of this miserable cycle, she is slaughtered.[15] This is the suffering in a slice of bacon.

An egg-laying battery hen spends her 18–24 months of life crammed into a small wire cage with four to ten other hens. This leaves each bird with less than a sheet of paper's worth of space. None of them can even spread their wings. Thousands of wire cages are stacked on top of each other in huge sheds without adequate ventilation or sunlight. To reduce the severe harm caused by stress-induced pecking at each other, the tips of their sensitive beaks are seared or sliced off without pain relief.[16] This is the suffering in an egg.

Further harm from egg production extends to the male chicks. As valueless "by-products" who won't produce eggs or grow as large as chickens bred for meat, they are typically disposed of as newborns. Each year, more than 250 million male chicks are killed in the United States alone. That's more than 600,000 every day, more than 25,000 every hour. These baby birds are literally thrown away in dumpsters to suffocate on top of each other, poisoned with gas, electrified on "kill plates," or ground alive in industrial macerators.[17] Imagine the horror and public outcry if these were puppies or kittens.

Regardless of farm size or ownership type, intensive production methods are nearly universal in the United States and many of these cruel practices are standard operating procedures.[18] Agribusinesses have usurped and greenwashed terms like "humane," "free-range," and "family farm," but humane labels are riddled with loopholes that still allow many of the worst factory farming cruelties.[19] Such everyday practices include castration, dehorning, debeaking, tail-docking, and branding—all without pain relief. Severe confinement and crowding are also routine. Ultimately, regardless of which type of food product or which production process, the animals face a gruesome slaughter-house end—generally hung upside down by their feet to have their throats slit.[20] This is the suffering in using animals for food.

Tangible Connections — The Inefficiency of Meat

Overwhelmingly, it is not the case that we must choose between feeding people or saving animals. On the contrary, animal consumption is generally a matter of preference based on factors such as habit, acquired taste, convenience, and custom. It is important to distinguish eating meat for survival from eating meat for preference. This is especially relevant as the former is often used to justify the latter, even when healthful plant-based options are abundant.

There are many tangible ways in which the production and consumption of animal-based foods negatively impact global hunger and food security. For our purposes here, we'll focus on meat consumption for preference, especially among wealthy and high-consuming populations. We'll also focus on one of the most obvious ways in which meat consumption contributes to global hunger—the inefficiency of using animals as food.[21]

Simply put, animals eat much more food than they produce. Most of the caloric energy they consume is used to fuel their metabolism and to form bones, cartilage, feathers, fluids, and other non-edible parts.[22] As such, animals raised for food take more from the global food supply than they provide. Even meat proponents acknowledge many of the inefficiencies inherent in cycling plant-based feed crops through animals to produce animal-based foods.[23]

Compared to consuming plant-based foods directly, eating crop-fed animals yields only a small fraction of the total available calories *and* protein.[24] Raising animals for food is thus not only resource-intensive—requiring massive amounts of land, water, and energy—it is also specifically crop-intensive, requiring far more crops than would be needed to feed people directly.

A recent scientific report, "Redefining Agricultural Yields: From Tonnes to People Nourished Per Hectare," found that existing crop-lands could feed up to four billion more people globally. The analysis specified that by reallocating crops used for animal feed and biofuels toward direct human consumption, the availability of global food calories could be increased by as much as 70%.[25] With this, we see not only the magnitude of food that could be conserved, but also a path with which we could feed far more people, while harming far fewer animals. Coincidently, 70% more food is also the amount researchers predict will be needed to feed our expected population of more than nine billion people in 2050.[26]

Obviously, hunger is a deep-seated and extraordinarily complex problem. The point is not that eliminating animal-based food production and consumption will *solve* world hunger. The point is that any viable strategy to provide meaningful, long-lasting hunger solutions and improve global food security must include reducing animal-based food consumption as an essential part of the equation.

Supply and Demand—Outbidding the Poor

Beyond its negative impact on crop use, resource use, and other environmental concerns, let's consider how meat consumption affects supply and demand, and how supply and demand affects food prices and food availability.[27]

Because farmed animals consume massive amounts of crops, the global demand for food crops is high. High/increasing demand relative to supply increases food prices, thus decreasing purchasing power. A counterargument can made for technology increasing food yields, but resource limitations, population growth, climate change, and biofuel competition are grave threats likely to tighten future food supply beyond the scope of tech-driven yield increases. As such, high demand for animal feed crops puts upward pressure on global food prices, as those who can pay more for food, feed, and fuel crops outbid those who cannot even afford their basic food requirements.[28]

We saw this play out during the 2007–2008 food crisis in which the increased use of biofuels is considered a leading contributor.[29] Growth in the biofuel sector increased global demand for food crops, which elevated food prices. The wealthy paid high prices to purchase tremendous amounts of extra crops for animal feed and biofuel. In doing so, we outbid the poor for even their basic food needs. In a system where having enough food is deeply dependent on income, higher prices drove access to food out of the reach of the poor, resulting in skyrocketing malnutrition, hunger, starvation, and death.

While there are perilous trade-offs related to *fuel vs. food*, a more serious concern for a variety of reasons is *feed vs. food*. With 75% of all agricultural land used for animal production—and more than a third of global calories and half of global protein inefficiently used as animal feed[30]—the impact of increasing or decreasing global meat consumption is monumental even outside of price fluctuations.

Meat as Overconsumption, Redistribution, and Waste

To the extent that meat requires more calories and resources to produce than plant-based foods of equal or superior nutritional value, meat can be considered a form of overconsumption. Similarly, to the extent that vast amounts of food are diverted away from feeding people directly, meat can be considered a form of redistribution.

To provide some perspective of the scale at which meat is a form of overconsumption, commonly cited Feed Conversion Ratios (FCRs)[31] for beef cows range between 6:1[32] and 16:1.[33] These FCRs indicate that cows consume 6–16 pounds of feed crops for every pound of weight gained or pound of ready-to-eat meat produced. There are many factors to consider in determining specific conversion ratios.[34] Smaller ratios often refer to the live weight gain of the animals. Larger ratios more accurately represent inefficiencies based on edible meat after slaughter and processing.[35]

Yet, even the high-end of these commonly cited FCRs are conservative based on newer, more comprehensive calculation methods that have been recently published. According to the World Resources Institute (in conjunction with the United Nations and World Bank), "even poultry, the most efficient source of meat, convert only around 11 percent of gross feed energy into human food."[36] And it's not a matter of "trading-up" carbohydrate-based grain for protein-based meat. In terms of protein, eating animals is also a highly inefficient net loss.[37] This is why even a small amount of meat can be an overconsumption that draws unevenly or unfairly from the global food supply.

To illustrate the concept of meat as a form of overconsumption, let's say that the production of a 100-calorie hamburger patty requires 1,000 calories of crops used for animal feed (assuming a conservative 10:1 ratio). As such, the 100-calorie hamburger patty can be seen as an overconsumption of 900 calories. Over the course of a day, 2,000 calories consumed from an animal-inclusive diet could easily carry a global cost in excess of 5,000 calories. Multiply this by two or three billion of the world's heaviest meat consumers, and the result is a massive redistribution of calories within the global food system.

So, while there may be technically enough calories produced to feed the world's current population—about 2,800 daily calories per person,[38] with caloric need for normal activity ranging between 1,800 and 2,800[39]—the high demand for animal-derived foods distributes crops in ways that exacerbate regional disparities. Regional food disparities are sometimes missed from a global perspective, but despite significant macroeconomic improvements between 1990 to 2012, the 45 "least-developed countries" have almost 60 million more undernourished people suffering from extreme caloric deficiencies in both quantity and quality.[40]

Such food disparities, and hunger more generally, are likely to worsen as our population expands, diets become more animal-centric, natural resources dwindle, and climate disruptions intensify. If, however, those of us in wealthy, high-consuming countries, and the high-consuming sectors of low- and middle-income countries, reduce (or better yet eliminate) our meat consumption, we could greatly reduce our enormous "foodprint" to help reverse these trends.

Finally, let's consider the recent push to reduce consumer food waste in high-income countries as a means of increasing food availability for the world's poor.[41] To the extent that reducing food waste in high-income countries is important, then reducing crop-intensive meat consumption is even more pressing for the same reasons of conserving global food and environmental resources. Similar to the ways in which meat is a form of overconsumption and redistribution, it is also a form of food waste. Couple its inherent feed-to-food inefficiency with its highly perishable nature, and meat can easily be considered a "multiplier form of food waste."

Focusing on reducing food waste is important, but it is popular in part because it allows people to express their altruism without calling into question deeper issues of justice or threatening the basic tenets of our longstanding abuse of animals for food. As a standalone issue, it's just not asking much of people to eat leftovers and ugly produce. Reducing food waste has great potential benefit, but given the magnitude of threats to global hunger and food security, it needs to be implemented in addition to minimizing animal consumption, not instead of it.

Conclusion—Normalizing Justice and Compassion

More attention and details have been provided here about animal suffering relative to human suffering because even though our efforts to reduce world hunger are inadequate, at least it is widely accepted that hunger is a tragedy. With regards to animals, however, meat consumption is encouraged and celebrated, while the cruelty is defended and denied.

The casual killing and near universal consumption of animals by billions of people around the world continuously reinforces and normalizes the atrocities we commit against them. Justice, compassion, and global well-being would be dramatically increased by conceptually reframing meat away from something that is sought after to something that is shunned.

When we ignore or justify the routine horrors of animal farming and slaughter, we are complicit. Even if we are emotionally distressed by and opposed to the suffering of animals, our compassion and empathy are diminished by our active participation as we purchase the products that perpetuate the abuse. While we may be able to suppress our empathy and fragment our compassion to a degree, the process of normalizing one type of atrocity bolsters the routinization of injustice and violence more generally.

Fortunately, the reverse is also true. What we choose to eat can instead reinforce and normalize justice and compassion. Our food choices are influential beyond the individual resources we conserve and animals we spare. Research has shown that a minority opinion can reach a "tipping point" when just 10% of a population adopts it.[42] After that, an idea can speed through society and create widespread behavioral change. The choices we make about our food can bring us closer to such a tipping point by popularizing plant-based foods among our friends, families, social institutions, and increasingly businesses and political decision-makers.

In this way, plant-based food choices and plant-friendly food policies become normalized. This increases plant-based food accessibility and desirability, which then creates a positive feedback loop capable of reinforcing itself up to and beyond progressively beneficial tipping points. The ripple effect of popularizing plant-based foods and reducing pro-meat biases can also create sweeping improvements on a global level, especially when new attitudes, policies, and priorities are adopted and promoted by nations with substantial amounts of power and influence.

Social justice cannot exist without food justice. The world is full of abuses beyond our control, but the immense, unnecessary, and unconscionable suffering of people and animals that results from our food system is something that we *can* positively affect by making better food choices.

If we want to reduce hunger, conserve natural resources, and mitigate climate change, removing animal products from our shopping carts is a powerful step we should take. If we want to end atrocities committed against animals, removing animal products from our shopping carts is an essential step we must take. If we are in leadership positions, prioritizing a shift away from animal-based foods through advocacy, policy, and personal example moves us toward the structural changes and tipping points necessary for widespread social justice.

Change is challenging, but it is important that we shift from compassion as a *feeling* to compassion as *action*. With power and privilege come ability and responsibility. For reasons of both justice and practicality, it is imperative that we acknowledge the ways in which our meat-centric consumption and meat-biased policies contribute to world problems. Abstaining from animal consumption is not a panacea, but it is a fundamental part of the social justice web, and a concrete way we can remove the most immediate, violent, and unjust actions from our daily lives. 🐾

[1] The term "meat" is sometimes used here as shorthand for animal-derived foods: meat, dairy, and eggs.

[2] Christopher Delgado, Mark Rosegrant, Henning Steinfeld, Simeon Ehui, and Claude Courbis, *Livestock to 2020: The Next Food Revolution*, Food, Agriculture, and the Environment Discussion Paper 28 (Washington, DC: International Food Policy Research Institute [IFPRI]; Rome: Food and Agricultural Organization of the United Nations [FAO]; Nairobi: International Livestock Research Institute [ILRI], 1999), http://www.ifpri.org/sites/default/files/publications/pubs_2020_dp_dp28.pdf.

[3] Ibid., 65.

[4] FAO, International Fund for Agricultural Development (IFAD), and World Food Programme (WFP), *The State of Food Insecurity in the World 2013: The Multiple Dimensions of Food Security* (Rome: FAO, 2013), 8, www.fao.org/docrep/018/i3434e/i3434e.pdf.

[5] FAO, IFAD, and WFP, *The State of Food Insecurity in the World 2012: Economic Growth Is Necessary but Not Sufficient to Accelerate Reduction of Hunger and Malnutrition* (Rome: FAO, 2012), 55, http://www.fao.org/docrep/016/i3027e/i3027e.pdf.

[6] Enough Food for Everyone IF, *The Need for UK Action on Global Hunger*, January 23, 2013, 6, www.enoughfoodif.org/sites/default/files/IF_policy_report.pdf.

[7] Compassion in World Farming, Strategic Plan 2013-2017: For Kinder, Fairer Farming Worldwide, 2013, 3, www.ciwf.org.uk/includes/documents/cm_docs/2013/c/ciwf_strategic_plan_20132017.pdf.

[8] Henning Steinfeld, Pierre Gerber, Tom Wassenaar, Vincent Castel, Mauricio Rosales, and Cees de Haan, *Livestock's Long Shadow: Environmental Issues and Options.* (Rome: FAO, 2006), XX, ftp://ftp.fao.org/docrep/fao/010/a0701e/a0701e.pdf.

[9] "Overview," Fish Feel, accessed 2014, http://www.fishfeel.org/.

[10] "Farm Animal Statistics Slaughter Total for 2013," The Humane Society of the United States (HSUS), accessed 2014, http://www.humanesociety.org/news/resources/research/stats_slaughter_totals.html.

[11] Frances Moore Lappé, Jennifer Clapp, Molly Anderson, Robin Broad, Ellen Messer, Thomas Pogge and Timothy Wise, "How We Count Hunger Matters," *Ethics & International Affairs*, 27, no. 3 (2013): 3, http://dx.doi.org/10.1017/S0892679413000191.

[12] Hannah Arendt, *Eichmann in Jerusalem: A Report on the Banality of Evil* (NY: The Viking Press, 1963).

[13] Carol Adams, *The Sexual Politics of Meat: A Feminist-Vegetarian Critical Theory* (NY: Continuum Press, 1990), 46.

[14] "The Welfare of Cows in the Dairy Industry," HSUS, accessed 2014, http://www.humanesociety.org/assets/pdfs/farm/hsus-the-welfare-of-cows-in-the-dairy-industry.pdf.

[15] "The Welfare of Breeding Sows," HSUS, accessed 2014, http://www.humanesociety.org/assets/pdfs/farm/welfare_breeding_sows.pdf.

[16] "The Welfare of Animals in the Egg Industry," HSUS, accessed 2014, http://www.humanesociety.org/assets/pdfs/farm/welfare_egg.pdf.

[17] Ibid.

[18] "Factory Farming," Farm Forward, accessed 2014, www.farmforward.com/farming-forward/factory-farming.

[19] "Labels and Loopholes," Humane Facts, accessed 2014, http://www.humane-facts.org/labels-loopholes.

[20] L.A.H.M. Verheijen, D. Wiersema, L.W. Hulshoff Pol, and J. De Wit International Agriculture Centre, "Slaughterhouses," *Management of Waste from Animal Product Processing* (Wageningen, The Netherlands: FAO, 1996), http://www.fao.org/wairdocs/lead/x6114e/x6114e04.htm.

[21] The focus here is on grain-fed animals as they represent the overwhelming majority of animal agriculture, especially in high-income countries. Grass-fed animals pose other threats related land use, deforestation, and greenhouse gases, which are beyond the scope of this essay.

[22] Humane Society International (HSI), *An HSI Report: The Impact of Industrialized Animal Agriculture on World Hunger* (HSI, 2009), 3, http://www.fao.org/fileadmin/user_upload/animalwelfare/HSI--The%20Impact%20of%20Industrialized%20Animal%20Agriculture%20on%20World%20Hunger.pdf.

[23] Ryan Rueter, "Supplement Conversion Ratio," *Beef Magazine*, November 3, 2009, www.beefmagazine.com/nutrition/1104-supplement-conversion-ratio.

[24] David Pimentel, "Livestock Production: Energy Inputs and the Environment," *Food, Energy, and Society: Third Edition* (Boca Raton, FL: Taylor and Francis Group, 2008): 68.

[25] Emily S. Cassidy, Paul C. West, James S. Gerber, and Jonathan A. Foley. "Redefining Agricultural Yields: From Tonnes to People Nourished Per Hectare," *Environmental Research Letters* 8 no. 3 (September 2013): 1, doi:10.1088/1748-9326/8/3/034015.

[26] Tim Searchinger, Craig Hanson, Janet Ranganathan, Brian Lipinski, Richard Waite, Robert Winterbottom, Ayesha Dinshaw, and Ralph Heimlich, *Creating a Sustainable Food Future: A Menu of Solutions to Sustainably Feed More than 9 Billion People by 2050* (Washington, DC: World Resources Institute [WRI], December 2013), v, http://www.wri.org/sites/default/files/WRI13_Report_4c_WRR_online.pdf.

[27] This basic explanation of supply and demand principle holds constant a wide range of context-dependent factors that affect the overall price to greater or lesser degrees. Also note, food cost is more relevant to increasing urban populations than rural communities.

[28] Patrick Westhoff, *The Economics of Food: How Feeding and Fueling the Planet Affects Food Prices* (Upper Saddle River, NJ: Pearson Education/FT Press, 2010), 97.

[29] ActionAid, *Fueling the Food Crisis: The Cost to Developing Countries of US Corn Ethanol Expansion* (Washington, DC: ActionAid, October 2012), 6, http://www.ase.tufts.edu/gdae/Pubs/rp/ActionAid_Fueling_Food_Crisis.pdf.

[30] Cassidy et al., "Redefining Agricultural Yields," 2-3.

[31] The range of 6-16:1 represents commonly cited beef FCRs. Some meat industries report smaller ratios. Others, like researcher Vaclav Smil, report higher ratios. See also *Creating a Sustainable Food Future*, p. 4 for extremely high inefficiency ratios based on new calculation methods. http://www.wri.org/sites/default/files/WRI13_Report_4c_WRR_online.pdf.

[32] See note 23 above.

[33] Jeanne Yacoubou, "Factors Involved in Calculating Grain:Meat Conversion Ratios," Vegetarian Resource Group, accessed 2014, http://www.vrg.org/environment/grain_meat_conversion_ratios.php.

[34] Ibid.

[35] Ibid.

[36] Tim Searchinger et al., *Creating a Sustainable Food Future*, 4.

[37] Cassidy et al., "Redefining Agricultural Yields," 2-3.

[38] Lappé et al., *How We Count Hunger*, 5, interpreting FAOSTAT, "Food Balance Sheets" (Entry: World+2009), http://www.faostat.fao.org/site/354/default.aspx.

[39] "Calories Chart," *WebMD*, accessed 2014, http://www.webmd.com/diet/calories-chart.

[40] FAO, IFAD, and WFP, *The State of Food Insecurity in the World 2012*, 46.

[41] FAO, *Food Wastage Footprint: Impacts on Natural Resources* (Rome: FAO, 2013), 8, http://www.fao.org/docrep/018/i3347e/i3347e.pdf.

[42] J. Xie , S. Sreenivasan, G. Korniss, W. Zhang, C. Lim, and B.K. Szymanski, "Social Consensus Through the Influence of Committed Minorities," *Physical Review E* 84, no.1 (July 2011), http://pre.aps.org/abstract/PRE/v84/i1/e011130.

Animal Rights Equal Human Rights:
Domesecration and Entangled Oppression

by David Nibert

When animal rights advocates speak even to socially and environmentally-conscious people about the oppressive treatment of animals, we usually get the cold shoulder. Our concerns are dismissed with claims that using other animals as food and other resources is necessary and has been integral to the development of human society and social progress. We are frequently advised to get our priorities straight and focus on more important, *human* problems. "When human problems are solved," the refrain goes, "*then* we can worry about animals." In reality, however, it is impossible to resolve the pressing problems of our world without addressing the subjugation of other animals. Human use of other animals has undermined the development of a just and peaceful world for all species, and their continued oppression—especially for use as food—constitutes one of the most significant threats to both human rights and environmental sustainability.

Few people are aware that, for most of our time on the planet, our species foraged and lived primarily on plant-based diets. Our communities were egalitarian and there was ample time for leisure and social activities. This long period has been referred to by anthropologists as "the original affluent society."[1] However, this era ended when humans began to routinely hunt large animals—primarily a male pursuit. As our species does not have the biological make-up of a predator, this hunting could only be accomplished through the creation of weapons. Those men most successful at such killing exerted growing power. Social hierarchy began to emerge, and the status of women began to decline.[2]

The beginning of systemic human exploitation and social stratification can be traced to the advent of agricultural society in Eurasia roughly 10,000 years ago. Agricultural systems were tied to the exploitation of large social animals—including cows, horses, sheep, pigs, and goats—who were captured and exploited as laborers and for their hair, skin, body fluids, and flesh. By their confinement, exploitation, cruel treatment (and, over time, their biological manipulation) these animals were desecrated. However, the true effects of such use of other animals, and the implications for our species, have been masked by the apparently-benign term, "domestication."

Language is a powerful tool in rationalizing and naturalizing injustice, and we should always seek to expose phrases and words that serve as ideological supports for oppressive systems. It is important to reject the term "domestication," a word that sanitizes and normalizes a violent practice and that serves to naturalize the oppression of other animals. Because these other animals were desecrated, the word used here to refer to the injustice and violence they experience is *domesecration*.[3]

As early agricultural society proceeded, the possession of large numbers of domesecrated animals became a sign of power and wealth, and elite males' treatment of them as property came to be extended to women and devalued people. Countless people were relegated to the socially constructed positions of "peasant," "serf," and "slave."[4] Growing numbers of men armed with weapons—weapons created for killing other animals but soon used on other humans—were dispatched by elites to raid other people for their domesecrated animals and other sources of wealth. Violent attacks on distant societies were made possible by the exploitation of horses as instruments of war.

Some societies relied almost entirely on animal exploitation for their subsistence, such as the patriarchal and highly aggressive nomadic pastoralists of the Eurasian steppe. They rampaged across the continent for centuries in search of the fresh grazing land and water needed to sustain enormous numbers of domesecrated animals.

Invasions led by such murderous men as Attila the Hun and Chinggis Khan destroyed countless communities and entire societies; people not murdered outright by nomadic warriors—or forced into slavery—died from zoonotic diseases like smallpox, diseases that developed due to the crowding together of large numbers of domesecrated animals. Sexual violence against women became a standard military practice, and countless women were enslaved by privileged warriors.[5]

Empires were also made possible by the use of other animals as laborers, rations and instruments of war. Elite rulers of settled societies like Rome invaded weaker societies while battling for supremacy. This large-scale warfare and violence was both enabled and promoted through the oppression of domesecrated animals.

Notably, such widespread violence and destruction did not take place in regions of the world that lacked populations of large mammals to exploit, such as the pre-Columbian Americas. Before contact with Europeans, conflict between human societies in the Americas primarily took the form of small-scale raids and skirmishes. Until the European invasions, the Americas were the home of some of the world's most advanced civilizations, with impressive systems of crop cultivation. Development and social progress occurred in these sophisticated societies without the exploitation of domesecrated animals.[6]

The Europeans' ability to conquer the Americas was possible only because of the Eurasian custom of exploiting other animals as laborers, rations, and instruments of war. However, even with the use of domesecrated animals and the invaders' long experience with large-scale warfare and weapon-making, effective conquest would have been unlikely had it not been for the deadly effects of smallpox and other zoonotic diseases brought by the Europeans, which dramatically reduced indigenous populations and increased their vulnerability to invasion.

Exporting the skin and body fat of animals to Europe was very profitable in the Colonial Era,[7] driving the continual expansion of ranching operations in Latin America and the ongoing murder, displacement, and enslavement of indigenous peoples. The Spanish forced enslaved peoples—both Native Americans and, increasingly, enslaved people from Africa—to work on sugar plantations and in gold and silver mines. The exploitation of domesecrated animals as laborers and as rations for the enslaved, and the use of their body fat for making candles were essential for the day-to-day operation of profitable plantation and mining enterprises.[8] The oppression of indigenous peoples and of domesecrated animals was deeply intertwined.

Eurasian customs and institutions, debauched by incessant and widespread violence—and promoted and enabled by animal oppression—overwhelmed the Americas and much of the rest of the world. The wealth derived from the entangled oppression of indigenous people and other animals was central in producing the change from the highly exploitive European feudal system to an even more exploitive and destructive capitalist system.

For example, the quest for profit, the primary characteristic of capitalism, led to the first military campaign of the newly established United States in 1794. Federal forces would eventually wipe out Native Americans' resistance in the Ohio territory, and much of their land fell into the hands of elite ranchers known as the "cattle kings," who dominated regional economic and political decision-making. Native Americans were continually pushed west with ranchers on their heels. Tragically, when ranchers and investors decided to populate the Great Plains and Western states with cows, Native Americans were subjected to even more state violence, and survivors were sequestered on largely barren reservations.

Free-living animals, including grazers such as the buffalo, also stood as obstacles to ranching profits. Encouraging the slaughter of millions of buffalo, the commander of US forces in the West, General Philip Sheridan, boasted that buffalo hunters would eliminate "the Indians' commissary," and he declared, "Let them kill, skin, and sell until the buffalo is exterminated. Then your prairies can be covered with speckled *cattle* and the festive *cowboy*."[9]

Buffalo were not the only animals slated for extermination. Ranchers and their government supporters declared war on prairie dogs, wolves, coyotes, and any other animals perceived as posing a threat to ranching profits. Similarly, free-living animals in Australia such as kangaroos, wallabies, and dingoes; many animals in Africa, including antelope, lions, zebra, and leopards; and in Latin America, animals such as cougars and jaguars, were all ruthlessly hunted or poisoned. Such carnage, promoted by ranchers and supported by government policy, continues to this day.

Railroads, privately-owned and constructed by oppressed immigrants, connected the newly established western ranching operations to eastern markets, and led to the rise of giant slaughterhouses, infamous for the cruel, rapidly-paced killing and disassembly of enormous numbers of domesecrated animals—jobs performed by hyper-exploited workers. The profits accruing to powerful capitalists were enormous.

It was during the Great Depression, a calamity produced largely by the greedy and self-interested pursuit of wealth, that a grain surplus caused farm revenues to fall. The solution eventually proposed by agribusiness and government officials was to offer subsidies to grain producers, while diverting much of the surplus for use as feed for domesecrated animals, and to promote increased public consumption of "meat," "dairy", and "eggs."[10] Over time, this strategy facilitated the rise of the fast-food industry that would spawn ubiquitous advertisements pushing public consumption of "hamburgers" and related fare. Citizens socially engineered to consume increasing amounts of animal products paid with their lives. Growing numbers died prematurely, and many today continue to die in large numbers, from heart disease, stroke, and various forms of cancer related to diet.

While such treatment of other animals was occurring in the United States, and as the North American "hamburger culture" grew, food retailers began to seek low-cost cow flesh for "hamburgers" from Latin America. This practice was strongly supported by the US government, which with the assistance of the World Bank, loaned hundreds of millions of dollars to Latin America for the expansion of privately owned ranching operations. This policy—popular with elite landowners in the region and US commercial "meat" sellers—was calculated to place Latin American economies and governments more firmly under US control, especially after US capitalism and hegemony were challenged by the 1959 revolution in Cuba.[11]

As a result, Latin America was plagued by more domesecration-related violence. For instance, lands in Central America occupied by subsistence farmers and indigenous communities were aggressively expropriated for the expansion of ranching operations. Rural jobs connected to coffee and other export crops were reduced as many land owners switched to more profitable ranching enterprises. People who resisted the taking of their land and the loss of their jobs were violently suppressed by repressive US-backed governments. Central America was engulfed in brutal repression and warfare for decades, as all the while the consumption of cheap "hamburgers" in the United States grew steadily. Although the widespread violence in Central America in the latter half of the 20th century drew worldwide attention, few connected the carnage to ranching or to the growing consumption of products derived from domesecrated animals.

Today, as a result of Colonial Era land theft and policies like those of the United States in Latin America, 70% of all of the world's agricultural land is used to generate products derived from domesecrated animals for people in wealthy countries.[12] Such appalling use of land, which contributes to the fact that chronic hunger currently afflicts a nearly a billion people, occurs under capitalism because it is profitable. And dwindling vital resources such as fresh water, topsoil, and fossil fuel—all essential for supporting a growing human population projected to reach 9.6 billion by 2050—are being massively squandered in the oppression of tens of billions of domesecrated animals throughout the world as food.[13]

These dire circumstances are both contributing to and exacerbated by climate change. As early as 2006, a report by the UN's Food and Agricultural Organization (FAO) estimated that raising animals for food is responsible for the creation of 18% of anthropogenic greenhouse gasses.[14] A 2009 report by two scientists associated with the World Bank, Robert Goodland and Jeff Anhang, criticized the FAO study for not going far enough and for discounting that fact that tens of billions of farmed animals are exhaling carbon dioxide while the earth's capacity to trap carbon through photosynthesis is declining, especially as forests continue to be destroyed for ranching and feed grain production.[15] Moreover, 37% of human-induced methane—a much more powerful greenhouse gas than carbon dioxide—comes from domesecrated animals, while fluorocarbon refrigerants (required for cooling meat and related products) have a global warming potential several thousand times higher than carbon dioxide. Taking such factors into account, Goodland and Anhang estimated that the farming of animals is responsible for 51% of human-generated greenhouse gases.[16]

Such reports on the impact that growing numbers of domesecrated animals have on climate change are largely neglected by environmental activists and policy makers, even as the production of animal products is projected to double by 2050.[17] The result will be the existence of roughly 120 billion intensively confined, farmed land animals throughout the world by mid-century; one byproduct of their suffering will be the emission of alarming amounts of carbon dioxide and methane.

Current actions to limit or counteract climate change mainly center on reducing emissions. However, as the mainly-overlooked 2009 report points out, replacing products derived from oppressed animals with plant-based food would not only reduce the greenhouse gas emissions created by farming domesecrated animals, but would also allow for large-scale reforestation, including much of the land mass that is currently used to produce feed crops. Reforestation would trap carbon dioxide and ameliorate the climate crisis much faster than the current conventional (mostly anemic) efforts.[18]

Compounding the danger of ignoring the growing numbers of domesecrated animals are the additional perils that the practice will have as climate change advances. Climate change-related violent storms, floods, severe droughts, wildfires, and record temperatures already are upon us. Climate change will adversely affect crop harvests in the United States and throughout the world, and will make future food shortages all but certain.

As the globalization of the Western diet continues, and as critical finite resources become scarce and climate change unfolds, powerful nations like the United States and Britain—with long histories of imperialistic and chauvinistic foreign policies—will unquestionably use military force to control critical fresh water, arable land, and other valuable resources, as foretold by the unprovoked and disastrous invasion of oil-rich Iraq.

These dangers are compounded by the increasing risk of a deadly influenza pandemic. While smallpox thankfully appears to have been eradicated, widespread influenza outbreaks emerged three times during the 20th century, including the deadly pandemic of 1918 that took an estimated 50 million lives. Due to the expansion of large-scale factory farms throughout the world, public health advocates fear the emergence of new, highly infectious strains of influenza.[19] The intensive confinement of tens of billions of domesecrated animals today could hardly have been better designed as breeding grounds for deadly zoonotic diseases.

In the face of such enormous problems, some people believe they are behaving responsibly by consuming local, "humanely-raised" or "free-range" products. I applaud them for eating local plant-based foods, but the continued consumption of products derived from domesecrated animals is more harmful than they know. The reduction in "food miles" from consuming such products is overshadowed by the energy and resources necessary for their production and refrigeration. Oppressing domesecrated animals locally is still land and water-intensive, it does little to mitigate the effect on climate change, and cannot feed a human population racing to 9.6 billion by mid-century (of whom an estimated 6.4 billion will live in urban areas).[20] While the more affluent among us can afford the costlier "grass-fed" products and thus avoid eating domesecrated animals plied with pesticides, antibiotics, and hormones, the vast majority of people will continue to eat the cheapest fare that industrial agriculture can profitably produce. And even if the world were more equitable (leaving aside the moral and environmental issues of animal oppression), there simply is not enough land and water to "free-range" the tens of billions of domesecrated animals necessary to meet the growing, socially-engineered demand.

As we have seen, large-scale human violence and warfare began with the systemic oppression of other animals 10,000 years ago. Human societies were debased and social progress was stymied. The capitalist system emerged and the resulting terrible, entangled oppressions were fodder for profits, creating wealth largely concentrated in the hands of global elites. Today, the oppressive and destructive practice of treating other animals as food is causing chronic disease and premature death, depleting vital resources, polluting the environment, furthering climate change, and increasing the threat of regional and global violence and warfare.

So, contrary to what many people have been taught, the truth is that the oppression of other animals is unnatural and has undermined human social progress and the advancement of human rights. We must not let the devastating practices tied to animal oppression—practices that corrupted the past and the present—determine the future. Social justice activists of all stripes need to work together to promote a global movement for a democratic, just and peaceful world, one that includes urgent calls for the transcendence of the capitalist system and the global transition to a vegan diet. ✺

Notes

[1] Marshall Sahlins, *Stone Age Economics* (Chicago: Aldine, 1972).

[2] Peggy Reeves Sanday, *Female Power and Male Dominance: On the Origins of Sexual Inequality* (Cambridge: Cambridge University Press, 1981), 64-68.

[3] David A. Nibert, *Animal Oppression and Human Violence: Domesecration, Capitalism and Global Conflict* (New York: Columbia University Press, 2014), Introduction and Chapter One.

[4] Words and expressions that are disparaging to devalued groups (such as "cattle") and euphemisms that tend to disguise the reality of oppression (such as "meat," which disguises the reality that other animals' dead bodies are used for food) are placed in quotation marks, or in italics when included in quoted material.

[5] Elisabeth Young-Bruehl, *The Anatomy of Prejudices* (Cambridge, MA: Harvard University Press, 1996), 382.

[6] Nibert, *Animal Oppression and Human Violence*, 34-42.

[7] Ibid., Chapter Two.

[8] Ibid., Chapter Two.

[9] Ian Frazier, *Great Plains* (New York: Picador, 2001), 59.

[10] Bill Winders and David Nibert, "Consuming the Surplus: Expanding 'Meat' Consumption and Animal Oppression," *International Journal of Sociology and Social Policy* 24, no. 9 (2004): 76–96.

[11] Nibert, *Animal Oppression and Human Violence*, Chapter Seven.

[12] Henning Steinfeld, Pierre Gerber, Tom Wassenaar, Vincent Castel, Mauricio Rosales, and Cees de Haan, *Livestock's Long Shadow: Environmental Issues and Options.* (Rome: FAO, 2006), XX, ftp://ftp.fao.org/docrep/fao/010/a0701e/a0701e.pdf.

[13] "World population projected to reach 9.6 billion by 2050," *UN News Centre*, accessed August 8, 2014, http://www.un.org/apps/news/story.asp?NewsID=45165.

[14] Steinfeld et al., *Livestock's Long Shadow*, xxi.

[15] Robert Goodland and Jeff Anhang, "Livestock and Climate Change," *World Watch* 22, no. 6 (2009): 10-19, http://www.worldwatch.org/files/pdf/Livestock%20 and%20Climate%20Change.pdf.

[16] Ibid.

[17] Steinfeld et al., *Livestock's Long Shadow*, iii.

[18] Goodland and Anhang, "Livestock and Climate Change," 15.

[19] Avid Benatar, "The Chickens Come Home to Roost," *American Journal of Public Health* 97, no. 9 (September 2007): 1545.

[20] "Urban Population Growth," World Health Organization, accessed on August 7, 2014, http://www.who.int/gho/urban_health/situation_trends/urban_population_ growth_text/en/.

Building an Animal Advocacy Movement for Racial and Disability Justice

by Anthony J. Nocella II

Having been involved in animal advocacy for about 20 years, I have worked on numerous grassroots campaigns, collaborated with national and international organizations, and tried a variety of tactics—from lobbying to civil disobedience. At the beginning of my activism, I tried to be involved in everything at all times. People always asked what I *didn't* do and if I ever slept. In the last 5 years, I have started being less of a leader in campaigns such as fur and anti-vivisection, and have become more involved in building bridges between movements, organizing intersectional conferences, and providing activist, group-building, and conflict transformation workshops.

Because I am still involved with animal liberation, however, I have seen inspiring growth within the animal advocacy movement from the assistance of social media. Globally, more people are aware of what veganism is; there are more animal protection laws than ever; the movement is more socially accepted; conflicts within the movement are managed more constructively; and feminist and queer perspectives have become interwoven and embraced. At each organization, conference, and lecture, we need to promote hope and acknowledge our accomplishments, even if they are small, to emphasize that we are making positive changes. We also need to acknowledge that no global change occurs overnight. Moreover, we must note that when working for animal liberation, we are arguing that nearly all facets of human life must change. No other movement has ever asked so much. If the goal is to end all animal exploitation, that could potentially mean no computers, cell phones, or any other electronics, no cars or mass travel, no pharmaceuticals, no war, and certainly no animal agriculture, amongst many other things. We are asking for the end of oppressive acts against other species. This affects us too; for it means even the most dedicated, radical animal liberationists would have to change their lives drastically.

With so many major changes to accomplish, there are two that are pivotal but often overlooked: embracing racial justice and embracing disability justice. People of color and those with disabilities are the two largest groups on this planet crossing age, gender, sexuality, religion, nationality, and economic status, so if we want to liberate nonhuman animals, we must first end racism and ableism within the animal liberation movement (and society in general). As a person with disabilities involved in Hip Hop activism, prison abolition, and anti-racism work, I am highly concerned about these two issues.

Challenging Racism

Since the rise of Western animal rights ideologies—developed to rebuild the relationship between humans and nonhuman animals strategically destroyed by colonialism—this movement has launched witch hunts, and stigmatized those of color as unethical savages when they oppress animals. For example, Michael Vick is vilified for dog fighting, Native Americans for hunting, and the Chinese for eating dog meat. These campaigns have been launched by both radical grass-roots groups as well as corporate international nonprofits within the animal advocacy movement. There are two reasons beyond simply wanting to protect animals that these targets were chosen. First, the animal rights movement is historically racist because it arose out of colonialism; second, targeting the oppressed leads to easily winnable campaigns (a.k.a. the low-hanging fruit). Of course, this does not mean there are no people of color in the animal rights movement, as focus on whiteness might lead one to conclude. In the last decade, more people of color have joined the cause, and many of them are challenging racism within the movement and from a de-colonial perspective such as Sarat Colling, Breeze Harper, David Pellow, Alma Williams, Kevin Tillman, lauren Ornelas, Riaz Sayani-Mulji, Nekeisha Alexis-Baker, Federico Alfredo Berghmans, Daniela Romero Waldhorn, Anastasia Yarbrough, Alka Chanda, Veronica Guevara-Lovgren, Rosie Little Thunder, Linda Fisher, Tiffany Frost, Miyun Park, Tracy Veg, JRey Crow, and Sinem Ketenci.

An argument from those within the movement is that Michael Vick is wealthy, as if that removes race from consideration, and the more important issue at hand is he was running an illegal dog fighting ring and abusing canines. As one might expect, the law and race are inherently connected here when considering that argument. If we look at illegal animal entertainment in the United States, we find cock fighting associated with Latino communities and dog fighting with African-American communities. Compare that to *legal* animal entertainment such as bull riding, zoos, rodeos, and marine aquariums, which are seen by many as mere family fun and often advertised with the depiction of smiling white parents and their excited white children.

What makes zoos acceptable entertainment? Besides their history in Euro-American popular culture, zoos have roots in exoticism. We do not often see deer or squirrels in zoos. We mainly see animals who are foreign. Historically, this has meant people as well as other species: "Throughout the late 19th century, and well into the 1950s, Africans and in some cases Native Americans, were kept as exhibits in zoos. Far from a relic from an unenlightened past, remnants of such exhibits have continued in Europe as late as the 2000s."[1] Zoos have racist roots, which is why organizations such as MOVE (a black liberation group based in Philadelphia that was bombed by police in 1985) protested them.[2]

Animal advocates also argue that despite a past in which hunting was needed for survival, Native Americans now use modern weaponry in their hunts. The critique arises from the supposition that indigenous cultures victimized by American genocide should remain static and not employ new technologies. Once they shook off the "primitive," "savage" image of throwing spears, perpetuated by their white oppressors, they were seen as fair game for activists to protest. Here one sees a paradoxical double bind. If native people do not modernize, they are depicted as savages. If they do modernize and keep certain traditions that include killing other animals, they will be vilified and protested.

Finally, eating dogs in China is no different than eating any other animals in the United States, but because Americans have deemed dogs pets, companions, and family members, it is seen as barbaric. Moreover, with China an economic and political threat to the Western world, it is socially acceptable to cast it as an exotic enemy with backwards ways that must be defeated by the civilized West.

Race and Eco-Terrorism[3]

One example of white domination of the animal rights movement is the treatment of activists arrested or imprisoned for their role in the modern Green Scare, a term used to address the political repression of environmentalists and animal advocates. Not a single radical animal liberation activist has been assassinated, put on death row, shot by police, or given a life sentence. While activists have certainly been repressed, most of the animal and eco-activists who have been arrested are privileged, white, able-bodied males who have paid lawyers, college degrees, and socioeconomic dispensations. I suspect that if a group of black youths destroyed a McDonalds by bombing it for political reasons in the name of the Animal Liberation Front (ALF), they would likely receive life sentences. Examining the history of repression of people of color leads me to this conclusion.

It is for this reason that many black liberationists claim all black individuals in prison are de facto political prisoners because prison is a modern form of slavery. We only need to read the Thirteenth Amendment to prove that slavery in the US exists and is only allowed in prisons.[4] Along with the usual targets, these forms of repression should be challenged by animal activists who acknowledge the webbed nature of oppression. They should protest unjust laws, police-imposed curfews, surveillance cameras in predominantly poor communities of color, and the daily police sweeps that are traumatizing marginalized communities.

The Green Scare, concerned as it is with a few select animal and eco-activists, is simply not comparable to the repression that people of color and people who are poor face daily. Ida Hammer cogently explains the dilemma of comparing the oppression of the vegan movement to that of oppressed racial or sexual groups:

> As such, I believe it is inappropriate when we use how other groups are the targets of oppression to describe being vegan or to use their struggles against oppression as a metaphor for the vegan movement. I say this for the simple reason that vegans as a group are not ourselves the targets of oppression.[5]

Animal advocates may be politically repressed, but we are not ourselves oppressed. Animal rights activists must remember that their activism is voluntary. People choose to join the animal advocacy movement. They are not forced to join this movement to survive, hence this is not a struggle for them, but a movement for other species. Their children will not grow up to be incarcerated, beaten, or given a second rate education because their parents are animal advocates.

Prisons and Racism

Another example of how the animal advocacy movement perpetuates racism is the support of the current punitive criminal justice system in the US. With the rise of animal advocacy as an intersectional social justice cause, advocates need to address what should be done with those who illegally abuse nonhuman animals. Rather than call for imprisonment, they should advocate for transformative justice, mediation, and conflict transformation. This question of "punishment" is critical for anti-racist animal advocates because anyone who opposes racism and slavery must also oppose prisons and the current criminal justice system. After hundreds of years, social slavery officially ended in 1865 with passage of the Thirteenth Amendment. However, institutionalized slavery now exists for any individual who is "duly convicted of a crime," which allowed for cheap labor to occur in prisons.[6] Therefore, anti-racist animal advocates should not support the conviction, sentencing, and incarceration of those who abuse nonhuman animals. While many individuals and organizations advocate for harsh prison sentences for animal abusers, this in effect promotes slavery, a social injustice inherently connected to mainstream views of nonhuman animals as products and machinery. With so many organizations and individuals supporting the current criminal justice system, the same system that labels animal advocates terrorists, it must be asked: Why do we support such an oppressive, repressive, violent structure?

The answer is simple. Many animal advocates fail to critique the criminal justice system because they do not understand that this system and the oppression of nonhuman animals are interconnected. Just as nonhuman animals are cheap labor and often property of the State, so too are human prisoners. Beyond just providing free labor to corporations, prisoners are also forced to work in slaughterhouses and on dairy farms. Finally, the criminal justice system protects the very corporations that animal advocates contest. Animal advocates' protests and boycotts, once protected under the First Amendment, are now considered illegal and domestic terrorist threats under laws such as the Animal Enterprise Terrorism Act (AETA).[7] Those activists who adopt such once-legal tactics now frequently find themselves arrested, charged, and convicted as criminals and sometimes even as terrorists. As a result, many animal advocates have begun to educate themselves about political repression and unjust laws such as the AETA, but many still support the current US justice system via their calls for the imprisonment of people who abuse nonhuman animals.

Challenging Ableism[8]
Similar to the roots of racism, ableism emerged out of the philosophy of normalcy that divides the world into a socially constructed binary of abnormal vs. normal. The normal are civilized, white, able-bodied, Christian, wealthy, domestic, formally educated, heterosexual, men; the abnormal are savage, primitive, interdependent, disabled, economically

disadvantaged, non-formally-educated, People of Color, women, non-Christian, animalistic, wild, and queer. Those who are normal construct the binary, while those who have been killed, tested on, tortured, and oppressed are abnormal.

The first phase of marginalizing a group into the abnormal category is stigmatizing them. Western culture is replete with comments meant to demean humans through their comparison to nonhuman animals: "you are such a pig," "you are acting like an animal," "stop acting like a bitch," "he's a dog," "you are as fat as a whale," etc. Similarly, people with disabilities are stigmatized and marginalized with popular comments such as: "you are retarded," suggesting a person is not cool; "you are a freak," suggesting a person has uncommon sexual behaviors or simply acts outside the norm; "why are you acting so lame?," suggesting a person is boring; and "you are acting crazy," suggesting a person is not in control of their actions.[9] Many ableist conversations also occur in the animal advocacy movement. Meat eaters are referred to as "psychos," "crazy," "stupid," "dumb," "idiotic," or "retarded." I have personally overheard such conversations, and when I question the speaker's word choice, the individual will more often than not be defensive rather than reflective.

Most of the leaders within the animal advocacy movement, from queer/trans scholar-activists to anarcho-ALF supporters, use ableist language and strategies. On blogs and on Facebook, fellow activists call animal abusers—and each other—"idiots," "blind to the truth," "psychotic," etc. Another example is Rory Freedman and Kim Barouin, authors of *Skinny Bitch* (2010), who in the marketing of their book wrote: "Stop being a moron and start getting skinny." However, using these outdated medical terms without any sense of self-reflection suggests that those individuals are being reactionary and, albeit unintentionally, oppressive. They likely do not have any expertise in medicine, psychology, or psychiatry, but they borrow terminology in a futile attempt to fight oppression from those industries that have aided in the construction of normalcy. In other words, they are attempting to fight oppression with a form of oppression that they cannot or will not acknowledge.

Academics, Facebookers, and bloggers are not the only ones using ableist language. At a fur protest recently I heard two classic chants: "When animals are abused, what do you do? Stand up! Fight back!"; another chant was "Stop the murder! Stop the pain! [Insert company name here] is insane!" The first chant is ableist because of its lack of inclusion of those that are not able to physically stand. The second chant is ableist because of use of the term "insane," which stigmatizes those with mental disabilities as being violent.

This critique of ableism within the animal advocacy movement would not be complete without mention of Peter Singer, author of *Animal Liberation*, the book that launched the modern animal advocacy movement. I argue that because Singer is the founding philosopher of modern animal advocacy, the movement is, by nature, ableist. Singer reinforces the stigmatization of people with disabilities and suggests that being a nonhuman animal is more valuable than being an individual with disabilities. For example, as Ida Hammer of *The Vegan Ideal* blog notes, Singer (1996) writes the following in *Rethinking Life and Death*:

> To have a child with Down syndrome is to have a very different experience from having a normal child. It can still be a warm and loving experience, but we must have lowered expectations of our child's abilities. We cannot expect a child with Down syndrome to play the guitar, to develop an appreciation of science fiction, to learn a foreign language, to chat with us about the latest Woody Allen movie, or to be a respectable athlete, basketballer or tennis player.[10]

With these words, Singer reinforces the value of normalcy by stressing that children with disabilities are deficient, and that parents raising such children will not have a complete parenting experience because of all the activities they will miss out on (i.e., talking about Woody Allen). However, children with Down syndrome *can* excel in music, sports, education, language, art and, as even Singer admits, they are capable of love and warmth.

Introducing Eco-ability

In challenging ableism within the animal advocacy and environmental movements, a group of individuals came together to come up with a community, theory, and movement called eco-ability. Eco-ability is similar to other interventions within the animal and environmental movements such as environmental justice, which addresses racism, and eco-feminism, which addresses patriarchy. Eco-ability challenges and resists speciesism, ableism, and unrestrained cultural "civilization," while also dismantling the socially constructed binaries of human vs. animal, normal vs. abnormal, and domestic vs. wild. Eco-ability is not welfarist, reformist, or conservative. Eco-ability opposes the views and work of Temple Grandin, a professor and doctor of animal science with autism who has became famous for her design of so-called humane slaughterhouses and livestock farms. Eco-ability acknowledges the inherent contradiction within the idea and practice of humane slaughter. Eco-ability is against normalcy and standardization, two theoretical concepts needed to buttress capitalism, which are commonly promoted in the packaging and processing of standard products within a factory. Eco-ability is against any medical or digital technology modifications for economic profit or socio-political control. I have developed eight values of eco-ability: (1) difference and diversity, (2) holistic transformation through dialogue and education, (3) inclusive social justice and a total liberation movement, (4) intersectional, solidarity, and alliance politics, (5) being against all forms of oppression and domination, (6) engagement in critical theory and practice, (7) techno-digital justice, and (8) a collaborative and interdependent web of life.

Conclusion

To challenge racism and ableism within and outside of the animal advocacy movement, we must first take accountability and responsibility for the historical and modern theories and practices that are perpetuated therein. Next, we must genuinely, with no hidden agenda, listen to those with disabilities and to people of color, and also become involved in their movements. Being involved, however, does not mean joining a cause to promote veganism or animal advocacy, but to put those issues aside completely and really listen to others' stories, and to become involved in another cause. Finally, one must be willing to become an ally, and that means a willingness to be challenged and to challenge others, rather than waiting for a person with disabilities or a person of color to address racism and ableism. Organize events to speak to fellow able-bodied and able-minded people about ableism, and white people about racism. Here are 14 strategies for being an effective ally:

1. Make sure to be invited to the movement, rather than entering it and taking up space.
2. Listen without giving advice or questions, until they ask for your opinion.
3. Make sure to articulate your level of commitment and follow through on all commitments to build trust.
4. Explain your skills that can be used for their cause, such as website design, etc.
5. Explain your motivation and personal goals so others understand why you are there and interested in them.
6. Be willing to follow, and never lead. Take directions and be delegated rather than telling others what to do and controlling the agenda. Be willing to not get credit, but to give credit to others. This will be difficult because we enjoy feeling appreciated and valued.
7. Be willing to take accountability and own one's supremacy and domination. This is difficult, and you must be willing to listen if others call you out on your privilege and domination.
8. Be willing to be challenged and be called out.
9. Be willing to learn new processes and cultural practices; sometimes the best way of getting from Point A to Point B is not always the most familiar route.
10. Be willing to take more risks than those that are oppressed do, because you have more social mobility and cultural capital because of your privileges.

11. Be willing to do more because you are responsible indirectly and directly for their oppression and benefit from it.

12. Be willing to refuse money or other benefits, because that would reinforce inequity and construct a savior relationship with the oppressed.

13. Challenge acts by white, able-bodied/minded individuals and agencies that seem to tokenize, patronize, and/or co-opt. These are covert acts of oppression.

14. Be willing to leave, and do not blame others for being asked to leave. Often oppressors strive to publicly and privately justify why they were asked to leave, which includes suggesting that the oppressed are not knowledgeable or experienced.

To know more about racism or ableism, do not wait for a person of color or an able-bodied/minded person to knock on your door. Instead, go out to the library, Google, and join organizations focusing on these issues and begin sharing and reflecting. Animal advocates in the United States are asking people with disabilities and people of color to go vegan, while not addressing that a large segment of these populations live in poverty with little if any local access to healthy produce and non-processed foods. If we have criticisms of a movement or group, it's important that we not just speak or write about it, but rather join and support this movement. Criticism without action is unhelpful, stigmatizing, and oppressive. ❧

Notes

1 Staff, "Deep Racism: The Forgotten History of Human Zoos," *Popular Resistance,* accessed July 26, 2014, http://www.popularresistance.org/deep-racism-the-forgotten-history-of-human-zoos/.

2 Mumia Abu-Jamal, *All Things Censored* (New York: Seven Stories Press, 2000).

3 Parts of this section have been reprinted with permission from "Challenging Whiteness in the Animal Advocacy Movement," *Journal for Critical Animal Studies* 10, no. 1 (2012), http://www.criticalanimalstudies.org/wp-content/uploads/2012/10/JCAS+Volume+10+Issue+1+2012+FINAL.pdf and "Animal Advocates for Prison and Slave Abolition: A Transformative Justice Approach to Movement Politics for an End to Racism," *Journal for Critical Animal Studies* 10, no. 2 (2012), http://www.criticalanimalstudies.org/wp-content/uploads/2012/10/JCAS-Vol-10-Isse-2.pdf.

4 Evelyn Williams, *Inadmissible Evidence: The Story of the African-American Trial Lawyer Who Defended the Black Liberation Army* (Chicago: Lawrence Hill Books, 1993).

5 Ida Hammer, "Why 'Vegan Oppression' Cannot Exist," *The Vegan Ideal* (blog), February 3, 2010, paragraph 1, http://veganideal.mayfirst.org/content/why-vegan-oppression-cannot-exist.

6 U.S. Const. amend. XIII.

7 S. Best and A. J. Nocella II, *Igniting a Revolution: Voices in Defense of the Earth* (Oakland, CA: AK Press, 2006).

8 Parts of this section have been taken from "Challenging Ableism in the Animal Advocacy and Environmental Movements Introduction".a chapter in the forthcoming book *Animals and Subject 2.0* (forthcoming) edited by Jodey Castricano and Lauren Corman.

9 S. L. Snyder and D. T. Mitchell. *Cultural Locations of Disability* (Chicago: IL: University of Chicago Press, 2006).

10 Peter Singer, *Rethinking Life and Death: The Collapse of Our Traditional Ethics* (New York: St. Martin's Press, 1996), 213.

Our Lifeline Revealed Through the Eye of Justice

by Richard A. Oppenlander

Connecting Sustainability and Justice

In April of 1967, at Chicago's New Covenant Baptist Church, Martin Luther King, Jr. delivered a sermon titled "The Three Dimensions of a Complete Life." Dr. King's discussions that day continued to strengthen his message regarding the necessity of reaching beyond self-interest where intolerance and imposed injustices tend to form. He described one of the valued dimensions of a "complete life" in this manner:

> Somewhere along the way, we must learn that there is nothing greater than to do something for others. And this is the way I've decided to go the rest of my days. And don't forget in doing something for others that you have what you have because of others. Don't forget that. We are tied together in life and in the world.[1]

Whether or not Dr. King intended this message to apply strictly to our own human species, it certainly has unequivocal implications and relevance as we take a step back to view our relationship with planet Earth and all other life with which we share this planet.

True sustainability of our species is inextricably intertwined with the sustainability of our planet, its resources, and other life forms. Therefore, we must adopt a new paradigm of viewing matters and of managing our actions outside of self—as stewards of all other animals, plants, and Earth's multitudinous ecosystems. We are linked to all other life here, and to future life as well. Therefore, as we seek justice everywhere, we will establish a higher level of morality and consciousness that will circle back to ensure balanced long-term wellbeing for our own species. This translates into peace, health, harmony, and sustainability.

At the time he gave this sermon in 1967, Dr. King was likely unaware of the ecological devastation and massive slaughtering that was occurring throughout the world, caused by something as simple as food choice. To be sure, just a few years later, by 1973, we were to begin a tumultuous slide downward from a 1:1 global footprint relationship with our planet (requiring one Earth to keep up with the resources we were using in production and consumption). In 2014, just 41 years later, we now require the resources of nearly two full Earths to sustain what we are taking from and doing to our planet.[2] We are in a drastic overshoot mode, conducting our lives in a state of unsustainability, and most of this ecological debt is a result of our choice to eat animals, and the demand that this choice places on our planet, its resources, and other species.

"We are tied together": The Scope of the Problem

With 70 billion raised each year globally, livestock now consume 45% of the entire landmass on Earth and 77% of all coarse grains grown annually.[3] The land-based animal agriculture industry uses 27% of all freshwater withdrawals,[4] and is one of the leading contributors to climate change, producing between 14.5%[5] and 51%[6] of all human-derived greenhouse gas emissions. Another estimated 1.7 trillion chickens (unaccounted for in the 70 billion figure quoted above) and over 1 trillion fish by way of aquaculture, are also raised and slaughtered annually[7]—all this while we fumble with blaming fossil fuels and non-specific "overconsumption" for our woes, and allow nearly a billion people to go hungry and 3.1 million children to starve to death each year.[8]

Raising livestock on land has caused warming, acidification, and deoxygenation of our oceans that our planet hasn't seen in 250 million years. At that time, 95% of all sea life became extinct, and it took 30 million years to rebound.[9] Over 80% of all Amazon tropical rainforest loss since Dr. King's sermon in 1967 has been due to livestock and the crops we feed them.[10] As we raise animals to eat on land, we are destroying interdependent ecosystems and fragile habitats for other life.

Similarly, as we commercially extract animals out of our oceans, we are slaughtering not only massive amounts of target fish, but also other life by way of bykill, as we destroy oceanic habitats and ravage natural resources that other sea life depends on. With our demand to eat fish, we have plundered our oceans to the point where 85% of all fish species are considered overexploited and on the verge of collapse,[11] causing the irreversible destruction of ecosystems, and imbalances beyond comprehension that are irreparable in our lifetime.

Loss of biodiversity (plants and animals, including insects) is occurring at an annual rate as high as 10,000 times what we've seen for the past 65 million years (scientists' estimates range that from 2,000-40,000 species are now becoming extinct per year).[12] The primary cause of these massive extinctions is loss of habitats, which is a result of our insatiable desire to eat animals. Secondary causes include the effects of climate change, invasive species, and pollution—all of which derive, in large part, from what we put on our plates, specifically animal products.

Most researchers predict that our oceans will be effectively devoid of life by the year 2048,[13] and that the majority of tropical rainforests will be destroyed. The fractions of rainforests that remain will be way past their tipping point by 2050, and will die shortly thereafter.[14] Our oceans and tropical rainforests perform vital climate regulatory functions. They serve as eternally devoted and humbly silent moderators for us—sequestering excess carbon and heat while producing 90% of the atmospheric oxygen we breathe. So, our oceans and tropical rainforests form the life support mechanisms for every life-form on Earth. When our oceans and rainforests die, we will die. We are indeed, as Dr. King stated, "tied together in life and in the world."[15]

Injustice and Humane Food Choices

"True peace is not merely the absence of tension: it is the presence of justice."
—Martin Luther King, Jr.,
Montgomery Bus Boycott speech, 1955

When we think of injustice, we typically view it within a human-to-human context—how we, through variations of bias or self-interest, inflict an unkind, unfair, violent, hurtful, or otherwise unjust action or situation upon another human being. However, that is quite a limited view. With growing concern for how we treat food animals raised in factory farm settings, there is now a considerable movement for more humane principles to be applied to nonhuman species. But this, also, is not enough. To realize justice everywhere in the world, we must extend our concern well beyond the realm of the human-to-human context, or that of grass-fed, pastured, cage-free, sustainable seafood, or any other form of certified humane-raised animal or animal product.

Whenever there is a slaughter involved, as is the case with all animals or animal byproducts that are consumed as food, there is a calculated, inhumane, and unjust act—the slaughter itself, the willful taking of another living being's life—regardless of how the victim was treated while living. Whether we choose to eat a terrestrial or an aquatic animal, and whether or not a certified humane label has been stamped on its carcass, killing is killing—an act that is neither peaceful nor consistent with an approach that seeks justice for all.

Fish, whether wild caught or raised in captivity (in aquaculture or aquaponics settings), cannot be excluded in our conception of justice. Similar to mammals, including humans, fish are known to have numerous polymodal nociceptors (sensory neurons) in and around their faces, heads, and necks. These are nerve cells that allow them to perceive and experience pain.

Additionally, we must extend our view of justice to encompass other living beings (non-target species on sea and land) that are *indirectly* involved and sacrificed in our pursuit of consuming food animals. Finally, we must expand the scope of our human concerns to include future generations that will inherit a grossly depleted, unhealthy planet that deteriorated on our watch, while we thoughtlessly conducted our eating habits and food production systems under a veil of myopia.

Any time we eat an animal, it has undergone both a raising process *and* a killing process. Slaughter has to take place with all animal operations, a fact that may seem obvious...but for those who support urban agriculture and animal products labeled as local, grass-fed, pastured, sustainable, real-food, cage-free, organic, or certified humane, the ubiquitous murder as well as unnecessary, unsustainable resource depletion seem to be mysteriously overlooked.

Doing Something for Others: Redefining Ethics

The concepts of sustainability and "doing something for others" are further bound together in the sense that becoming sustainable is a multidimensional, multilayered state—one that must include not only humanity, but all other life on Earth also. By all counts, we cannot reach a state of true sustainability alone or collectively by perpetuating violence and injustice. We must surely do something good for others—*all "others"*—if we intend to survive as a species. In fact, it is time we view ethics or conscious eating in a much different and larger context than simply in terms of the rights or welfare of the particular domesticated or farmed animals raised for us to eat.

Is it ethical, for instance, for any of us to eat food that causes the extinction of other species if we don't need to? Is it ethical for the vast majority of humans on Earth to cause irreversible climate change, devastated ecosystems, and resource depletion, while less than 2% of us, by way of our choice to eat only plants, are living our lives in ways that better protect the Earth? Is it ethical for any of us to use our planet in a way that exacerbates world hunger, and diminishes the potential for future generations of humans or any other species to survive?

If we are to survive as a society or species, we must recognize our role as stewards of this planet, identify those forces that imperil us, and then act responsibly and quickly to create needed change. We must make the correct choices—for our own well being, for other living beings with whom we share this planet, and for all those who will come after us. It's time to realize our role in requiring so many sentient beings to be killed every minute of every day as we consume them. We need to seek a higher level of conscious eating, a more comprehensive level of justice. This is the ethos with which we need to live and by which we will be remembered.

Delegitimizing an Unjust Habit and Imminent Timelines

Raising animals on land and extracting sea life out of our oceans, then slaughtering and eating them, creates a tremendous depletion of resources and loss of other species—which negatively affects our health and that of planet Earth. This is an imposition on all life that is unparalleled in the history of our planet. As such, I call for the consumption of all animal products to end—effective today. Much like secondhand smoke from cigarettes in public places, apartheid, or even slavery, eating animals may eventually be delegitimized as a burden on society and a clear display of both unsustainability and injustice throughout the interconnected web of life.

In addition to horrific current statistics like the aforementioned annual extinction of 2,000–40,000 species and the starvation deaths of 3.1 million children each year, various imminent timelines associated with global depletion are now generally recognized by leading researchers, including the following:

- Irreversible climate change if human induced GHGs are not drastically reduced by 2017.[16]
- 40% shortage in freshwater supply by 2030.[17]
- Extinction of all major oceanic fish species and loss of most coral reef systems by 2048.[18]

With the global human population expected to near the 9 billion mark by 2030,[19] and the effects of climate change worsening, it is imperative that we recognize the link between sustainability and justice everywhere. Then, we must take the necessary steps to live our lives from a perspective beyond the self, which has to include food choice.

Eat only whole, organically grown, purely plant-based foods, thereby attaining the highest level of relative sustainability and inspire others to do the same. This will set us on a course toward greater peace and health, and toward justice everywhere.

Perhaps nowhere has Dr. King's prescient 1967 sermon applied so aptly as it does in the context of our future as a species: "…there is nothing greater than to do something for others," and, "We are tied together in life and in the world."[20]

Human Characteristics Needing an Adjustment

Certain innate, consistently-found qualities define a species and perhaps its role in the complex web of life on Earth. Beyond genetically transmitted DNA coding, and physical and mental capacities such as locomotion and communication that typically characterize all mammals, human beings are also known to demonstrate a number of social traits that are generated by complex thought processes. These traits—such as compassion, peace, love, understanding, tolerance, and ability to interpret just, kind, and fair actions—are guided by emotion and discernment. Human beings are also able to differentiate between what is right and wrong, to anticipate the effects of our actions on others, and to display an inherent sense of altruism.

But we also know that humans can be characterized by intolerance, unkindness, and violence, and we often actively participate in or tacitly condone inequities and injustice. These characteristics become stumbling blocks to progress, and this is especially true with respect to food choice.

Regarding the all-too-often heard food choice arguments that eating meat is "natural," or that "we've always eaten this way," or that "we can't take away our cultural heritage"—it's time we recognize that the food choice landscape has changed. We have stripped away the base of natural resources that once so easily sustained us, to the point where we *must* change. It is a necessity.

When considering world hunger and inequities found in food security, global demand for meat and dairy products in developed countries drives resource depletion, reduces food availability, and increases food prices in developing nations where poverty, illiteracy, human sickness, soil infertility, and gender inequalities all spin off the wheel of food choice.

Our survival as a species will be predicated on the comprehensive application of justice everywhere. The practice of raising and consuming animals generates injustices on many levels:

- Targeted animals: intentional slaughter of those raised or extracted for food
- Ecosystems: damage of habitat and loss of non-target species
- Humans: widespread hunger due to food distribution inequities
- Future generations: compromised quality of life for both humans and other species

The massive extinctions we have wreaked upon other species might be seen as a prophetic glimpse of the tragic fate we have laid out for our own species.

Ultimately, we will be judged by future generations according to how we treat our planet and all life it harbors. These same daily decisions will also form the lifeline by which our own human species will either survive or perish.

Navigating the Anthropocene Era: Connections to Justice

"Injustice anywhere is a threat to justice everywhere. We are caught in an inescapable network of mutuality, tied in a single garment of destiny. Whatever affects one directly, affects all indirectly."

—Martin Luther King, Jr.,
Letter from Birmingham Jail, 1963

We humans have reached a critical and fragile point in our evolutionary journey as a species. Just in the past 100 years—a blink of an eye in terms of time—we've reached what some scientists have termed the Anthropocene Era, where we have acquired the power to affect our biosphere—the lithosphere, hydrosphere, and atmosphere—in both positive and negative (but mostly negative) ways. These are the very environs that sustain us and all other life on Earth. Unfortunately, we haven't acquired the wisdom or maturity to be able to manage this power in a sensible or beneficial manner. We're essentially in the adolescent phase of our place in the Big History, and have reached a bottleneck of sorts, one that many experts predict we may not be able to work our way through as a species.

But there is a way. It begins with applying Dr. King's imperative to seek justice everywhere. This imperative weaves its way through our food choices—the profound effects we have on our planet and the other living plants, animals, and insects that we share it with—and ultimately, it circles back to us as a species and as individuals.

As we begin to view our existence outside of self and with love, peace, and concern for "others"—other humans, other species, other generations, and our planet—we will find our way. In a collective manner, perhaps in a cosmic sense, our task now is to forge a path toward true sustainability—with a lifeline to the future of our species, woven through a network of many dimensions, and firmly embedded in compassion. It may very well be what saves us.

Notes

[1] Martin Luther King, Jr., "The Three Dimensions of a Complete Life," (sermon, New Covenant Baptist Church, Chicago, IL, April 9, 1967).

[2] "World Footprint," Global Footprint Network, last modified March 28, 2014, http://www.footprintnetwork.org/en/index.php/GFN/page/world_footprint/.

[3] Philip Thornton, Mario Herrero, and Polly Ericksen, "Livestock and Climate Change," *Livestock Exchange Issue Brief* 3, International Livestock Research Institute, November 2011, https://cgspace.cgiar.org/bitstream/handle/10568/10601/IssueBrief3.pdf.

[4] M. M. Mekonnen and A.Y. Hoekstram, "A Global Assessment of the Water Footprint of Farm Animal Products," *Ecosystems* 15 (2012): 401–415, doi: 10.1007/s10021-011-9517-8.

[5] P.J. Gerber, H. Steinfeld, B. Henderson, A. Mottet, C. Opio, J. Dijkman, A. Falcucci and G. Tempio, *Tackling Climate Change Through Livestock: A Global Assessment of Emissions and Mitigation Opportunities* (Rome: FAO, 2013), 14, http://www.fao.org/docrep/018/i3437e/i3437e.pdf.

[6] Robert Goodland and Jeff Anhang, "Livestock and Climate Change," *World Watch* 22, no. 6 (2009): 10-19, http://www.worldwatch.org/files/pdf/Livestock%20and%20Climate%20Change.pdf.

[7] Stefania Vannuccini (FIPS) and Nicolas Sakolas (ESS) (FAO officials), in interviews with the author, from June 30 through August 12, 2012.

[8] "Hunger Statistics," World Food Programme, accessed August 16, 2014, http://www.wfp.org/hunger/stats.

[9] Sarda Sahney and Michael J. Benton, "Recovery from the Most Profound Mass Extinction of All Time," *Proceedings of the Royal Society* 275, no. 1636 (2008): 759-765.

[10] Sergio Margulis, "Causes of Deforestation of the Brazilian Amazon," *World Bank Working Paper no. 22* (Washington, D.C.: The World Bank, 2004).

[11] Food and Agriculture Organization of the United Nations Fisheries and Aquaculture Department, *The State of the World Fisheries and Aquaculture 2012* (Rome: FAO, 2012), http://www.fao.org/docrep/016/i2727e/i2727e.pdf.

[12] Richard Oppenlander, *Food Choice and Sustainability: Why Buying Local, Eating Less Meat, and Taking Baby Steps Won't Work* (Minneapolis: Langdon Street Press, 2013), 396-404.

[13] Boris Worm, Edward B. Barbier, Nicola Beaumont, J. Emmett Duffy, Carl Folke, Benjamin S. Halpern, Jeremy B.C. Jackson, Heike K. Lotze, Fiorenza Micheli, Stephen R. Palumbi, Enric Sala, Kimberley A. Selkoe, John J. Stachowicz, and Reg Watson, "Impacts of Biodiversity Loss on Ocean Ecosystem Services," *Science* 314, no. 5800 (2006): 787-790, doi: 10.1126/science.1132294.

[14] Organisation for Economic Co-operation and Development (OECD), *OECD Environmental Outlook to 2050: The Consequences of Inaction* (OECD Publishing, 2012), doi: 10.1787/9789264122246-en.

[15] See note 1 above.

[16] International Energy Agency (IEA), *World Energy Outlook 2011* (Paris: IEA, 2011).

[17] Mike D. Young, "Water: Investing in Natural Capital," *Towards a Green Economy: Pathways to Sustainable Development and Poverty Eradication*, United Nations Environment Programme, UNEP, 2011: 110-149, http://www.unep.org/greeneconomy/Portals/88/documents/ger/4.0_Water.pdf.

[18] See note 13 above.

[19] World Bank, "Developing World's Share of Global Investment to Triple by 2030, Says New World Bank Report," press release, *The World Bank*, May 16, 2013, http://www.worldbank.org/en/news/press-release/2013/05/16/developing-world share-of-global-investment-to-triple-by-2030-says-new-world-bank-report.

[20] See note 1 above.

A Hunger for Justice

by lauren Ornelas

Social injustice continues to haunt our world today, and it's clear that there is a common link when we look at oppression. It's the vulnerable who get exploited. It's nonhuman animals, women, workers, the poor, children, communities of color and/or low-income communities; it's those who are seen as having no power and no voice.

As someone who has dedicated more than 25 years to the animal rights movement and started Food Empowerment Project—a vegan food justice organization that encourages food choices that reflect a more compassionate society by spotlighting the abuse of animals on farms, the depletion of natural resources, unfair working conditions for agricultural workers, and the unavailability of healthy foods in low-income areas—I cannot ignore the similar ways in which both humans and nonhuman animals are exploited. My inability to extricate the two is why I started Food Empowerment Project.

Animal Rights

I got involved in the animal rights movement when I was in high school in Texas, but I had also been aware of and involved in two different campaigns: one that addressed the rights of farm workers, and another in support of the anti-apartheid movement in South Africa. I definitely came across as different from my peers, and I was very aware that animals were not the only ones being oppressed.

Decades later, I was asked to be the director of Viva!USA, a national nonprofit vegan advocacy organization that created campaigns focused on factory farming issues to bring about change for the animals. I conducted factory farm investigations to expose the dire circumstances of pigs, turkeys, ducks, and chickens raised for "meat" and eggs, cows used in the dairy industry, and even calves raised for the "veal" industry. I can attest to the absolutely horrific and unacceptable conditions under which these animals are forced to live and die.

Despite the prevalence of online videos these days, most people are still not aware of the suffering of animals who are killed for food. Many don't even think of where their food comes from—I imagine all of us are guilty of this to some extent.

Factory Farms

I knew when I first began my investigations of factory farms that it would be difficult. I remember seeing my first undercover video of animal exploitation in 1987 and thinking, "I could never do that." But I did—I had to. My first investigation was at a "veal" farm. I felt awful leaving the baby male calf kicking at the front of his wooden crate; it was painful. Running away (as to not get caught), it was hard to bear the thought that he could hardly move his legs; he couldn't even turn around. I felt like a speciesist. Imagining he was a person, I questioned whether or not I would have left him behind. But I knew how important it was to get the images out to the public, to bring awareness of the plight of these baby calves, to get people to do something—to not contribute to the suffering, to not eat them or drink the milk from their mothers. Informing the public is what I continued to keep in my mind for every investigation, and I'd remember who I was doing it for. At each farm I investigated, I picked an individual animal to remember, one whom I would think of and speak out for when I gave talks to like-minded individuals, or when I was advocating for change to corporations.

The investigations at pig farms were just as difficult. Pregnant pigs are kept in tiny crates so small they can't turn around, and right before they give birth they are moved to another form of confinement. On these farms, you could see the frustration and boredom in their eyes.

The sound of them constantly banging their heads on the crates will always be in my head. One investigation I will never forget was in North Carolina. The place was covered in cobwebs and flies. There were thousands of pigs housed in sheds. Many were dead or dying—one actually died right in front of me. This was the same for the piglets being housed in what the industry so frightfully terms a nursery! The dying and dead pigs were still in the pens with the living pigs. A revealing insight on how this industry views animals is offered by its treatment of the dead and dying. They were tossed in the aisles, some barely alive, some rotting. Sick or injured pigs who were still alive could not reach food or water, and were sure to die a painful death. There was a pig so thin he barely looked like a pig at all. He had some type of rupture protruding from his stomach; in addition to this, his ribs were showing. He was in desperate need of veterinary care, but apparently none was being provided, if he was being monitored by anyone at all. The absolute disregard for these animals was obvious. Death accompanies them at every stage of their short 5- to 6-month lives. These losses are built into the economics of pig farming. Animals may not even survive the transport to slaughter (dying from heat stroke, or freezing to death, depending on the time of year).

It is shocking to realize the cruelties inflicted upon these living and sentient beings. Chickens are killed when they are mere babies at 6–7 weeks of age. Their bodies are forced to grow at an unnaturally rapid rate, but they still have the tiny little peeps of baby chicks. This atrocity occurs as if it were a right of ours to kill and eat them, and many of these gentle birds are boiled alive during the slaughtering process. Approximately 285 chickens are killed every second in the United States. That is almost 24 million a day![1]

I was also involved in a rescue at a facility where hens are forced to lay eggs in what is called a battery cage. Hens are housed in cages so small they are unable to spread their wings or turn around without stepping on their cage mates. Because they are packed so tightly together, the birds have the tips of their beaks cut off (without pain-killers) to prevent them from pecking at each other. As I attempted to walk down the aisles of the shed, I made it about halfway down when the powerful stench became truly overwhelming. I could only imagine that these horrific fumes also affected the health of the birds. Rows and rows of cages of birds filled the shed with about three rows stacked on top of each another. We were allowed to go in and rescue as many of the birds as we could, because the facility was shutting down. I will never forget how it was a time of both joy and intense sadness. Although I was rescuing many lives, I was looking into the faces of all of the thousands we had to leave behind.

I tell all this because people need to be aware of it. We need to know what happens to animals, and we have a right to know, and I feel a need to tell my stories. More than likely, most people have heard about or seen other investigations on television. These aren't random situations or just the "bad apples;" this suffering is pervasive in the animal agriculture industry. During every investigation, I witnessed incredible suffering: those hens raised for eggs kept in such small cages they could barely move in, and living with a dead cell mate; turkeys, the most curious critters I encountered, who would peer into my video camera with complete interest, trembling—*trembling*—in the shed during the summer. It was heartbreaking.

Understanding Injustice

Although many people have not been able to have a close relationship with an animal—to notice fear in their eyes, boredom, or even sick-ness—many of us do understand injustice. Unfortunately, many of us have experienced it ourselves due to our skin color, our religion, or our sexual orientation. Animals seem to be overlooked on this level of injustice, but my hope is that by acknowledging the connection of this oppression, we can all work together to stop it.

A system that is based inherently on exploiting one being sees no problem in allowing this mistreatment to extend to others, and this includes abuse to humans and the environment. I think the animal agriculture industry paints this portrait clearly.

As the treatment of animals in a variety of arenas continues to be made more transparent to the public, it too will not stand up to scrutiny by the majority of people. Unfortunately, billions of animals continue to be oppressed and exploited for food, clothing, entertainment, and medical research. Looking at animals in factory farms, we don't find much of a difference in how they are treated when compared to the treatment of workers in this industry.

Agricultural Workers

Animals are considered to be mere commodities, their needs not met, with "acceptable" death rates figured into the bottom-line profit. This is not unlike the compromised health of workers in industrial animal factories and the "acceptable" injury (possible death) rates in large slaughterhouses. Workers' needs are not considered (in fact, I am often amazed at how little workers in most industries are considered) as they are often exposed to numerous hazards, work excessively long hours under dangerous conditions, are threatened for attempting to organize, and frequently find themselves denied compensation for injuries.[2] The bottom line is making a profit at any expense. Like the animals, they usually have no recourse for standing up for their rights!

Animals' voices are silenced in our society, and immigrant workers are often either not able to communicate in English or are fearful of speaking up because of threats of being fired or reported to immigration.

The 2008 raid on Agriprocessors, a kosher meatpacking plant in Iowa, gave the public the opportunity to peek into a world of oppression that also includes children! At least 57 child labor violations were uncovered at this particular slaughterhouse.[3] In Iowa, minors under the age of 18 are not allowed to work in this industry because it is excessively dangerous, having one of the highest injury rates of all public sector industries in the US.[4] Like animals in factory farms, these workers do not have a voice, and are instead just a means to an end.

Profit and Exploitation

Most of us know that the biggest incentive for exploiting others is profit. Profit is a force that drives many to look the other way or approve of actions that would not normally stand up to scrutiny. Under capitalism, both humans and nonhuman animals are typically working (and being killed) for the profit of others under a system that sees no problem with exploiting others and keeping them oppressed.

Exploitation is rampant in the fields where farm workers are subjected to the spraying of agricultural chemicals, as if they are not impacted by these toxic materials. In a famous example, endosulfan is part of the same family of chemicals as DDT, which the EPA banned in 1972. It is persistent in the environment and can be found in regions far from where it was applied. The EPA's own analysis confirmed that the agricultural chemical poses severe risks to humans with only minimal benefits to growers. Approximately 1.38 million pounds of endosulfan were used annually in the United States as of 2002.[5] By 2010, after years of protest, the EPA reversed course and announced a phase-out of the chemical, and countries like Australia and New Zealand banned it outright. Its effects, however, persist.

Driving along Highway 101 in California, you can see many farm workers along the sides of the highway picking fruits and vegetables. Some are US citizens and others are not. Many do not speak English, and often it's the migrant workers' children (who speak some English) who bear the brunt of any verbal abuse by the grower. It is here where men, women, and even children are forced to work under the harshest of conditions. In fact, a number of workers have died in California due to the heat. One pregnant 17-year-old was 10 minutes away from the water station. Walking over there to quench her thirst would have used her entire 10-minute break, not to mention that she wouldn't have had time to walk back. She toiled under that sun, pruning grape vines in 100-degree heat, for more than eight hours. Her body, now dehydrated, could function no more. She collapsed, and two days later was dead, from heat stroke. The findings: Merced Farm Labor had denied her proper access to shade and water![6] Unfortunately, this was not an isolated incident, and because the voices of the people are not yet loud enough, farm workers are continuing to suffer and even perish.

I know why this happens, and yet cannot understand the senselessness of it. It pains me greatly, but at the same time, I am glad I know. I am glad not to be ignorant of the true cost of food in this country and of who pays the price. This is what allows me to make better choices and to help others understand the need for them to do the same.

Chocolate

In 2002, I saw a BBC program about workers on the Ivory Coast who pick cocoa beans for chocolate. They spoke of not being paid, being locked indoors, not being allowed to leave, and being beaten if they tried to leave. When a worker was asked what he would say to a Westerner who ate chocolate, he said, "[When they eat chocolate,] they are eating my flesh."[7] This made me think that if an animal could speak in our language, she would say something very similar. I gave up chocolate for a long time until I discovered I could purchase chocolate that is not sourced from the worst forms of child labor, including slavery, and therefore not contribute to this suffering.

But this type of suffering isn't just limited to West Africa. It is happening here to our farm workers in the United States. In fact, those stories of farm workers in Florida being chained and locked in overnight for the tomato industry seemed to go unnoticed for too long.

Working for Social Justice

Throughout the years, I have been fortunate to use my voice, time and again, to share the need for all of us to recognize the oppression around us. While speaking at the World Social Forum in Caracas, Venezuela, I realized that many of the issues I felt passionately about—farm worker justice, the environment, people of color, and animals—all had something in common: food! So, I began Food Empowerment Project as a way to combine my interests by working on behalf of injustices against vulnerable populations, which include both animals and people. I realized that as consumers we indeed have power, and that is probably why the tagline to Food Empowerment Project is that our food choices can change the world. At present, Food Empowerment Project is an all-volunteer nonprofit organization. Up until recently, I also had my regular day job as the Campaigns Director for the Silicon Valley Toxics Coalition (SVTC). One of the issues SVTC works on is the exportation of electronic waste (e-waste) from the US to developing countries all over the world, including China, Nigeria, and India. People are completely unaware of not only what happens to their TVs and computers when they no longer have use for them, but also that these products contain thousands of toxic chemicals.

During the summer of 2008, a few of us from SVTC traveled to Hong Kong, India, and China. Our task was to witness firsthand the communities there who dismantle the e-waste. We observed workers dismantling computers, televisions, and other electronics full of toxic chemicals right where they lived. A majority of the workers in this industry are Muslim—a people discriminated against in India. Their neighborhoods did not have paved roads, running water, a sewer system, or proper electricity. These people were some of the most generous and kind I have ever met in my life. With unpaved roads that even our taxi would not drive down, and potholes full of water with mosquito larvae in a country where malaria has not been eradicated, the people would offer us tea, soda—anything—to welcome us, their guests.

I had often heard about the poverty in India, but I honestly do not think I could have ever prepared myself for what I was seeing. Of course, we were going specifically to the areas where the waste pickers lived. And here, the poor dismantled the e-waste of our TVs and computers, while the CEOs of some of the corporations producing these products lived in the most expensive areas of California without any worry about what was happening to that electronic product when it reached the end of its life cycle.

I tell this story because it seems that there is no escape from those who are in power and seek to make a profit at the expense of the workers as well as the environment.

"Food Deserts"

Another issue that has gained some understanding in the US is that of what I call "food apartheid" or what some call "food deserts." Many communities of color, and low-income communities do not have access to healthy foods.

What is incredibly ironic about the entire situation is the fact that farm workers rarely ever benefit from the fresh fruits and vegetables they are picking. Most live in areas where liquor stores and fast food restaurants are more plentiful than the healthy foods they pick almost every day.

Food Empowerment Project conducted its own survey of over 200 locations of supermarkets, convenience stores, liquor stores, etc., in Santa Clara County in the areas of the most advantaged and least advantaged based on income, education, and ethnicity. What we found was no different than other studies.

We released our report, "Shining a Light on the Valley of the Heart's Delight: Taking a Look at Access to Healthy Foods in Santa Clara County's Communities of Color and Low-Income Communities," and we found that, on average, higher-income areas have twice as many locations with fresh fruits and vegetables compared to the lower-income areas. The disparity for frozen produce was even higher, with higher-income areas having 14 times more locations with frozen fruit and 6 times more locations with frozen vegetables. Access to canned goods was about the same, though organic was almost non-existent in low-income communities. "Meat" alternatives were available in more than 22% of the locations in higher-income areas, but in only 2% of the low-income areas, and only 3% of the low-income locations had vegan dairy alternatives, whereas these alternatives could be found in 21% of the higher income areas.[8] For us, this raises concerns, because individuals who want to make healthier and more ethical choices are limited. According to the US Department of Health and Human Resources, 95% of Asians, 60-80% of African Americans and Ashkenazi Jews, 80-100% of American Indians, and 50-80% of Latinos are lactose intolerant; only a very small proportion of individuals of northern

European descent experience any pain as a result of consuming lactose-filled milk products.[9]

When you consider that a diet high in fruits and vegetables decreases your chances of Type 2 diabetes, heart disease, and some types of cancer, it is no wonder that many minorities are so at risk for many diseases that could be easily prevented.

The following facts were published in a report by the California Legislature's Legislative Task Force on Diabetes & Obesity in January of 2009:

> African Americans are 1.8 times more likely to have diabetes as non-Hispanic* whites. It is estimated that 2.5 million of all Hispanic/Latino Americans aged 20 years or older have diabetes. Mexican Americans are 1.7 times more likely to have diabetes as non-Hispanic whites." "Approximately 1.8 million Californians (7 percent) have diabetes...prevalence of diabetes is higher among Latinos, African Americans and American Indians compared to Caucasians. Almost 37 percent of Latinos with diabetes are diagnosed before the age of 40. This compares to only 20.4 percent of their Caucasian counterparts.[10]

The report also shows that there is a much higher prevalence of diabetes among low-income Californians:

> Mortality rates associated with obesity and diabetes are also higher within minority populations. Of all racial and ethnic groups, Native Americans and Alaskan Natives die at the earliest age due to diabetes, 68.2 years. This is 6.4 years younger than Caucasians. African Americans die from diabetes at a rate of 97.6 per 100,000, much higher than for any other racial/ethnic group.[11]

(*Please note that I am using terms associated with the report—such as "Hispanic"—not a term I use or would ever consider myself.)

Unfortunately, these issues are not as easy to solve as making a call, sending out an email, or even protesting. Part of the solution comes from understanding and having empathy, and through community action. All forms of oppression, such as racism, sexism, homophobia, and speciesism, need to be pointed out and addressed by everyone.

Urban Gardens

At Food Empowerment Project, we know that there is not one answer to the food apartheid question. More than likely there will be a variety of solutions for different people, different areas of the country, etc. Of course, an ideal solution would be one that does not penalize the victim and, for example, allows single parents the ability to support themselves and their children with one job, where they have time to shop for and cook healthy meals—where they can make a living wage.

Until then, one way we could see people reconnecting with each other, the land, and with their culture is by growing their own food. Urban gardens have become more common, as information about the distance that our food travels, the unknowns regarding genetically modified organisms, and agricultural chemicals in and on our food have been made public. To us, this is a side benefit; we just truly want people to feel empowered by growing their own food and being able to sustain themselves.

In a country of more than 11 million people, Cuba found a way to ensure that everyone has access to healthy food. This small country, whose existence for many decades has been impacted by US sanctions, recognized that the challenge facing them was the difficulty of transporting food grown in the rural areas to the major cities, which, in essence, put the health of their people in jeopardy.

According to D. Barav in "How Environmental Conservation Helped Save Cuba,"

> With the rise of organic and low-input garden lots, or 'organoponicos,' built through the city on overtop unused parking lots or any space available, citizens began to grow

their own vegetables. This secured access to health food for city-dwellers and reduced the energy burden of transporting it from rural areas. Due to the same economic and political constraints as rural agriculture, urban vegetable plots also were, and continue to be, mostly farmed organically because chemical fertilizers or pesticides [sic] are simply unaffordable. This type of agriculture is more labor intensive than its large-scale counterpart, but it is also more sustainable.[12]

It seems obvious that urban gardens could help people in the US sustain themselves, and also empower them. However, we know we live in a country very different than Cuba, and attaining land can be difficult, but being creative with small plots of land in urban areas can be an effective way to begin having access to healthy foods.

The South Central Farmers in Los Angeles created a 14-acre urban farm and community garden in industrial Los Angeles, which fed around 350 low-income (mostly Latino) families. Unfortunately, the farm was torn down for development, but the farm instilled pride in the community as well as self-reliance and power.

These are the seeds that Food Empowerment Project wants to plant. We consistently strive to offer ideas that will instill pride in people; we attempt to remind everyone that they do have the power, and most importantly, we help people understand the need to eat in a way that is compassionate to other people, themselves, the planet, and the animals.

Equality

Underlying most oppression in this country are issues dealing with ethnicity and class. As much as we would like to say that this country has gained ground on issues such as race, I believe that we have just worked harder to push it out of view. We may currently have a black president, but we still have a long way to go when it comes to equality.

All communities are still not created equal. Some neighborhoods, communities, and regions are still dumping grounds for all kinds of toxins. Communities of color and low-income neighborhoods and their residents suffer from greater environmental risks than the larger society. For example, a 1993 CDC report found that lead poisoning was the number-one environmental health threat to children in the United States, especially poor children, children of color, and children living in older housing in inner cities.[13]

When I started to do research on environmental racism while I ran Viva!USA, we found studies reporting similar findings, such as one in *Environmental Health Perspectives* that reported in North Carolina, large pig farms are about 7 times as likely to be in very poor areas versus higher income areas. The excess of pig farms is greatest in areas with both high poverty and a high percentage of non-whites. Farms run by corporations are more concentrated in poor and non-white areas than those run by independent farms.[14]

In addition to this, a study was also done on the health problems experienced by people living near these farms in North Carolina. The results showed that residents living near large pig farms had increased occurrences of headaches, runny noses, sore throats, excessive coughing, diarrhea, and burning eyes. People exposed to odors from intensive animal operations experience more tension, depression, anger, fatigue, and confusion than unexposed people, and groundwater contamination is also not uncommon.[15]

Solutions

As with many of these issues, there are no easy solutions. Obviously, people can and should go vegan if they care about animals and ecosystems, and want to do their part in reducing some of the human suffering in our world. We can all strive to support our local farmers markets and Community Supported Agriculture, where we can talk to the farmers ourselves. And we can try to be conscientious and aware shoppers. Think of every dollar you spend as speaking for you and your values.

I have often felt that those of us in this movement would have been the same ones who would have strayed from the beaten path and joined the likes of John Brown, Harriet Tubman, Malcolm X, Martin Luther King, Jr., and Stephen Biko to speak out and shake the earth with our opposition to such injustices.

I do recognize that times are different and that often forms of racism, oppression, and exploitation are a bit more hidden or more easily justified by blaming the victims. But those of us who are striving to make this world a better place, owe it to all of them to speak out.

Food Empowerment Project recognizes that there are far more injustices taking place in the world besides those relating to food. However, we feel that this is an area where we want to shine the spotlight and remind people to endeavor to take the opportunity to lessen the suffering somewhere—whether it be choosing to not participate in the bloodshed that takes place every day in slaughter-houses, buying organic produce when going grocery shopping, or not buying chocolate that is sourced from the worst forms of child labor in West Africa.

For me, the key is working toward consistency in our beliefs and recognizing that oppression is oppression, no matter what form it takes. Even if we work in only one movement, we can use that experience to bridge the gap between other social justice issues. When it comes to personal choices, ethical changes in our own diets are a way to address many of these important issues at once, including making food choices that are both compassionate and good for the planet.

Sometimes when I feel alone in my desire to be consistent in my food choices—when I don't eat a vegan brownie because I cannot determine if the chocolate is from West Africa, or when I get teased for boycotting companies that are involved in some of the most cruel labor policies—I try to remind myself of Martin Luther King, Jr. Not that I liken myself to him in any way, but I try to think of those who expanded their understanding beyond the issue in which they got involved and began to recognize that they needed to do more to make a difference. Martin Luther King, Jr. became most dangerous when, in addition to speaking about civil rights, he spoke against the war in Vietnam, and the poor people's plight.

The establishments that hold power over and exploit many can be rocked to their core if we make the connection, enlarge our circle of compassion, and become conscious of our own privileges and the changes that we need to make in order to live a more consistent life with a bent toward justice. ☯

Notes

[1] "Chickens," United Poultry Concerns, accessed August 15, 2014, http://www.upconline.org/chickens/chickensbro.html.

[2] Human Rights Watch, *Blood, Sweat, and Fear: Workers' Rights in U.S. Meat and Poultry Plants* (New York: Human Rights Watch, 2004), http://www.hrw.org/sites/default/files/reports/usa0105.pdf.

[3] Associated Press (AP), "57 child labor violations at Agriprocessors in Postville," *Iowa State Daily*, August 8, 2008, http://www.iowastatedaily.com/news/state/article_138dc3bc-e2ac-5481-98aa1cb550f0f50c.html.

[4] Bureau of Labor Statistics, "Employer-Reported Workplace Injuries and Illness – 2012," news release, U.S. Department of Labor, USDL-13-2119, November 7, 2013, http://www.bls.gov/iif/oshsum.htm#12Summary_News_Release.

[5] "Lawsuit Asks EPA to End Use of Hazardous Pesticide in USA," *Earthjustice*, July 24, 2008, http://earthjustice.org/news/press/2008/lawsuit-asks-epa-to-end-use-of-hazardous-pesticide-in-usa.

[6] Gosia Wozniacka, "California: Plea bargain for supervisors in farmerworker's death Death of 17-year-old worker from heat stroke sparked outrage," *LegalNews.com*, March 10, 2011, http://www.legalnews.com/detroit/896065.

[7] Brain Woods and Kate Blewett (directors), *Slavery: A Global Investigation* (London: True Vision, 2000), video, 1:19, http://truevisiontv.com/films/details/90/slavery-a-global-investigation.

[8] lauren Ornelas, "Shining a Light on the Valley of Heart's Delight," *Food Empowerment Project*, August, 2010, http://www.foodispower.org/documents/FEP_Report_web_final.pdf.

[9] National Institutes of Health (NIH), "Lactose Intolerance: Information for Health Care Providers," U.S. Department of Health and Human Services, NIH 05-5305B, January, 2006, https://www.nichd.nih.gov/publications/pubs/Documents/NICHD_MM_Lactose_FS_rev.pdf.

[10] M.R.C. Greenwood, P.B. Crawford, and R.M. Ortiz, "Legislative Task Force on Diabetes & Obesity Report to the California Legislature," January 23, 2009, 10, http://nature.berkeley.edu/site/forms/pdf/diabetes-obesity.pdf.

[11] Ibid., 11.

[12] D. Barav, "How Environmental Conservation Helped Save Cuba," US-Cuba Cooperative Security Project, January 2008, http://www.wsicubaproject.org/resourcemanagment.cfm.

[13] National Research Council, *Measuring Lead Exposure in Infants, Children, and Other Sensitive Populations* (Washington, D.C.: National Academy Press, 1993).

[14] Steve Wing, Dana Cole, and Gary Grant, "Environmental Injustice in North Carolina's Hog Industry," *Environmental Health Perspectives* 108, no. 3 (2000): 225.

[15] Steve Wing and Susanne Wolf, "Intensive Livestock Operations, Health, and Quality of Life among Eastern North Carolina Residents," *Environmental Health Perspectives* 108, no. 3 (2000): 233.

Veganism: A Path to Non-Violence

by Colleen Patrick-Goudreau

I was raised in a typical American family eating the typical American fare: pretty much anything that had once walked, swum, or flew. I wore leather, wool, and fur; slept under down comforters; went to the zoo; attended the circus; and even tried my hand at fishing and falconry. Nightly dinners in our home consisted of a rotation of pork chops, lamb stew, meatloaf, veal cutlets, and ground beef, with vegetables on the side, smeared with butter or covered in cream sauces. With a father who owned ice cream stores and kept a separate freezer just for the gallons of frozen treats he brought home, desserts were a daily (sometimes twice-daily) staple for my sister and me. Milkshakes and hot chocolate flowed from our very own countertop machines, and a year-round supply of gelatin- and milk-laden candies filled our kitchen cabinets and bureau drawers. There was no dearth of animal products in our home, and I ate them all with great enthusiasm. What I know now is that much of my bliss was due to my ignorance about what—and who—I was actually eating.

As a child, I cared deeply for animals, and intervened whenever they needed aid. My affection for and connection with them was fostered by my parents and the adults around me: I was dressed in clothing that featured images of baby animals; I had stuffed animals all over my bedroom; I sang songs, read books, watched movies, and played games that used animals not only to teach me how to be polite, generous, and kind but also how to read, how to spell, and how to count. I was the child who saved injured birds, sheltered stray animals, and stayed up whole nights comforting my dog when she was a scared puppy or sick adult. My parents commended and supported me for demonstrating such kindness, even when it was inconvenient or unreasonable. In every area of my life, I was given the message that animals played an integral role in the shaping of my identity and in the creation of my worldview.

In fact, empathy for and kindness toward animals is one of the barometers we use to measure the emotional and mental health of both children and adults, and we're justifiably concerned when someone is overtly unkind to—or derives pleasure from harming—an animal. It's not that children don't have to be taught that it hurts an animal when you pull his fur, but we shield children from participating in or witnessing animal suffering because we are aware of the trauma it causes both to the observer as well as to the victim. Although I believe that all humans have the capacity to be violent and cruel, I believe also that we have the capacity to be fiercely compassionate, and I think most of us are inclined in the direction of the latter rather than the former. Not everyone necessarily has the desire to spend time in the company of animals, but almost everyone has an aversion to animal cruelty, and we are wary of those who can look upon it—or partake in it—without empathy or remorse. In fact, lacking either is indicative of antisocial behavior.

Most of us can't even look at a dead animal lying on the side of the road without turning away, and it's not merely disgust that forces us to avert our eyes. It's the awareness that a life has been cut short and possibly in a manner that may have caused pain and distress, and in those moments, we're faced with the choice to either close our eyes and suppress our discomfort with (and sometimes our complicity in) animal suffering, or to face it full on and take responsibility. And so, when I was 19 years old, I made the connection between the animals and animal products I was consuming, and the violence I was contributing to—and stopped eating them. But I didn't stop eating animals because I was an "animal lover," as I had been so called as a child. It was much less sentimental than that. It also wasn't altruism. It was something much deeper, something fundamental. It was justice. It was compassion.

I had just read John Robbins's groundbreaking book *A Diet for a New America* and for the first time faced the violence that I had been contributing to. I stopped eating land animals, then all aquatic animals, and after a few more years stopped buying, eating, or wearing anything that came off of or out of an animal or that in any way contributed to animal exploitation. I "became vegan." I wasn't looking for a club to join or a label to wear, and I certainly wasn't looking for anyone's approval, but I didn't expect the negative reactions I elicited from society in general and my parents in particular. I was hurt and surprised, but mostly confused.

The compassion that compelled me to save an injured bluebird when I was a child was the same compassion that now compelled me to want to spare the helpless millions we call "food animals." The only difference was the recipients to whom I extended that compassion. And then it hit me. That difference was not insignificant at all. That difference was a massive chasm between what I realized was the *selective* compassion I had been indoctrinated in, and the *unconditional* compassion I had always been inclined toward.

Demonstrating kindness to dogs, cats, songbirds, and other wild animals is acceptable in our culture, but extending that same compassion to the chickens, turkeys, pigs, cattle, and fish we kill and eat is viewed as an entirely different thing. And so we are taught—implicitly—to temper our compassion, and to compartmentalize animals into arbitrary categories of those we love and those we eat, those we live with and those we exploit, those deserving of our compassion and those unworthy of it simply because they are of a particular species or bred for a particular use.

Couched in the defensive reactions to my veganism was the message that the injured birds who were lucky enough to fall into my yard were worth saving, but the chickens and turkeys whose boneless, featherless bodies lay lifeless on my plate were valuable only in so far as their flesh was tender and juicy. The consequences of this cognitive dissonance are certainly grave for the victims of our appetites, but I would argue that they're equally grave for us. Going from innately compassionate children who identify deeply with animals to desensitized adults who justify our violence against them cannot but affect us at the most basic level—both individually and as a society. And in this thinking, I am certainly not unique.

Ethical vegetarianism—outside of religious doctrine—is not a newfangled, novel idea. It harkens back thousands of years, and at its core is compassion, a universal principle grounded in religions and secular philosophies, resonating with men, women, and children all around the world, all across the ages. We tend to think of "veganism" as a new reactionary trend against what we call factory farming, but for centuries, men and women have been thinking about, writing about, and expressing distress over the violence inherent in killing animals for human use and consumption. My veganism is part of a long continuum of men and women—from ancient times until today—who stopped eating animals (and their eggs and milk) not because they witnessed a modern, mechanized, industrialized factory system, but because they didn't want to be part of the brutal and unnecessary process of turning sentient animals into butchered bodies.

In the 6th century BCE, the Greek philosopher Pythagoras abstained from the flesh of animals—and advised his followers to do the same—out of a sense of justice not only for ourselves and our ancestors (he fervently believed in the transmigration of souls), but also for the animals themselves. Though we have no primary written texts by Pythagoras, his beliefs were well documented in secondary sources. Ovid's 9th century poem "Metamorphoses" tells us that Pythagoras urged his acolytes to eat "food that requires no bloodshed and no slaughter." Pythagoras was the first of many secular philosophers to contend that the killing of animals for consumption desensitizes us to human suffering as well. Greek historian and essayist

Plutarch (c. 46–120 AD) saw no difference between sadistic cruelty and routine butchery, declaring that the person who "tortures a living creature is no worse than he who slaughters it outright." Similarly, it wasn't factory farms that 3rd century Greek philosopher Porphyry had on his mind when he wrote about the "injustice of carnivorism" in his essay "On Abstinence from Animal Food." Recognizing the fact that we have no physiological requirement for the flesh of animals, he lamented that we "deliver animals to be slaughtered and cooked, and thus be filled with murder, not for the sake of nutriment and satisfying the wants of nature, but making pleasure and gluttony the end of such conduct."[1]

These anti-violence, pro-vegetarian sentiments did not preoccupy only our ancient predecessors. Modern Western figures have been equally disturbed by the slaughter and consumption of animals, from Renaissance scholars and Enlightenment philosophers to Romantic artists, 20th century scientists, and 21st century politicians.

All that is to say it is not *how* we breed, keep, and kill animals for human consumption that has been the impetus for vegetarianism for thousands of years; it is *that* we kill animals for human consumption. Throughout the centuries, the common thread in the arguments against eating animals is the fact that because we have no nutritional requirement for the flesh or fluids of animals, killing them simply to satisfy our taste buds—or habits or customs—amounts to senseless slaughter, and senseless slaughter is no small thing.

And so I recognized, as so many others have before and around me, that the most rational, merciful, and obvious way to reflect my compassion for animals was to not eat them. The same compassion that penetrated Plutarch's heart penetrates mine; it is different neither in substance nor degree. The only difference between me and my compassionate forebears is the word we use to describe our desire to avoid causing someone else to suffer when we have the power to do so.

From the time of Pythagoras in the 6th century all the way up to the 19th century, a "Pythagorean diet" signified one that that was based on plants. In the 18th and 19th centuries, proponents of the

Pythagorean way often referred to it as a "vegetable diet" or a "vegetable regimen" (although these are somewhat misleading phrases in that adherents did not subsist on vegetables alone, but also on grains, fruits, nuts, seeds, legumes, and fungi). The word "vegetarian" first appeared in print in the *Healthian* magazine in 1842, though it is clear from its context that it would have been familiar to its audience by that time, leading etymologists to surmise that it was in use by at least the 1830s. And then, in the middle of the 20th century, in reaction to the word "vegetarian," a young British animal activist named Donald Watson conceived a new word to better convey the ethics behind the diet.

Watson was born in 1910 and died 95 years later in the northern region of England called Yorkshire. Intentional vegetarianism was not exactly widespread in the rural, meat-eating community in which he grew up, but when asked about his journey to "becoming vegan," Watson would speak of his childhood memories of seeing and hearing animals slaughtered or being dragged along alleyways to the butcher. He would talk about his visits to his Uncle George's farm, where various animals were kept and used:

> One thing that shocked me was that my Uncle George, of whom I thought very highly, was part of the crew. I decided that farms—and uncles—had to be reassessed: the idyllic scene was nothing more than Death Row, where every creature's days were numbered by the point at which it was no longer of service to human beings.[2]

And so, repelled by violence and compelled by compassion, Watson became vegetarian (and eventually vegan)—a sensible response to the violence he witnessed on the small farms characteristic of his time and locale. That is to say, Watson didn't stop eating animals because of industrialized slaughterhouses and the "Concentrated Animal Feeding Operations" that define today's meat, dairy, and egg industries. He saw even small-scale animal agriculture for what it is: exploitative, ugly, messy, unpredictable, difficult, cruel, and bloody—not as the romanticized thing we've made it out to be when we talk about returning to family farms.

Watson went on to co-found The Vegan Society (vegansociety. com), the first vegan organization in the United Kingdom, which is still active today. A group called The Vegetarian Society was already in place by that time, having been founded in 1847, and was responsible for popularizing the word "vegetarian," which originally referred to a plant-based diet that excluded all animal products—both flesh and secretions. Over time, however, diets called "vegetarian" began to include and embrace the consumption of eggs and animals' milk. Disheartened by this, Donald Watson set out to create a more concise word to describe ethical vegetarians who ate and used no animal products at all, and so in 1944, he, along with his wife, Dorothy, decided on the word "vegan" by taking the first three and last two letters of "vegetarian," because, as Watson explained, "veganism starts with vegetarianism and carries it through to its logical conclusion." Watson emphasized its pronunciation as VEE-gun (not VAY-gun, VEE-jun, or VAY-jun), and wrote its definition: "a philosophy and way of living which seeks to exclude—as far as is possible and practical—all forms of exploitation of and cruelty to animals for food, clothing, or any other purpose." The word was accepted by the *Oxford English Dictionary*, and there it remains, alive and increasing in recognition.

The word has gained traction in the public consciousness, especially in recent years, but misunderstandings still prevail about what it actually means, particularly the misconception that being vegan is about striving to be perfect, as if there is such a thing as a 100% pure certified vegan. Even Watson anticipated this when he clarified: "as far as is possible and practical." I think one of the reasons people tend to equate veganism with perfection is that they're operating under the mistaken idea that being vegan is an *end* in itself, and so you find non-vegans trying to *catch* vegans in all the ways they're imperfect— stepping on insects while walking, driving a car whose tires contain animal products, wearing leather shoes leftover from their pre-vegan days—and vegans, too, beating themselves up for accidentally eating something that contains eggs or for not being able to afford to replace the leather couch they bought just before becoming vegan. But all of this entirely misses the point about what it means to "be vegan." Being vegan is not an *end* in itself; it's a *means* to an end. And that *end* is compassion: doing our best to not contribute to violence against animals when it is possible and practical. Being vegan is a powerful and effective means toward attaining that end, but it is not the end itself.

Had I been asked before I was vegan if I considered myself a compassionate person, I would have answered with a definitive "yes!" I perceived myself to be a compassionate, empathetic, and nonviolent person. But looking back, my perception of myself was not in alignment with my actions, and my actions were not in alignment with my values. Paying people to do things to animals that I would never dream of doing myself was not a reflection of my compassion. Supporting an industry that is by definition violent was obviously not an expression of nonviolence. It's not that there weren't areas in my life where I displayed compassion; of course there were. But compassion when it's convenient or prudent is not really compassion. True compassion doesn't have boundaries or conditions. It is without prejudice and doesn't play favorites according to who the recipients are.

In supporting an industry defined by killing, I simply wasn't immersed in the fullness of my compassion. How could I have been? I was supporting the very things that are antithetical to my core ethics. When I became vegan—which is just a succinct way of saying that I removed the barriers to the compassion that had been inside me all along—unexpectedly, the guilt and hypocrisy I had experienced while I was reveling in the fat and flesh of animals just disappeared. No longer did I have to make excuses about who and what I ate, and any conflict I had felt about how I perceived myself and how I was actually living just melted away. My behavior became consistent with my values, and the sense of peace I experienced was palpable.

I'm tempted to say that I returned to the unconditional compassion of my childhood, but I don't think that's the entire truth of it. As I write in the introduction to my first book *The Joy of Vegan Baking,*

"When I was a child, I acted compassionately without any thought—as if I didn't know any better than to respond to those who needed my help. It just came naturally."[3] As a conscious adult, "I act compassionately *with* thought, and I regret only that the innocent kindness of a child is valued more than the informed kindness of an adult."[4] It was only when I was willing to look at how I contributed to violence against animals that I became awake, and in doing so, I have not so much returned to the innocent compassion of my childhood but instead have found a deeper place, where my eyes and heart are open not because of what I don't know, but because of what I do know. ✆

Notes

[1] Porphry, "On Abstinence from Animal Food," trans. Thomas Taylor, http://www.animal-rights-library.com/texts-c/porphyry01.htm.

[2] "Interview with Donald Watson - Vegan Founder," Foods for Life, http://www.foodsforlife.org.uk/people/Donald-Watson-Vegan/Donald-Watson.html.

[3] Colleen Patrick-Goudreau, *The Joy of Vegan Baking* (Beverly, MA: Fair Winds Publishing, 2007), 14.

[4] Ibid.

Climate Change and Injustice Everywhere

by Sailesh Rao

"The one who says it cannot be done should not interrupt the one who's doing it." —Chinese Proverb

Climate change is a searing indictment of our entire way of life in the industrialized world. Almost everything we do in our global industrial society causes the Earth to heat up. What we wear, what we eat, what we do, and how we live spew greenhouse gases into the atmosphere. It's no wonder that the governments of the world have been punting on this issue for the past two decades even as they meet annually in their Conference of the Parties (COP) at the UN. They have made it abundantly clear that they are unwilling to implement a top-down solution to climate change. At the recent COP19 conference in Warsaw, Poland, the Filipina Climate Chief Mary Ann Lucille Sering said, "It feels like we are negotiating on who is to live and who is to die."[1]

At its core, climate change is a symptom of pervasive injustices that have seeped into industrial societies everywhere. When gross inequity is common, and the strong prey on the weak routinely, both economic and ecologic systems become unbalanced, and climate change happens. In a brilliant article entitled, "Are We on the Verge of Total Self Destruction?" Professor Noam Chomsky of MIT wrote, "At one extreme, you have indigenous tribal societies trying to stem the race to disaster. At the other extreme, the richest, most powerful societies in world history, like the United States and Canada, are racing full-speed ahead to destroy the environment as quickly as possible."[2]

The indigenous tribal societies all have one thing in common: they consider the Earth to be sacred. The richest, most powerful societies in the world all have one thing in common: they are effectively ruled by transnational banks and corporations who consider the Earth to be composed of resources to be processed for economic profit. And therein lays the source of the conflict, as well as the source of the injustices. Nurturing elements within the richest, most powerful societies (women, for example) get caught up in the conflict. They face a double bind: either submit to the corporate-sponsored, dominant, exploitative view of the Earth, or face discrimination and oppression. Even grandmothers are branded as "eco-terrorists" and are thrown in jail for daring to oppose this exploitative paradigm.[3]

While pervasive discrimination and oppression can be classified as economic colonialism, sexism, racism, etc., the underlying motivation is mostly just business. It is no coincidence that four of the richest societies, the United States, Canada, Australia, and New Zealand, are the only four countries to have voted against the UN Declaration on the Rights of Indigenous People in 2007. Even as they reluctantly ratified the Declaration after it was overwhelmingly adopted at the UN, these countries passed legislative resolutions stating that the UN Declaration was non-binding on them.[4] These four countries all happen to be colonized countries, majorly populated by immigrants, where symbols of overt racism towards their indigenous populations are still prevalent even in the 21st century. For example, the mascots of national sports teams use pejorative terms for indigenous people, even today.[5] It is also no coincidence that these four countries along with the United Kingdom are the "Five Eyes" nations implementing a total surveillance state, where there is a mere semblance of privacy for the general public, but total secrecy for governments and corporations. As Bruce Schneier, a security expert wrote:

Both government agencies and corporations have cloaked themselves in so much secrecy that it is impossible to verify anything they say; revelation after revelation demonstrates that they've been lying to us regularly and tell the truth only when there's no alternative... All of us are being watched, all the time, and that data is being stored forever. This is what a surveillance state looks like, and it is efficient beyond the wildest dreams of George Orwell.[6]

And so the battle lines for global sustainability are drawn. Will the indigenous tribal societies and their supporters succeed, or will the corporate powers in the rich societies crush them, along with our collective future? Those of us who live in the richest, most powerful societies have a choice to make: either continue supporting the worldwide destruction of the environment through our consumer choices, or vote with our wallets to make a difference. For therein lies the Achilles heel of the global corporate empire: it depends on our continued consumption to fuel its destruction of the environment. The corporate empire needs us to continue believing in its false promise of packaged happiness in a soda bottle, in a Botox injection, in a block of cheese, while ignoring the connection to our suffering from diabetes, cancer, stroke, and heart disease. It is this brainwashed belief in the pursuit of happiness through external means that sustains the destruction of the environment. If we, instead, wake up to the truth that there is an infinite source of happiness within ourselves, then we can take steps to address climate change, from the bottom up.

Of course, one standard response to this observation is that this is really a population problem, that we can continue believing in the corporate story on the pursuit of happiness while sustaining the consumer society that we've all become accustomed to, if only there were a lot fewer people on the planet. But according to the UN Human Development Report, 91% of the world's consumption is done by the top one-third of humanity.[7] Therefore, the required reduction in population is truly draconian to achieve sustainability, unless those of us in the rich societies constitute the bulk of the reduction. This is simply unthinkable!

Another response is that this is really a global policy issue since "You are not going to get a lot of people to take voluntary action at once," as an eminent climate scientist was quoted as saying recently.[8] But voluntary action is precisely what Mahatma Gandhi spearheaded in the early 20th century by writing magazine articles and by just plain people-to-people persuasion, without the internet, without cellphones, and without social media. It is very instructive to study how he got hundreds of millions of people to take voluntary action at once.

The year was 1914. Gandhi, a middle-aged lawyer, dressed in a finely tailored British suit and tie, embarked on a ship to travel from South Africa to India via England. He was an accidental activist, thrust into that role when he was thrown off the first-class compartment of a train in South Africa for being colored. But now he was sailing out to join and possibly spearhead the Indian independence movement, to take on the mightiest empire that the world had ever seen until that time.

After visiting the villages, towns, and cities of India over the next three years, Gandhi announced his grand idea for taking on the British empire: Indians must change their clothes from British clothes manufactured in the mills of Manchester to simple, home-spun "Khadi" clothes.

At first, Gandhi's plan was met with some ridicule in Indian intellectual circles, as some magazine articles from those times show. How could the bitterly divided people of India take on the mightiest empire the world had seen by just changing their clothes? But he had the backing of a few key intellectuals, including Rabindranath Tagore, a poet Nobel Laureate, who saw the wisdom of concerted action, which could unite the people of India as well as undermine the British textile industry and thus, the economic might of the British Empire. At that time, the textile industry was one of the largest industries in Great Britain. And thus the Khadi movement was born in 1918.

The colonial rulers ignored the Khadi movement, even as Gandhi waged a tireless campaign. Gandhi wrote in the Navjivan magazine in 1925, "It is my duty to induce people, by every honest means, to wear Khadi."[9] And to the consternation of the colonial rulers, within a dozen years after it was founded, by 1931, the Khadi movement had managed to bankrupt the textile mills of Manchester, paving the way for the eventual independence of India 16 years later, in 1947. Gandhi was a genius for framing the Indian freedom struggle, not as one between peoples, but as one between the people of both India and Great Britain versus the ruling corporate elites. He rightly observed that the textile mill workers of Manchester were also the oppressed victims of industrialization and that it was the English East India Company (not the people of Great Britain) that began the colonization of India. Gandhi was also a genius for recognizing that it is only concerted personal actions that can lead to a social transformation. The Khadi movement united the people of India in a common bond, helping them tide over their other vast differences.

Now, almost a century later, we are faced with a similar situation, but on a global scale. Gandhi was fighting for the independence of India. We are now fighting for the survival of our children and grandchildren, and indeed, for the survival of all life on Earth as we know it. Gandhi inspired the people of India to make that one simple change, to take that voluntary step of changing their clothes. We need to inspire people in industrial societies—specifically, all people who have access to the internet—to take that voluntary step of changing what we eat and buy, to go vegan. The food industry of the early 21st century is the global equivalent of the textile industry of the early 20th century in Great Britain. It is one of the largest industries in the world with, by far, the largest footprint on nature. As George Wuerthner points out, in the continental US alone, more than half the land, around 1 billion acres, is used for livestock production, while half the vegetables and fruits eaten in the US, along with three-quarters of the almonds consumed worldwide, are grown on just 3 million acres of land in the state of California.[10] Globally, the International Livestock Research Institute (ILRI) reports that 45% of the land area of the planet is currently used for livestock production.[11] Thus, a mass transition to veganism in the industrial societies would make a huge, positive impact on the environment, and strike a blow against the corporate culture angling for its destruction, while alleviating the suffering of billions of our fellow creatures.

Thus the vegan movement, without a doubt, has the same potential for personal and social transformation in the 21st century globally, as the Khadi movement did in 20th century India. Just like the Khadi movement, it is simple to join; it is simple to implement; it is utterly empowering, and it is totally democratic. It is a far more practical step than foregoing the use of fossil fuels in our daily lives. Is it any wonder that countries like Germany have seen an 800% increase in vegans in the last three years alone? [12]

Our indigenous brothers and sisters will thank us today if we join the vegan movement, because if enough of us embrace veganism, they can stay in their forest communities and continue to protect the environment. And our children and grandchildren will thank us later for saving the forests and the oceans, for saving the planet for them.

Meanwhile, "What good is it to save the planet, if humanity suffers?" said Rex Tillerson, the CEO of ExxonMobil! [13]

Poor man, perhaps he really does suffer much when his bank balance slims a bit! Such is the lot of those who have bought into the false story that happiness can only be pursued and captured through external means. ❧

Notes

[1] "Filipina Climate Chief: 'It Feels Like We Are Negotiating on Who Is to Live and Who Is to Die,'" *Democracy Now!* November 20, 2013, http://www.democracy now.org/2013/11/20/filipino_climate_chief_it_feel_like.

[2] Noam Chomsky, "Are We on the Verge of Total Self-Destruction?" *AlterNet*, June 4, 2013, http://www.alternet.org/news-amp-politics/noam-chomsky-nuclear?paging=off.

[3] "Darryl Hannah and East Texas Great-Grandmother Arrested Protesting Keystone XL Pipeline," *Ecowatch*, October 4, 2012, http://ecowatch.com/2012/10/04/daryl-hanna-arrested/.

[4] Four Arrows, "The US 'Rethinks' the UN Declaration on Indigenous Rights, Maybe," *Truthout*, January 23, 2011, http://truth-out.org/archive/component/k2/item/94044:the-us-rethinks-the-un-declaration-on-indigenous-rights-maybe.

[5] New Mexico PBS, "Colores: False Traditions, False Idols," YouTube video, 27:52, uploaded by "knmedotorg" on December 7, 2009, https://www.youtube.com/watch?v=QeNn1Am2svc.

[6] Bruce Schneier, "NSA Secrets Kill Our Trust," *CNN*, July 31, 2013, http://www.cnn.com/2013/07/31/opinion/schneier-nsa-trust/index.html.

[7] United Nations Development Programme (UNDP). *Human Development Report 1998* (New York: Oxford University Press, 1998), http://hdr.undp.org/sites/default/files/reports/259/hdr_1998_en_complete_nostats.pdf.

[8] Frank Jotzo, "Climate Change – Economics and Policy: A/Prof Frank Jotzo Interviewed by Dr. Jan Libich," by Jan Libich, YouTube video, 1:00:10, uploaded May 13, 2014, https://www.youtube.com/watch?v=oLsMav4FbwQ.

[9] Divya Joshi, comp., *Gandhiji on KHADI* (Mumbai: Gandhi Book Centre, 2002), http://www.mkgandhi.org/ebks/gandhijionkhadi.pdf.

[10] George Wuerthner, "Livestock and the Environment," Vimeo video, 1:31, from a speech presented by Northwest Veg in Portland, OR, 2012, uploaded by "NWVeg.org," http://vimeo.com/29989350.

[11] Philip Thornton, Mario Herrero, and Polly Ericksen, "Livestock and Climate Change," *Livestock Exchange Issue Brief* 3, International Livestock Research Institute, November 2011, https://cgspace.cgiar.org/bitstream/handle/10568/10601/IssueBrief3.pdf.

[12] Fabio Chaves, "Veganismo cresceu 800% nos últimos 3 anos na Alemanha," *Vista-se*, June 10, 2013, http://vista-se.com.br/veganismo-cresceu-800-nos-ultimos-3-anos-na-alemanha/.

[13] Ryan Koronowski and Joe Romm, "Exxon CEO: 'What Good Is It to Save the Planet If Humanity Sufffers?'" *ThinkProgress*, May 30, 2013, http://thinkprogress.org/climate/2013/05/30/2076751/exxon-ceo-what-good-is-it-to-save-the-planet-if-humanity-suffers/.

Injustice Everywhere

by Anteneh Roba

While sitting in a Birmingham, Alabama jail in 1963, Dr. Martin Luther King, Jr., wrote a letter in which he said, "Injustice anywhere is a threat to justice everywhere. We are caught in an inescapable network of mutuality, tied in a single garment of destiny. Whatever affects one directly, affects all indirectly."[1]

These prophetic words, written decades ago by a man sitting in jail, confirm what I have witnessed throughout my travels across the globe. Although Dr. King focused on the human condition, I am sure if he were with us today, he would have expanded his sphere of concern to recognize that injustice to any sentient being anywhere is an injustice to every sentient being everywhere.

The intertwining of injustice and violence that nonhuman animals suffer at the hands of humans, and the injustice and violence that humans deliver to their fellow human beings, is displayed every day across the globe. This is also evident when one travels in Africa.

A vast and beautiful continent with a long history of colonialism, massive exploitation, unending poverty and hunger, and, most recently, ecological destruction, Africa can be seen as the prototype for the commonality of oppression in its various forms, such as speciesism, sexism, racism, classism, and other hierarchical ideologies.

In 2009, I traveled to Accra, Ghana, to attend the second West Africa Vegetarian Congress and to speak on behalf of International

Fund for Africa, a non-profit organization I co-founded in 2006 and for which I serve as president. Accompanied by my cousin, I visited the Elmina Castle on the Gold Coast of Ghana. Built by the Portuguese in 1482 as a trading post, the castle later became a major stop in the Atlantic slave trade.[2]

When we arrived at the castle, situated on a beach, the beauty of the area belied the place's hidden history. It was a very warm day. Our guide spoke about the history of the castle, and as we walked around the halls, my mood began to change. At one point, we reached a courtyard where young slave girls had been displayed, naked, as a commanding officer of the Dutch army stood on a balcony overlooking the yard. After he selected a girl, that poor soul would then be hosed down and taken upstairs to be raped. A sinking feeling overcame me, and I saw the color drain from my female cousin's face. It did not take long before we both realized that the reality of this place would only become grimmer as we continued on the tour.

Passing through another hallway, we reached a large closed door. When we opened the door and walked inside, we found ourselves in a large, windowless dungeon, very humid and damp, with no light penetrating the darkness. There was an indescribable odor, which I had never experienced before. Our guide explained that up to 400 women were stored in this filthy place not meant to hold more than 100 people. Slave traders kidnapped these people inland, sometimes with the assistance of the locals, before shipping them to the Americas. They shackled their human merchandise in the dungeon, where the slaves had to defecate, urinate, and menstruate where they were held in place until the time came for their shipboard ordeal. Some even gave birth in that dark and filthy dungeon.

While our guide spoke of events three centuries past, I felt myself transported to that time. I could smell the dungeon's fetid stench, feel the captives' terror and agony. My chest tightened, and I experienced difficulty breathing. I became sweaty and dizzy as if I were about to pass out. I regained my composure in time to exit the dungeon with the group, soon after which our guide showed us an opening in the castle's exterior wall, only inches wide, opening onto the beach. The guide explained that after a few weeks at the castle, the captives would lose so much weight that they could pass through such an opening to board the slave ships.

We made our way to a second dungeon, a bit larger than the first, where the male captives were held. As I stood in this dungeon, which could not comfortably house more than 150 people but had held 600, something even more profound happened. While in the first room of doom I had grieved for the innocent human lives lost and ruined, in the dungeon that held the men I saw mental images of animals in factory farms: hundreds of pigs, cows, chickens, turkeys, and other miserable beings similarly reduced to property-of-humans status and crammed into cruel, ugly places, terrified and crowded together with no space to move, no clean air to breathe, and no access to the outside world. I had seen countless scenes of animal abuse in the food industry in documentary films through the years, and now they flooded my mind.

The depth of sadness I felt was indescribable when I realized that although what had happened to those enslaved human beings might be over now, billions of nonhuman animals were experiencing similar mistreatment right now, with no end to their plight on the horizon. Worse, I thought, while human slavery at least was always deemed wrong by large segments of the human population, the vast animal abuse system hardly stirs controversy, although it afflicts living beings with feelings, emotions, and families—sentient beings with no less moral right than humans to live unmolested on this planet.

Every day throughout the industrialized world, and in many "developing" countries as well, these concentration camps attest to the immense injustice and violence that human beings perpetrate against their fellow beings and to the deep and far-reaching hatred and violence that still exist in our society. We human beings have made great strides in science, technology, and the humanities. We pride ourselves on becoming more civilized, on being governed by the rule of law, and feel content that barbarism is in our past. Despite such assumptions, the ongoing mistreatment of nonhuman animals, the endless wars for control of resources disguised as liberation or humanitarian intervention, the exploitation of countless millions of humans, and the thoroughgoing abuse of our Earth tell a different story.

My exposure to the horrors of Elmina Castle opened my heart and soul to what happened to Africans then and what happens to farm animals today. I became better able to connect on a deep level with the plight of farm animals, yet also expand my understanding of the complex ways that racism, sexism, and speciesism are all interconnected. And I can see why most people avoid this knowledge—"For in much wisdom is much grief, and he that increaseth knowledge increaseth sorrow" (Ecclesiastes 1:18).

My road to compassion began in 1999 when I adopted a fur-ball called Nikita. This little Maltese dog became my teacher, my "guru," my "Buddha." His unconditional love for me, and mine for him, reopened a door that had locked itself close in the deepest parts of my heart when I lost my mother at a very young age. Nikita opened the floodgates of compassion that I never thought I had, and because of him, I became vegan and decided to dedicate my life to alleviating the suffering of both nonhumans and humans.

After adopting Nikita, I became involved with dog rescue in my home of Houston, Texas. Dogs became my guide to the world of nonhuman suffering, which I learned much more about in the following years. Yet despite rescuing many dogs from terrible living conditions, watching countless documentaries on animal suffering, and intellectually understanding the enormity of the problem, nothing prepared me for the profound level of understanding I was to gain from standing in the dungeons of Elmina Castle.

After my tour of Elmina, my heart and mind were even more prepared to see what my eyes had refused to see and my ears had refused to hear. For the next several years, as I traveled in Africa to speak at conferences or work on projects for my organization, I developed a more acute awareness of the suffering I was seeing, and a greater ability to grasp how violence against nonhuman animals, women, and impoverished human beings is manifested. I was even able to mentally go back and re-examine events I was involved in a few years back, like the one that occurred in 2007 when my organization helped rescue four dogs in Ethiopia who had been tossed alive into a cave and left to die. They later became known as the Gido Cave dogs. At the time, we were pleased to save these four animals, and place them in homes in the US. We prevailed upon the Ethiopian government to close this cave, where, for 20 years, some 20 homeless dogs per month had been thrown in to die a painful and untimely death.[3] What I had failed to realize about this travesty in 2007 was that the dogs were mostly females. In many African countries, female dogs are deemed dispensable, and are discarded at birth, or, as with the Gido Cave victims, thrown away with newborn puppies soon after giving birth. I started to recognize that discrimination against the female sex extends to nonhuman animals. Male dogs in many African countries are valued as protectors, and recruited as guard dogs, while females are devalued as weak, troublesome, and costly.

The connection between violence against nonhuman animals intertwines seamlessly with violence against female humans, poor people, and minorities throughout the world. The captives who were transported to the Americas during the Middle Passage were seen as less than human, and treated as such. The exploitation of nonhuman animals provided a framework which made it easy to dehumanize and enslave black people. American and European colonialists who came from a long history of dominating and exploiting other animals used their familiarity with these practices to castrate, chain, brand, and crop the ears of human captives, as well as to separate family members once they arrived in the Americas.

Indigenous African religions center on a hierarchical universe with "man" at the top, and "animals" at the bottom. This worldview comes perilously close to "The Great Chain of Being" articulated by Aristotle,[4] whose views on "natural slavery" were used by Europeans to justify slavery during the early days of American colonization. Aristotle's hierarchy of being had been incorporated into Christianity by St. Augustine in the 4th century.[5] The origins of this hierarchy are uncertain, but many anthropologists hypothesize that the enslavement ("domestication") of nonhuman animals at the dawn of agricultural society served as the prototype for systems that became ritualized, codified, and eventually articulated and promoted by religion and philosophy.

Thus, a predominant assumption throughout Africa is that nonhuman animals are innately inferior to humans, and therefore have no rights. Whatever consideration humans extend to other animals is based on their perceived utility to human beings and human societies. Through my many travels in Africa, from the west coast to the east coast, and from the south to the north, after meeting and talking with many intellectuals, common folk, and people of various religions who are charged with seeing to the welfare of nonhuman animals, I believe the concept of a hierarchical world order informs many African cultures just as it does Western ones. And the ramifications are enormous.

Perceiving women as existing one rung below men, and other animals as one step below humans, opens the door to the subjugation of *any* weaker group by a stronger group. Colonialism, flourishing in Africa today under the rubric of neo-colonialism, is an extension of human supremacy over the animal kingdom.[6]

Resource extraction, whether by force as in recent centuries, or by proxy wars (such as in the Congo, Liberia, the Sudan, Rwanda, Libya, and Sierra Leone), devastates ecosystems, kills innocent animals, puts children in harm's way, and subjects women to rape—sometimes in huge numbers, as in the Congo. "Big game" hunting, fishing, and the dumping of chemical waste off the coastal shores of Africa all manifest the same ideology. So I find it sadly ironic that so many African men do not place their own treatment of women and nonhuman animals on a continuum with white men's treatment of them.

Among many other abuses, this hierarchical worldview produces ritual killing. The ritual killing of nonhuman animals is viewed as an acceptable and even necessary action demanded by the gods. In South Africa, for example, Ukweshwama, an annual ceremony that celebrates a new harvest, includes some forty Zulu warriors physically tearing apart a bull in thanksgiving to their ancestors and the creator.[7]

This horrendous treatment of a defenseless animal, seen as a soul-less, emotionless, inanimate being, which occurs in the first part of December every year in Zululand, South Africa, starkly shows how even people who have a courageous history of fighting the worst kind of racism will readily perpetrate violence if their ideology places others beneath them. The pervasiveness of this violence is so deep that it cuts across race and religious lines. One is reminded of Descartes's mecha-nistic view of animals as simple automatons with no feelings who can see, hear, and touch, but have no conscious thought and do not feel real pain or suffering.[8]

The incongruity, the paradox, the cognitive dissonance reflected in such actions illustrates how disconnected we human beings have become from the natural world, and how conditioned to violence we are. Whether we discuss European or American colonialists involved in the transatlantic slave trade, or Zulu warriors involved in violent crimes against enslaved bulls, the crimes are just as brutal and terrible. The victims are first vilified, perceived as brutes, stupid beasts, not worthy of consideration, then seen as having no feelings and occupy-ing a lower evolutionary position, after which it becomes very easy to abuse them.

Despite the enormous level of violence inherent in such acts, groups that oppose cruelty to animals in African societies are often accused of racism and cultural imperialism. Members of one such organization, the now defunct Animal Rights South Africa, were severely criticized and accused of being racists because most of them were white.

While speaking about animal suffering in Africa, I am often asked, "What about human suffering? How can you talk about animal suffering when there is so much human suffering?" A vexing problem, I remind my audience that human and nonhuman suffering are intertwined, not mutually exclusive, and that they share common roots, and that environmental exploitation harms all animals, including humans.

Factory farming serves as an example, and it is rapidly taking root in Africa. Factory farming is extremely harmful to the environment, exacerbating fresh-water scarcity, rainforest destruction, desertification, and global warming. In Africa, land is cleared for factory farms, for grazing, and growing feed shipped to the animal factories, all to raise animals for overseas markets. The people who work at these massive, inhumane, and dehumanizing facilities never see any of the corporate profits generated from the sale of the animals. Thus, the nonhuman-animal trade worsens the inequality and food scarcities that plague the African continent, as monetary benefits of land, water, and vegetation are channeled to distant owners and shareholders.

Another phenomenon sweeping Africa, closely linked to factory farming, is a new form of agrarian colonialism called "land leasing."[9] China, India, countries in the Middle East, and wealthier countries as well as Western corporations buy up precious arable land in Africa for very little money, and then set up factory farms or cash-crop businesses that leave the land wasted beyond repair. The human inhabitants of the land are forcibly removed, and endure destitution, poverty, prostitution, crime, and hunger.

Because of the severe inequality and classism that predominate in Africa, rich Africans abuse poor Africans, and poor Africans abuse nonhuman animals considered one rung below them in the "natural" hierarchy. Likewise, men dominate and abuse women—an epidemic case being the Congo during the intractable violent conflict of recent years. Cursed with an abundance of prized resources like gold, tantalum, and coltran, a mineral needed for the functioning of electronic devices like cell phones, the Congo has been exploited for centuries with the colonization and brutal treatment of its people by Belgium under King Leopold II. Since then, the Congo has been a scene of human tragedy unparalleled in recent history. The exploitation of its mineral resources by foreign powers, and the continuous armed conflict waged by militias to control the mineral resources of the country, led to the death of an estimated 6 million people by the end of the 20th century,[10] and the holocaust unfortunately continues. In the Congo, as many as forty-eight women are raped every hour.[11]

Domestic animals suffer from the same conflict; they either starve to death due to the continuous armed conflict between opposing sides, or are intentionally killed to inflict psychological and financial trauma on the local people. Wild animals also suffer because the Congo rainforest, being cleared for logging and for grazing of exploited farm animals, exposes them to hunting for "bush meat." This is considered a delicacy in some parts of Africa, fetching an amount of money that is significant to poor people barely able to survive in a war-torn economy.

Traveling the world and witnessing many forms of social injustice and animal abuse has led me to conclude that until we humans abandon our hierarchical way of thinking, the belief that one group has a right to oppress another based on species, race, gender, class, or other invidious distinctions, will continue. No laws, legislation, or political edict will reverse the tide of violence. What's called for is a deep shift in consciousness, a psycho-spiritual awakening that rejects domination, subjugation, oppression, and violence. One cannot legislate indifference and prejudice out of existence. One cannot pass laws that stamp out some people's sense of superiority and disrespect for others.

The meme of hierarchical thinking and the need to dominate other beings, passed down through generations like a gene, cannot be wished away or criminalized. Nor can we eradicate oppression as long as we value material wealth over sentient beings. However, issues such as poverty; injustice; class stratification; corrupt political, legal and judicial systems; and wars of exploitation can all be addressed by changing politico-economic power structures that dominate the planet and too often value profit over people and nonhuman animals.

Compassion for all life must filter through our thought process and our relationship to other beings if we are going to truly stop the bloodshed we humans inflict on ourselves, on nonhuman animals, and on "Gaia" or Mother Earth, and to reiterate what the great civil right leader Dr. King once said, "injustice anywhere is a threat to justice everywhere."[12] Unless we make that connection, unless we realize that the suffering of any being anywhere on the planet diminishes us all, the violence we witness every day will continue unabated until the end of time. ❧

Notes

[1] Martin Luther King, Jr., "Letter from Birmingham City Jail," *African Studies Center* – University of Pennsylvania, 1963, accessed August 22, 2014, http://www.africa.upenn.edu/Articles_Gen/Letter_Birmingham.html.

[2] Jamila White, comp., "The Slave Kingdoms: Elmina Castle," *Wonders of the African World with Henry Louis Gates, Jr,* PBS, accessed August 22, 2014, http://www.pbs.org/wonders/Episodes/Epi3/elmina.htm.

[3] Amsale Gessesse Memorial Foundation, "Gido Cave," YouTube video, 8:18, posted May 23, 2008, https://www.youtube.com/watch?v=rv7Jai-WgN0.

[4] Aristotle, *Politics* 1.1254b6-21.

[5] Michael Mendelson, "Saint Augustine," *The Stanford Encyclopedia of Philosophy,* Winter 2012 ed., edited by Edward N. Zalta, last modified November 12, 2010, http://plato.stanford.edu/archives/win2012/entries/augustine/.

[6] Charles Patterson, *Eternal Treblinka: Our Treatment of Animals and the Holocaust* (New York: Lantern Books, 2002).

[7] Barry Bearak, "Spilling the Blood of Bulls to Preserve Zulu Tradition," *New York Times*, December 8, 2009, http://www.nytimes.com/2009/12/09/world/africa/09safrica.html.

[8] Mary Midgley, "Descartes' Prisoners," review of *Through Our Eyes Only?: The Search for Animal Consciousness*, by Marian Stamp Dawkins, *New Statesman*, May 24, 1999, http://www.newstatesman.com/node/134849.

[9] "A Global Rush for Africa's Land: Riskes and Opportunities," African Development Bank Group, October 17, 2012, http://www.afdb.org/en/blogs/afdb-championing-inclusive-growth-across-africa/post/a-global-rush-for-africas-land-risks-and-opportunities-9844/.

[10] "IRC Study Shows Congo's Neglected Crisis Leaves 5.4 Million Dead; Peace Deal in N. Kivu, Increased Aid Critical to Reducing Death Toll," *International Rescue Committee*, accessed August 22, 2014, http://www.rescue.org/news/irc-study-shows-congos-neglected-crisis-leaves-54-million-dead-peace-deal-n-kivu-increased-aid—4331.

[11] Fiona Lloyd-Davies, "Why Eastern DR Congo Is 'Rape Capital of the World,'" *CNN*, November 25, 2011, http://www.cnn.com/2011/11/24/world/africa/democratic-congo-rape/index.html.

[12] See note 1 above.

Becoming a Vegan Feminist Agitator

by Marla Rose

The summer before I left for college, I went out with a guy I worked with one warm night that I'm guessing was in July. He was tall with olive skin and dark eyelashes, as reserved in demeanor as I was outgoing. I was surprised when he asked me out. We met up with some other friends from work and drank screwdrivers out of orange juice bottles at Lake Michigan on a park bench, feeling giddy and sly as we, probably very conspicuously, turned away from the bike path and took swigs from our bottles. I don't remember his name or very much about that night, other than the intoxication of a new crush, of his arm draped behind me on the bench, of tipsy laughter, of a sticky lime paleta ice pop. As the sunset melted down into the skyline, this guy who was so very quiet and shy at work was suddenly hilarious. He read the obscene carvings on our bench with an absurd, stuffy British accent that I remember thinking was uproariously inspired.

How I look back at that night changes pretty quickly after I remember what happened after leaving the beach. When he drove me home, we stopped at a traffic light a few blocks from my house. We were just laughing about something when, out of nowhere, he stared straight ahead and said, "I could rape you right now and there would be nothing you could do about it." I looked at him, blinking—*was he joking?* He made eye contact briefly to let me know that he was dead serious, his face as icily devoid of expression as his voice had suddenly become, and in that moment, my eyes flashed to those big hands on the steering wheel that were easily twice the size of mine. We rode in silence the rest of the way home, my fingers gripping the door lock. He dropped me off at my house, the one where my parents slept upstairs, where I'd left for work that morning, and I dashed out without a word. Then I went to bed like it was any other night.

We didn't go out again; we never even made eye contact again or exchanged another word. What he said unnerved me but I didn't think much more about it. My relative nonchalance about sharing a workplace with someone who'd said this to me is more telling than the fact that somebody had actually said it. By that point, the threat of sexual violence was already pervasive and normalized in my life. What he said—the chillingly cold assertion of his power, and, implicitly, that my safety was entirely owing to his unnecessary benevolence—wasn't anything worth getting upset about. This was life. It could have been far worse.

After I went away to college, my latent feminist tendencies developed and flourished like thirsty seedlings that had finally gotten some water: in this case, the water was books, friends, and conversations. I thought back about that night in the car, about other experiences where I'd been harassed or threatened based on the fact that I was female and I realized for the first time how pervasive, destructive, and yet utterly commonplace this practice was in my life and those of my friends. Developing a lens that noticed, and a voice that spoke out against misogyny, had consequences that I hadn't anticipated. I was accused of taking things too seriously, of prudishness, of unfairly vilifying what was natural and normal. (Sound familiar to some vegans?) To me, though, I was finally coming into my own. These loose threads were coming together. I had become a vegetarian when I was 15, and it was in easy alignment with my burgeoning convictions about justice and compassion, as was the feminist outlook I now effortlessly embraced. It all clicked into place as gratifyingly as puzzle pieces fitting together. I thought that I had taken my convictions about justice and compassion to their ultimate conclusion, but as I grew by being challenged, I learned that my puzzle had several missing pieces. I had a lot of room for evolving.

Working in humane education at an animal shelter, my blinders started coming off, specifically about the brutalities of the egg and dairy industries. We had a small library at the shelter, and part of my job was to research and print out educational materials for people who called our hotline. In addition to the books, magazines, and films we would loan out, we also had a big file cabinet filled with a pretty extensive and well-organized collection of articles curated by the manager of our department. As a shelter for dogs and cats, most of the materials were about topics relating to them, but at least once a day, someone would call with questions about agribusiness, animals in captivity, the leather industry, and more, and we had to be informed about all of this. As I was gathering articles to mail out (that thing you did before there was the internet), I was also reading them. One day, I was standing at the printer waiting for my copies, and I glanced down at my leather shoes. Without warning, it was as if invisible webs cleared from my eyes and I could suddenly see the tortured cow in the shoes I had put on that morning without a second thought. In that moment, and in the weeks that followed, I had a disorienting sensation of being in two places at once: where I was, and where I was headed.

I remember being irritated at having my complacency jostled by what I was learning. Actually, truth be told, it wasn't irritation: it felt closer to resentment. Wasn't I doing enough? Did I ever promise anyone that I'd be perfect? My family already regarded me as a melodramatic extremist for being both a vegetarian and a feminist: was I really thinking about pushing things yet again? There was an awkward period of time before I went vegan, of knowing better but wishing that I didn't, of wanting to return to the person I was before, the person who did enough without tearing at her comfortable seams, without disrupting her life. I treaded there for a while, but as I learned more about the unnecessary horrors we inflict upon animals and how deeply they violated my core beliefs about justice, the tide pulled me in deeper every day, up past my chest, my neck, my chin. I realized that if I didn't want to drown, I needed to make a decision: to keep treading the waters that were comfortable and familiar, or to embrace the nerves that come with swimming into the unknown.

At some point, I gave up my resistance. I stopped paddling wildly. I wasn't going to drown. In accepting the truth about my complicit role in aiding and abetting cruelty, I had to leave the cycle of denial. As my options for self-deception narrowed in on me, I learned that the only time I felt like I was drowning was when I fought with reality. The waters of self-deception were, in truth, far choppier. As a feminist, I couldn't hide from the fact that what we do to animals to fulfill our consumer demands is profoundly un-feminist. We impregnate the animals against their will, breeding them into captivity, we imprison them, we control and violate their reproductive sovereignty and organs so we can take what we want out of them, and, when they have given us most of what they have, we toss them out to make room for more fertile ones. This is what feminists approve of and directly cause when we consume animals' stolen milk and eggs. We take the babies we have forced into them so we can have the products we want. The mothers get nothing. They are denied the pleasure of raising their babies. They are denied the comforts of being suckled and feeling their wings around their chirping young. Even in the rare cases where babies and mothers aren't separated and are allowed something resembling a decent life, we still decide how they live as well as how and when they will die. None of this challenges the status quo of ownership, of our "right" to their very physical bodies.

How can an avowed feminist accept these terms imposed on another female? At the bottom line, we do this because we *can*, and this is terrifyingly cold and unjust, rooted in the same corrupt mentality of hierarchy that accepts rape and violence as business as usual. As I made copies of articles in our little library, I flashed back to that simple statement made to me in the car years before: *"I could rape you right now and there would be nothing you could do about it."* How is this different from, "I can forcibly impregnate you right now and there is nothing you could do about it", "I can steal your babies right now and there is nothing you could do about it", or "I can kill you right now and there is nothing you could do about it"? Even if I didn't wish to inflict violence upon another, what was I tacitly and overtly supporting when I paid those industries that did do it? My little luxuries had been more important than the miseries imposed on animals to get what I wanted, and I could no longer live with that decision.

Years after I started becoming enlightened in that little library at work, I took my son home from the hospital after he was born. I had a long and complicated delivery that stretched over days, but I was surrounded by professionals who cared, people who minimized my pain, and by loved ones who held my hand and stayed by my side. I was able to briefly hold my son before he was transported to another hospital for six days. He was taken from me with my consent, and there were people at his side who wanted the best for him, who were available at every moment of the day and night. When my son was finally able to come home with us and I was able to nurse him in my own bed instead of being surrounded by machines and mechanical beeps, I could finally relax. My husband and I washed the hospital smell off of him, dressed him in the adorable little purple tie-dye onesie I couldn't wait to dress him in, and got to know our magnificent baby. I was grief-stricken in the weeks that followed the birth of my son though, because I also understood in my bones how many mothers are denied the basic right to love and raise their own babies, and how brutal the mentality of ownership is to all animals. I will never forget this feeling either.

I am a feminist. I am vegan for the same reasons that I am a feminist. It is really as simple as that. ✑

How We Hinder Children to Protect Them

by Ruby Roth

We require children to recite the Pledge of Allegiance for "liberty and justice for all." We teach kids that Abraham Lincoln, in sum, freed the slaves. We ensure that every child can recognize the icon of Martin Luther King, Jr., and summarize his achievements in one sentence— and then we take the day off in celebration of his life.

We tell kids that it only takes one person to change the world, but we don't tell them how it can be done.

Our promises are empty: the nod we give to achievements in social justice is void of substantive wisdom.

Why go through the motions at all if not to relay lessons of significance? It is *not* that children are too young to learn the whys and hows of social change. They are capable of much more than our culture gives them credit for. We leave out the grittier details behind achievements in social justice because we collectively believe that children should be sheltered from the "adult" world.

Without much thought, we accept a concept of childhood that sees children as fragile beings who require being kept ignorant of many basic realities. But there is no universally accepted concept of childhood. Notions of what is and isn't appropriate for children vary throughout history and the world. Kids are more competent and sturdy than we think. When we sugarcoat, oversimplify, or avoid truths, we hinder what our children are capable of, psychologically, spiritually, and morally. We hinder our progress as a society.

The path to a more sustainable and socially just future lies in bravely *engaging* our children in new ways of thinking and living—even if matters are challenging. Kids must know what's at stake, they must understand the power of the individual in a substantive manner, and they must be aware of how, *specifically,* they can help change the world.

A vegan education (there's no better curriculum encompassing environmental, health, and humane education) starts where kids are already interested—with animals—and leads to the kind of life-centered worldview critical to sustainable innovations and environmental and social policies. Think how the future of business, industry, and politics would look with such systemic thinkers at the helm.

In my experience, the resistance to the *notion* of a vegan education is more about adults' unwillingness to change than it is about kids' abilities to learn.

When my second children's book, *Vegan Is Love,* was released in 2012, major media outlets picked up the news. Not in celebration of a new resource for a new generation of compassionate kids, but because inviting children into an honest dialogue about meat and dairy products was being deemed outrageous and controversial—after all, most parents avoid the day their kid realizes that chicken nuggets do not, in fact, grow on trees. My book threatened to make kids more aware than was comfortable for adults.

While a slew of media talking heads judged *Vegan Is Love* to be propaganda, dangerous, brainwashing, and even child abuse, vegan families—who have all along been engaging in the work of social change—had a good laugh. After a child psychologist on television called *Vegan Is Love* "the most disturbing children's book" he'd ever seen, I received a note from a 10-year-old vegan girl who had seen the segment and asked, "Why is that expert so ignorant?" An even younger girl threw her hands in the air and asked me, "What's so scary about your book? It just tells the truth!"

Grownups were having a hard time with the concept of social change toward a life-centered, compassionate worldview, while children were understanding it easily.

"Children don't know the full story!" these skeptical adults argued. "Kids don't know about nutrient deficiencies or human history or food production or costs! They just want to be nice to animals!"

Precisely. Where better to begin an exploration of the world's unknowns than from a place of compassion and a sense of justice?

With animals as the centerpiece, my books address how even the youngest of children can put their love into action—through healthy food and cruelty-free choices that protect our bodies, the environment, and all living beings. I cover the emotional lives of animals—the *whys* behind veganism—and our choices, the *hows* of a compassionate lifestyle. They *are* picture books, but at their core, my books are about democracy, supply and demand, and engaging ourselves in the public realm. We *can* give kids this education—and it is one that lasts a lifetime.

To this day, I have never known any child to be overwhelmed by discovering the motives behind veganism—only adults. In this way, the media outrage over *Vegan Is Love* revealed the invisible forces that shape public thinking about children, food, health, and animals—hindering our growth toward a more sustainable and just world. If the public were aware of the level of disease and abuse caused by eating animals, the outrage would be directed at the pervasive cultural programming, not at a children's book about choices alternative to the status quo.

Corporations are well aware of the importance of marketing to kids in order to increase profits. But neither our educational systems, nor parenting magazines, nor children's literature takes the intelligence and abilities of kids seriously enough to help empower them to create substantive social change. Engaging kids is not just good for business—it's good for a sustainable and just future.

Those families who do engage with tough topics enough to discover the level of disease and abuse in the meat and dairy industries find a broad range of reasons to change their eating habits. But most people, including conventional nutritionists, doctors, and psychologists, have nary the slightest notion of what they are eating, of our corrupted food systems, of the relentless brutality they participate in, nor the cognitive and emotional capacities of animals. In most every major media interview I've had, the question of animals nearly disappears, leaving me with a profound sense of the pervasive bias toward anthropocentrism. Perpetuated in adulthood, it is this outlook that is precisely the root cause of the health, economic, and environmental crises we find ourselves in today, and which validates the very need to educate children early on about the effects of our choices on both animals and ourselves.

Our naive delusion of supremacy is a miseducation that begins in childhood—both on our plates and at the zoo.

Unlike adults, children respond to the revelation of society's harmful practices with curiosity, insight, and reflection, rather than defensiveness or fear of judgment. (Remembering their reactions often saves me from jumping off a cliff of hopelessness.)

Potential profit does not sway a child's moral compass and it does not for them suffice as a good reason for harmful behavior. When kids learn how much destruction we create by eating animals, they ask multitudes of "why?" questions. You can see their holy curiosity about *humankind* and *why* we would even have such a system when it hurts. I answer them with the truth—that most people have no idea what they're participating in, and others don't care, which is why it's ever more important that kids *do*.

Public outrage over promoting a vegan education only exposes the willful ignorance most parents feel content in imposing on their children. The diplomacy with which children consider the facts, on the other hand, is a profound mark of emotional intelligence—something that seems harder to implement as we grow up, and that we seem to lose as we gain ego. Because children love and recognize animals with a profound curiosity that transcends barriers of language or species, early education about veganism is the essential *key* in unlocking the potential we have to reverse the devastation we systematically inflict upon animals, the environment, and other nations.

And what if a child feels upset or saddened upon discovering the use and abuse of animals? These are perfectly healthy responses to confronting the harm humans inflict upon the earth and other living beings. Veganism inherently offers solutions at every turn, solutions that anyone at any age can implement immediately. We will be doing the future world a favor if we help children learn to manage their feelings instead of avoiding triggers to begin with.

We *can* share with kids the real history that preceded Martin Luther King, Jr.'s leadership. We *should* discuss the hardships that our celebrated historical icons faced, and the truthful stories about how they achieved social change. We *must* confront tough issues like animal agriculture and water shortages in order to face real solutions.

And we can teach children that they don't have to fear anything we have the power to change. Anyone can make vegan choices, and by doing so, we activate our personal agency and influence the public realm, reaching every major industry and every corner of the earth. In our commitment to the wellbeing of others, we can practice the embodiment of love. Herein lies the *tremendous* socially transformative power of veganism. By changing what we eat, we can change our minds and the world we live in. Kids need but little guidance to love deeply, think critically, and act responsibly. It is we adults who have something to learn...or rather, recall from our childhood. ✺

Connecting the Dots on Dietary Choices

by *Richard H. Schwartz*

Until 1978, I was a "meat and potatoes" person. My mother would be sure to prepare my favorite dish, pot roast, whenever I came to visit with my wife and children. It was a family tradition that I would be served a turkey "drumstick" every Thanksgiving. Yet, I not only became a vegan, but I now devote a major part of my time to writing, speaking, and teaching about the benefits of veganism. What caused this drastic change?

In 1973, I initiated and started teaching a course called "Mathematics and the Environment" at the College of Staten Island. The course uses basic mathematical concepts and problems to explore current critical issues, such as pollution, resource scarcities, hunger, energy, population growth, the arms race, nutrition, and health. While reviewing material related to world hunger, I initially thought that the problem was mainly due to the world having more people than it was able to feed. Reading *Diet for a Small Planet* by Frances Moore Lappé helped me connect the relevant dots. That book made me aware of the tremendous waste of grain associated with the production of beef at a time when millions of the world's people are malnourished. In spite of my own eating habits, I often led class discussions on the possibility of reducing meat consumption as a way of helping hungry people. After several semesters of this, I took my own advice and gave up eating red meat, while continuing to eat chicken and fish.

As I continued to consider dietary factors, I saw more and more connections. I learned that a major factor behind the epidemic of diseases that afflict so many people is the prevalence of animal-based diets. I also learned that the vast majority of animal abuses occur on factory farms.

As I learned more, I was increasingly attracted to vegetarianism and, on January 1, 1978, I decided to join the International Jewish Vegetarian Society. I had two choices for membership: (1) practicing vegetarian (one who refrains from eating any flesh); (2) non-vegetarian (one who is in sympathy with the movement, while not yet a vegetarian). I decided to become a full-practicing vegetarian, and since then have avoided eating any meat, fowl, or fish.

Since making that decision, I started seeing connections between the production of animal products and many of the environmental problems that threaten humanity. I learned that the raising for slaughter of billions of farmed land animals—over 65 billion in 2011—is a major factor behind soil erosion and depletion, the rapid loss of biological diversity, water pollution, the destruction of tropical rain forests and other valuable habitats, and many more environmental problems.[1] In an increasingly thirsty world, during what some are calling "the century of drought," animal-centered diets use up to 13 times as much water per person as vegan (completely animal-free) diets.[2] In fact, every environmental problem is worsened by animal-based agriculture.

More recently, I have been connecting dots between "livestock" agriculture and the greatest current threat to humanity: climate change. While most people are still unaware of it, a 2006 UN Food and Agriculture Organization report, *Livestock's Long Shadow*, indicated that animal-based diets cause the emission of more greenhouse gases than is emitted by all means of transportation worldwide combined. Making matters worse, that same UN report indicates that the number of farm animals is projected to double in 50 years, and that the increased greenhouse gas emissions would negate the effects of positive changes in other areas, making the avoidance of the worse effects of global warming very difficult, if not impossible.[3] Two environmentalists associated with the World Bank documented in a 2009 report in *World Watch* magazine, "Livestock and Climate Change," that the livestock sector is responsible for at least 51% of human-induced greenhouse gases.[4]

In addition to learning much about vegetarianism's connections to health, nutrition, ecology, resource usage, hunger, and the treatment of animals, I also started investigating connections between vegetarianism and Judaism. I learned that there are many connections that people generally overlook and, in fact, that the production and consumption of animal products violate six basic Jewish mandates (with slight modifications, this analysis can be adapted to other major religions, all of which are based on compassion, justice, sharing, and other positive values):

1. While Judaism mandates that people should be very careful about preserving their health and their lives, numerous scientific studies have linked animal-based diets directly to heart disease, stroke, many forms of cancer, and other chronic degenerative diseases.

2. While Judaism forbids *tsa'ar ba'alei chayim*, inflicting unnecessary pain on animals, most farm animals—including those raised for kosher consumers—are raised on "factory farms," where they live in cramped, confined spaces, and are often drugged, mutilated, and denied fresh air, sunlight, exercise, and any enjoyment of life, before they are slaughtered and eaten.

3. While Judaism teaches that "the earth is the Lord's" (Psalm 24:1), and that we are to be God's partners and co-workers in preserving the world, modern intensive livestock agriculture contributes substantially to climate change, soil erosion and depletion, air and water pollution, overuse of chemical fertilizers and pesticides, the destruction of tropical rain forests and other habitats, and other environmental damage.

4. While Judaism mandates *bal tashchit*—that we are not to waste or unnecessarily destroy anything of value and that we are not to use more than is needed to accomplish a purpose—animal agriculture requires the wasteful use of grain, land, water,

energy, and other resources.

5. While Judaism stresses that we are to assist the poor and share our bread with hungry people, over 70% of the grain grown in the United States is fed to animals destined for slaughter, while roughly one in eight of the world's people is chronically hungry.[5]

6. While Judaism stresses that we must seek and pursue peace and that violence results from unjust conditions, animal-centered diets, by wasting valuable resources, help to perpetuate the widespread hunger and poverty that eventually lead to instability and war.

In view of these important Jewish mandates—to preserve human health, attend to the welfare of animals, protect the environment, conserve resources, help feed hungry people, and pursue peace—and since animal-centered diets violate and contradict each of these responsibilities, committed Jews (and others) should sharply reduce or eliminate their consumption of animal products.

One could say *dayenu* (it would be enough) after any of the arguments above, because each one constitutes by itself a serious conflict between Jewish values and current practice that should impel Jews to seriously consider a plant-based diet. Combined, they make an urgently compelling case for the Jewish community to address these issues.

In addition, the first biblical dietary regimen (Genesis 1:29) is strictly vegetarian, actually vegan, and the Messianic period is also imagined as a vegetarian one, based on Isaiah's prophecy that "the wolf will dwell with the lamb...the lion will eat straw like the ox... and none shall hurt nor destroy on all of God's holy mountain" (Isaiah 11:6-9). Hence the two ideal times in the Jewish tradition are pictured as vegetarian periods.

To get this message to a wider audience, I wrote a book, *Judaism and Vegetarianism*, which was first published in 1982. (Revised, expanded editions were published in 1988 and 2001).

I gradually moved toward veganism, and became a practicing vegan in 2000. Increasingly, as I learned about the realities of animal-based diets and their inconsistency with Jewish values, I have come to see veganism as not only an important personal choice, but also a societal imperative, an essential component to the solution of many national and global problems.

I have been spending much time trying to make others aware of the importance of switching toward vegetarianism or, preferably, veganism, both for themselves and for the world. I am currently president emeritus of Jewish Vegetarians of North America (JVNA), president of the Society of Ethical and Religious Vegetarians, a board member of the Farm Animal Rights Movement (FARM), and a patron of the International Jewish Vegetarian Society (JVS).

In efforts to spread vegetarian messages, I have appeared on over 120 radio and cable television programs; had many letters and op-ed articles in a variety of publications; spoken frequently to community groups; given over 60 talks, and met with five chief rabbis and other religious and political leaders in Israel, while visiting my two daughters and their families. In 1987, I was selected as "Jewish Vegetarian of the Year" by the Jewish Vegetarians of North America, and in 2005 I was inducted into the North American Vegetarian Society's "Hall of Fame."

To help people connect the dots and become aware that a major societal move to vegetarianism and, preferably, veganism is an essential part of helping shift our imperiled planet to a sustainable path, I raised the funding for and was the associate producer of a one-hour documentary entitled *A Sacred Duty: Applying Jewish Values to Help Heal the World*. In striving to get the movie to as wide an audience as possible, we have given away about 40,000 DVDs and have placed the entire movie on YouTube and other websites. It can also be seen at www. ASacredDuty.com, along with 11 subtitled foreign language versions.

I have always felt good about my decision to become a vegetarian, and more recently, a vegan. Putting principles and values into practice is far more valuable and rewarding than doing hours of preaching. I feel strongly that my spirituality, sensitivity, and compassion have been enhanced by my dietary shifts and my efforts to share information with others. When people ask me why I gave up meat and other animal products, I welcome the opportunity to explain the many benefits of veganism.

Recently, I have noted signs of increased interest in veganism, and a growing number of people are concerned about dietary connections to health, nutrition, animal rights, and ecology. Yet, consumption of animal products seems to be increasing worldwide even as evidence increases that this is contributing to an epidemic of diseases, global warming, and other environmental threats that are moving the world rapidly toward a potential unprecedented catastrophe. So there is much that still needs to be done to get people to see the damage that their diets and other lifestyle choices are doing. My hope is to be able to keep learning, writing, and speaking about veganism, to help people connect dots between animal-centered diets and many of today's crises, to help bring closer that day when, in the words of the motto of the International Jewish Vegetarian Society, "no one shall hurt nor destroy in all of God's holy mountain" (Isaiah 11.9). ☙

Notes

[1] Farm Animal Rights Movement (FARM), "Report: Number of Animals Killed in US Increases in 2010," FARM, accessed August 22, 2014, http://farmusa.org/statistics11.html.

[2] John Robbins, *Diet for a New America* (Walpole, NH: Stillwell Publishers, 1987), 367.

[3] Henning Steinfeld, Pierre Gerber, Tom Wassenaar, Vincent Caastel, Mauricio Rosales, and Cees de Haan. *Livestock's Long Shadow: Environmental Issues and Options* (Rome: FAO, 2006), ftp://ftp.fao.org/docrep/fao/010/a0701e/a0701e.pdf.

[4] Robert Goodland and Jeff Anhang, "Livestock and Climate Change," *World Watch* 22, no. 6 (2009): 10-19, http://www.worldwatch.org/files/pdf/Livestock%20and%20Climate%20Change.pdf.

[5] "Global Hunger Down, But Millions Still Chronically Hungry," FAO, October 1, 2013, http://www.fao.org/news/story/en/item/198105/icode/.

Looking Behind the Curtain
to the Hidden Side of Justice Issues

by Kim Sheridan

Spiritually inclined people often proclaim that we are not human beings having a spiritual experience, but rather, we are spiritual beings having a human experience. I wholeheartedly agree with this statement. However, in the next breath, many people often go on to say matter-of-factly that humans are superior to other animals and are the only ones who have souls. Why? Because we're human. Wait a minute—I thought they just said we were spiritual beings and not human beings; we're simply having a human experience. If we are indeed spiritual beings having a human experience, then it could equally be said that animals are spiritual beings having an animal experience. The logical conclusion: we are all spiritual beings.

I find it interesting that we humans often like to put ourselves at the top of a spiritual hierarchy, claiming that we are the most evolved beings of all. A quick glance at the evening news gives us but a mere clue as to the acts of cruelty that humans are capable of. Therefore, if humans are the most evolved and are at the top of some sort of spiritual hierarchy, I'd say the world is in big trouble! Do humans fear that we will somehow become less important if it is discovered that we're not the only ones who feel or have souls? It is a common human trait to belittle others in an attempt to make ourselves appear more important. Perhaps it's time we understand that the true path to greatness is not in putting others down, but in bringing them up; not in focusing upon their weaknesses, but in acknowledging their strengths.

After researching the subject for many years now, I feel that the enormous amount of evidence of animal souls sheds light on the necessary leap we must make, from a purely logical standpoint, from a belief system that accepts the existence of human souls to one that includes all living beings. (Interestingly, the Latin word for soul is "anima").

Some of the people who have had near-death experiences claim to have witnessed animals on the other side, but equally convincing are the accounts of ordinary people who are the subjects of profound, life-changing encounters with the spirits of animals. Some of these experiences provide evidence to make even the most die-hard skeptics stop and think. I have had such experiences myself, which have absolutely convinced me of the spiritual nature of animals. In my research, I have been privy to numerous heartwarming accounts of companion animals who have died and then come back, returning to their people to continue the bond they share. These thought-provoking stories are, at times, extremely convincing, providing evidence that goes beyond chance or wishful thinking. I too have had quite a few experiences of this nature. Further, professional animal communicators, who engage in telepathic communications with animals themselves, are providing some reassuring insights regarding animal spirituality. My own experience with reputable animal communicators, and my personal experience communicating with animals, lends credence to the notion that animals are unquestionably sentient beings, and they have an afterlife in spirit, just as we do.

It is essential that we use this new understanding not to justify animal abuse (just as the promise of a better life in Heaven was once used to justify the enslavement and abuse of other humans here on Earth), but rather, to hold animals in the same light as we hold other humans. They are, after all, our spiritual brothers and sisters, and once the costumes are removed, we are all of the same essence. I feel that this understanding holds the key to furthering our spiritual progress and to co-creating a more harmonious world.

Many people have asked me about animals who suffer and die

the most horrific deaths at the hands of humans. They ask me why such things happen. People sometimes use karma as a rationalization, implying that the animals somehow deserve it for some past wrongdoing. In my opinion, this is dangerous thinking and often nothing more than an excuse for complacency.

Throughout most of my life, I've studied various spiritual philosophies in-depth and accept the teaching of karma and that we reap what we sow. However, in my understanding, the fact that something bad happens to us doesn't necessarily mean we're paying off a debt from a prior transgression.

What I've come to understand is that some people and animals come here to Earth not to work out bad karma—or even to learn a lesson—but simply to teach others. And if they suffer in the process, it's not because they did something wrong. Sometimes, it's because they are here to express innocence in a world that hasn't yet fully embraced compassion. Sometimes, it's because they are here to initiate change in a world that often doesn't take kindly to anything that upsets the status quo. Few, if any, would contend that Jesus of Nazareth was crucified because of some wrongdoing in his own past. Few would contend that those who die for a good cause do so because they did something wrong. One of my heroes is Martin Luther King, Jr., and few would contend that he was killed because he had bad karma. Quite the contrary, he was a very compassionate and enlightened soul who came here, stood up, spoke out, and demanded change because he saw injustice and sought to make things right. He died for a cause, and God bless him for it.

When people turn their backs on the suffering of animals and explain it away with so-called spiritual talk about how it's the animals' destiny or karma and we should just accept it, I simply remind them that people once said that about slavery—and then there were those who took a stand and did something about it.

It was not long after the passing of my first animal companion in my adult life that I began to realize what animals can teach us: honesty, innocence, and forgiveness; and the importance of expressing sorrow or pain, feeling it fully, and then letting it go. Humans tend to hold on; animals teach us how to let life flow. Most of all, animals offer us unconditional love. Through their example, many of us learn for the first time what unconditional love is. It's not about being perfect; it's about being ourselves and loving each other regardless of our faults.

While researching my book, *Animals and the Afterlife*, as I spoke with dozens of people about their departed companion animals, I noticed a common theme. As they spoke of these animals, it was as if they were speaking of an angel or a saint. These animals hadn't just brought them love and companionship; they had acted as spiritual teachers, bringing remarkable insights and inspiration to them. Many people had been so touched by an animal that they changed their thinking, their life direction, even their diet, and all were better for it.

I am certainly leading a completely different life than I would otherwise be leading if not for the love of animals and the profound spiritual experiences I have shared with them. For one, I changed my diet as a result of the love and inspiration I've received from animals. I decided at a young age that I wanted to become a vegetarian when I grew up. And that I did. In fact, I became vegan.

For me, it was a decision based solely on the desire not to cause suffering to my fellow beings. I later learned that this decision also had a powerful beneficial impact on our environment and on world hunger. An added and unexpected bonus was that my health benefited dramatically when I changed my diet. I was a relatively sickly child and young adult, but because of a decision that was solely inspired by the animals themselves, my health improved tremendously. I am ever grateful to them.

When I become a practicing naturopath and health researcher, I discovered the scientific reasons why my health had improved dramatically due to my vegan diet. When people came to my husband and me for nutritional guidance during the many years that we practiced together as naturopaths, we—and they—were always amazed at the dramatic healings that took place due to this simple change in diet, regardless of blood type, body type, or any other factor.

I feel fortunate to have known and loved many different types of animals. In fact, as a child, cows and chickens were my friends long before I realized they were my food. Spending my summers on thousands of pristine acres of wilderness at my grandparents' ranch gave me an opportunity early on to commune with a wide assortment of beautiful beings; it gave me the opportunity to get to know the animals who, unbeknownst to me at the time, were destined for my plate.

Something that always struck me as odd was the fact that the cows at the ranch, with whom I spent a lot of time, always had a distinct air of caution and fear. They were my friends and clearly trusted me, but I always noticed their lack of trust toward—and fear of—the adults on the ranch. When I communed with them, I always felt an impending sense of doom. It was almost as if they were awaiting some horrible fate, every day wondering if this would be the day their peaceful life would end—the day it would all change.

At the time, it struck me as odd. They were living on this beautiful ranch and grazing on the natural grasses of the land, surrounded by thousands of acres of wilderness, taken care of by these wonderful people known as Grandmother and Grandaddy, and protected by a saintly border collie named Duffy. It was an unusually large ranch, and an incredibly magical place; these were unusually lucky cows. They had it so good, and as far as I could tell, this was where they would remain for the rest of their lives. Yet, every day they lived with a feeling of despair and hopelessness. I was so confused at their seemingly inappropriate demeanor, given their lot in life, that I spent long hours just trying to understand.

The answer came the day I found out that some of my friends had been sent off to the slaughterhouse. That was only the first part of the answer. I didn't get the full answer until years later, when I learned what a slaughterhouse is really like, and of the electroshock prodding, crowding, pain, and excruciating deprivation of their terrifying journey to that ultimate fate. When I learned of the assembly line of horrors (or rather, *disassembly* line) that awaited them, I felt horrible, realizing that my friends had been forced to endure this, and that I hadn't done anything to help them. My realization that meat was actually the flesh of my friends was a turning point in my life.

I find it disturbing that the terms *free-range* and *organic* and *grass-fed* are terms often used to assure us that there was no suffering involved in the production of this product. If only that were true. Not only do these terms conjure up images that are often quite different from the reality behind the scenes, but ironically, it was the fate of animals who actually did live the epitome of a free-range, organic, grass-fed lifestyle that originally led me to give up meat. I learned from the animals themselves that no amount of grass or land could take away their fear and sense of doom and dread of the undignified death that awaited them at the hands of humans.

I think we all have certain key moments in our lives that we see as pivotal. One such moment in my life took place when I received some literature in the mail from the organization People for the Ethical Treatment of Animals. It was through this that I first learned of the tremendous amount of animal suffering that goes on in our world, often behind closed doors and with our unwitting approval—and usually with our own dollars.

I could hardly fathom it, and wanted to do something about it, so I sent for additional educational materials right away. I'll never forget the day they arrived. I sat and read every word of every page they sent. I learned of the horrors of factory farming and animal testing; of fur farms and leather production; of animals of all types used for food, clothing, and more. I learned of chickens and pigs being literally boiled alive in scalding tanks; of animals having their throats slit and their limbs cut off while fully conscious. I learned of such routine practices as debeaking and castration—and many other unthinkable acts—all done without anesthesia. I learned of the tremendous suffering that billions of animals endure at the hands of humanity 24 hours a day, 7 days a week—due to a dangerous combination of greed, arrogance, and ignorance. If people knew what was really going on, I thought to myself, they'd revolt.

When I finished reading, I was angry and upset at humanity

for allowing such things to happen, and then labeling those who attempted to do something positive about it as radicals trying to disturb the status quo. It occurred to me that we often get angry at the messenger rather than opening ourselves to the message. I began to realize that, sometimes, what is deemed good and decent in our world can be, behind the scenes, anything but; and those who work to change things for the better are often ostracized, punished, or vilified.

That night, I quietly wept as I deeply empathized with all of the animals who were suffering unnecessarily at the hands of human beings, for the sake of products we don't need and would be better off without. It occurred to me that the only reason more people weren't concerned was because they didn't know they had anything to be concerned about. I vowed that I would henceforth refrain from contributing to such senseless suffering, and that I would do everything in my power to make things right in my lifetime. And I felt in my heart that most people—if they only knew the truth—would undoubtedly do the same.

I began to think about humanity and our bloody history here on Earth. I began to wonder if perhaps we were missing the lesson, over and over, and were repeatedly being given the opportunity to do things differently, and to expand our minds and our hearts to show respect and kindness to others. The various colors, creeds, lifestyles, and abilities within our species have given us abundant opportunities to expand our circle of compassion and justice, and it seems that we have failed at almost every turn. Here on classroom Earth, history tends to repeat itself until we get the lesson. The animal kingdom provides us perhaps an even bigger opportunity to get the lesson, because the animals typically don't have the means—or the voice—to defend themselves. So, this time it's entirely up to us to speak up for them.

The links between the cruelties that humans inflict on each other and those imposed on animals are many. When we are a part of—or avoid becoming aware of—the horrors involved in non-vegan diets and cruelly-produced products, we become desensitized to the pain of others—animals and humans alike. Our natural sensitivity to our fellow spiritual beings is repressed. On a fundamental level, we know we are all one, and allowing cruelty anywhere allows its manifestation everywhere. The institutionalization of animal cruelty greatly contributes to the hunger, poverty, and violence among our fellow humans. Our existence is essentially an energetic one: a vibratory phenomenon. When the energy of exploitation, cruelty, terror, or indifference is generated, on an energetic level, the cause-and-effect reverberation is felt, perhaps unconsciously, in our exchanges as human beings. Energy is not species-specific, and our violence toward animals is a damaging and self-propagating cycle. This is no less true on an individual level. Those who consume animal products or use products produced unethically are directly both causing and taking in the negative energy of the process. Going vegan is one of the most powerful steps we can take to make a difference, three meals a day, but we cannot stop there.

We, as a society, agree, at least in theory, that cruelty to animals is wrong. Yet, unfortunately, we support unimaginable animal cruelty every time we purchase products from industries that exploit animals. Every time we shop, we vote with our dollars. If we consume products produced by those directly benefiting from the institutionalization of torture, we transfer wealth into the hands of those industries and owners. This wealth transfer tends to—directly or indirectly—support the corporations and entities linked to the military-industrial-medical complex that exploits and victimizes the population. Our dollars, when put in the wrong hands, empower those making the bombs, those making the policies that impoverish and starve, the chemical companies threatening the food supply, and those working to create a world without compassion. Just as those who abuse animals are more likely to commit crimes against their fellow humans, those who make decisions for and profit from an unethical industry are less likely to invest in ways consistent with the compassionate world we are striving to create.

In addition to the moral and spiritual issues, animal products contribute more to global warming, air and water pollution, destruction of the land, and even human starvation than most of the more obvious environmental violations. Adopting a plant-based diet and compassionate lifestyle is not only good for the Earth and the animals; it's good for your health on every level! So it's a win, win, win!

Of course, the animals will be taken care of in the afterlife, and their ultimate destiny is the same as ours. However, it's the journey that counts, and it is a journey we all share. Nonhuman animals have been born onto this Earth, just as we humans have—and they have a right to be here, just as we do, without suffering needlessly at human hands. Just as passing from the physical world into the world of spirit is a major event (known to us as *death*), I find that those who come to Earth from spirit are faced with an equally major transition. The birthing of spirit into physical form is no small matter, and one that must be respected for all living beings. All life is sacred.

Note

Excerpts taken with permission from *Animals and the Afterlife: True Stories of Our Best Friends' Journey Beyond Death* and other writings by Kim Sheridan.

The Gay Animal:
A Personal Exploration of Interconnections

by Jasmin Singer

A weekend trip to Chicago in February is nothing short of masochistic, even when you are coming from freezing cold New York City. Nonetheless, there I was, sitting in Nathan Runkle's apartment, wearing my winter coat and hat, all but shivering. Nathan, a friend and personal hero, not to mention the founder and executive director of the animal rights organization Mercy for Animals, sauntered in wearing shorts. "Are you insane?" I asked.

"You get used to it," he offered, pausing for a moment to take in my winter garb, and widening his eyes as if to imply that I was the crazy one.

My partner, Mariann, and I were visiting The Windy (and Icy, Snowy) City to film Nathan for a short video exploring the connections between gay rights and animal rights. The video was for Our Hen House, the non-profit that Mariann and I founded in January 2010 to produce independent multimedia resources for anyone who wants to change the world for animals.

I took my hands out of my pockets just long enough to set up our lighting equipment and camera. I was behind the camera, sitting pretzel-style on the floor, feeling like a child awaiting story time. "Action," I chirped.

Nathan didn't miss a beat, immediately and poetically describing the links between the animal rights movement and other social justice movements. "Equality and fairness and kindness and compassion—that's really what I think all rights movements are based on," he started. "It's just extending our circle of compassion beyond a certain sexual orientation or beyond a certain species or nationality."

I sat, transfixed. It became clear that cutting this video to a mere ten minutes was going to be near impossible.

Nathan discussed his heartbreaking story of being the victim of gay-bashing at a club in Ohio, a hate crime that left him with several broken bones in his face:

> You really feel violated that somebody else was able to do this to you against your will. I've thought a lot about how this translates into violence in our society towards other people, and also towards animals. [...] These are animals that are subjected to misery and mutilation—having parts of their bodies cut off without anesthesia, without their consent obviously, being crammed in cages where they can't move, being poked and prodded and beaten and punched onto transport trucks, and then having their throats slit at the slaughterhouses, all against their will, all while they're protesting. And really, just because of who they are. [...] It really goes back to our perceptions of others and how that can affect our behavior towards them and [other] innocent individuals—whether it be gay individuals, or animals, or African Americans, or women— being the target of violence and hatred and oppression. And it has to stop. It has no place in a civilized or ethical society.[1]

Nathan founded Mercy for Animals when he was a young teenager. Today, MFA is a leading farmed animal rights organization, advocating for change and producing undercover videos of animal cruelty that have been covered in nearly every major press outlet.

I looked at him, a handsome man in his late 20s, and wondered what on earth had conspired to create such a game-changer. What events in Nathan's life led him down the path of social justice?

And what about me? Did the events in my own life lead me to connect the dots of different social injustices and dedicate myself to opposing them?

That night in Chicago I became determined to find out what made me notice these interconnections in the first place, and whether a deeper understanding of my own misadventures and seminal moments would help me figure out how I could use that information to help others connect the dots too.

"You Don't Think She Could Be Gay, Do You?"

I stood outside of my mother's bedroom door and listened in on her phone conversation with my grandmother. I was 15—it was 1994. I was undoubtedly wearing a long, eccentric dress, attempting (unsuccessfully) to distract from my overly-endowed chest.

They were talking about me again, and I was not ashamed to eavesdrop. My mother said in a loud whisper that was not intended for my ears, "You don't think she could be gay, do you?" Clearly my grandmother replied, "No, no, not Jazz..."

I nearly guffawed out loud at the very idea, but slapped my hand over my mouth just in time to avoid unintentionally announcing my presence.

My mother, grandmother, and I had an indelible bond that still grounds me, twenty years later. Nowadays, my family considers my wife, Mariann, as much a part of the family as I do. But at the time, as an angst-ridden, depressed teenager who distracted myself with dreams of becoming a Broadway star, "gay" was something that happened to your distant cousin—not to your daughter. And certainly not to yourself.

The real reason for this conversation between Mom and Grandma wasn't my sexual orientation—I don't even know how that subject came up in the first place. Perhaps an unconscious, but accurate, anxiety haunted my mother. As I inched even closer to the door, cupping my hand and holding my breath, they started to discuss the actual issue at hand: it was, as Grandma called it, my "bosom," which, according to what I gathered from listening at the door, made me seem "matronly" (Mom's word), and perhaps should be "dealt with."

My body was, in fact, a thing that I loathed, that I cut into—not only by way of the breast reduction surgery that I wanted so desperately and finally had when I was 16, but with scissors, pencils, my nails. I detested the abundance of me. I wanted out. And I wanted out of my small provincial New Jersey suburb, too. This was not me.

I planned to become a star. My first step was an acting conservatory in Philadelphia. New York would be next, and only then would I be home. Plan in place, I stopped cutting myself and opted instead to drown myself in a world of pot, booze, and theatre class.

Self-cutting, drugs, and alcohol are all serious issues for gay teens. They can be both coping mechanisms for and rebellions against a difficult situation, but either way, they are self-destructive. Loathing one's body and wanting to change it is also common among gay youth, despite the stereotype that lesbian girls in particular are less vulnerable to what the media dictates women should look like. I felt like I was alone in my pain, but I was following sadly well-worn paths.

Following my plan to remake my life, I also started to become a bit more comfortable with the idea of gayness—as long as it applied to someone else. Emily, with her boy's haircut, became a friend. A portrait of a nude woman hung above her bed at her swanky Rittenhouse Square apartment. I remember being embarrassed by it. Emily—she was gay. Naturally, she was also a vegetarian.

Now vegetarian I could try on for size—just as long as I didn't need to kiss a girl. In acting class the week prior, after being assigned a scene that involved a kiss with another girl, I was too nervous to sleep for three days. Vegetarianism seemed easier.

It also seemed so much more acceptable. Approximately one million kids aged 5–17 are openly vegetarian, and it hardly invoked the same taboo as being gay. Plus, I was, after all, a theatre student, and ditching meat seemed a natural extension of that—like wearing all black (check!) or smoking clove cigarettes (double check!). I gobbled down my last Philly Cheesesteak and told Emily I was going to join her team. She curiously raised an eyebrow, and salaciously half-smiled. "No!" I protested, perhaps a little too vehemently, "I'm a vegetarian now, too!"

I had no strong moral impetus for becoming vegetarian. Mostly I thought it increased my cool-factor, and it also allowed me to embrace a new identity, something I craved intensely. And yet the shallow decision I made on the fly, to ditch meat, was in many ways the beginning of my life's journey. Soon enough, I began to discover the many links between the person I was creating by becoming vegetarian, and the strong lesbian inside of me who so longed to emerge.

But first I had to conquer the worst year of my life, and then I had to find my way home—to New York City.

Darkest Before the Dawn

Like so many kids who go off to college, woefully immature in some ways, yet pretending to be adults, I wasn't thinking clearly at all. My lingering depression and poor self-esteem led me to a therapist who prescribed "mood-stabilizing" medication that made me stop functioning pretty much altogether. I recall standing in my early morning jazz dance class as my classmates did the routine all around me. I just stared, unable to move. When my academic advisor expressed concern about my behavior, I told him that it wasn't that I wanted to die, but I didn't want to live.

I left school midway through my sophomore year with the goal of taking a semester off, moving back in with my mother and stepfather, and then resuming college somewhere in magical New York. A week after leaving Philadelphia, I was browsing in a used bookstore when I started chatting with the long-haired guy working behind the counter. His name was Joe; he was an "older man" (all of 35), and after some friendly chitchat, when he asked me out on a date, I jumped at the opportunity. My boyfriend and I had broken up in the midst of my latest depressive episode, and getting attention from a man felt validating. Referring to my then-plump frame, my secret source of shame, Joe told me that, had I been around in the 1940s, I could have been a model.

A week later, following our date and on an appropriately rainy and eerie night, I went to Joe's house. This became the scene of my date rape, a 2 a.m. struggle where I, at age 19, could not get him to stop penetrating me—despite yelling "no" several times. When he was finished, I threw on my clothes and staggered outside. Joe shut the door behind me, and when I squinted through my tears to look back at this house where a piece of me had been forever lost, I saw the sign on the front of his door. It read, "U.S. Army: Forever Straight."

In nearly two-thirds of rapes, the victim knows the rapist.[2] Although my trauma was deeply personal, it was also common to many others like me.

Somehow, the months passed. I got a part in a play and steadfastly auditioned for new schools where I could finish my BFA. The night with Joe lived in my nightmares and my body. Victims of sexual assault are 6 times more likely to suffer from post-traumatic stress disorder,[3] and I was no exception. I also blamed myself for the crime against me.

That fall, I moved to Brooklyn and started over at a new college in the City of My Dreams. I was in New York now, and it was time to create a new existence, and a new self.

Gay as in Happy

I met Clara in the costume shop at school. She was from Queens, with brownish-black spiral curls and dark eyes that bespoke wisdom beyond her 18 years. I confided in her about my rape. She listened intently, and hugged me fiercely. Clara took me to a presentation of Eve Ensler's *The Vagina Monologues* at Madison Square Garden. There, I was completely star-struck by the likes of Sarah Jessica Parker and Oprah Winfrey, two of the many famous performers who took to the stage that night. But only when Eve Ensler herself got to the microphone—welcomed by thunderous applause—did the evening begin to take shape.

Eve asked any woman in the audience who had been a victim of rape to stand up. All around me, thousands of women rose. Clara took my hand and gave me an encouraging nod, and I stood too, thus starting the process of recognizing that awful night as one I did not need to bury any longer. As I saw the women all around me allowing themselves to be seen and heard, and no longer ashamed, I firmly decided—at age 20—to plant a seed in myself which I promised I would nurture. This seed, I decided then, would eventually allow me to truly accept, and even love, not only my body—which I was deeply detached from—but also my true self, even though I didn't know for sure yet who that person was.

"You Don't Think She's Gay, Do You?"

Gay. I had an aunt who was gay, and two second cousins—both women. And, predictably, the theatre department at my school had its fair share of gay people, though they were almost all men. But me? Well, I did think about Clara quite a lot, and though I had had sex with several men, it was never satisfying.

Through the magic of AOL—which was still pretty much the only online dating service that existed then—I decided to try on "bisexual" for size. If nothing else, I thought, I could use my experiences for character study.

While I was moving toward a more compassionate relationship with myself, I had not yet really turned my thoughts and actions outward, to the world at large. That was soon to change, thanks to the first job I landed out of college, with an AIDS-awareness theatre company called Nitestar. With Nitestar, I would perform in several plays—all geared toward different ages—centered around issues involving AIDS-awareness, sexuality, teen pregnancy, bullying, domestic violence, and building communication skills. I had no idea then, but Nitestar would forever change the course of my life.

This "job" seeped into my soul. My colleagues became my best friends, my family. When we weren't rehearsing or performing, we were still together—dancing all night at clubs, taking day trips to meet one another's families, sleeping with each other. The cornerstone for our relationships was the work itself, work that represented a social justice issue that we all believed in deeply.

Seeking social justice is a strong thread woven throughout my life. Back when I was 13, studying to become a Bat Mitzvah, my rabbi told me to prepare a speech highlighting something meaningful to me. When it came time to give the speech, I confidently approached the Bima. I was wearing a fuchsia off-the-shoulder dress with matching heels—and yes, matching lipstick (it was 1992). "This speech is about Ryan White," I boomed, acting—as always—more sure of myself than I actually was. "Ryan White was a boy who died of AIDS two years ago," I continued, as my friends and family looked up at me, confused as to what this had to do with the Jewish tradition of becoming a woman.

With Nitestar, I was, for the first time in my life, able to explore that side of myself—my activist side—and turn it from talk to action. I would visit schools in the toughest neighborhoods in New York, schools where you had to go through a metal detector to get through the front doors. There, we got to teach incredibly interested, smart kids about accepting people who are perhaps different from them, and considering whether they are all that different after all.

During the beginning of a six-week program, the kids readily yelled words like "fag" and used "gay" as an insult. But we'd get them talking about their preconceived ideas of what "gay" meant, and soon enough—after the walls began to come down—they'd ask questions. It was seldom us, the adults in the room, who were the impetus for these kids to begin to practice tolerance and acceptance. All we had to do was mirror their behavior to them and pose a few questions. They took it from there. We just sat back and watched as these kids would come to pronounce homophobia and bullying "messed up!" Toward the end of the six weeks, it would not be unusual for a kid to come out herself, frequently to the massive support and back-patting of her peers. It was an incredibly magical and empowering thing to watch. It instilled in me the understanding that humans are capable of behaving ethically and with compassion. Sometimes, they just need someone to start that dialogue with them.

Finally, at 22, I realized just how badly I wanted to do my part to change the world. I also saw a glimpse of how badly it needed to be changed.

Yet I still didn't know what was about to hit me.

Discovering Hidden Horrors

One Sunday afternoon, I met my friend David—a comrade from Nitestar—in Central Park for a picnic with his friends. I recognized Marisa immediately, even though I had only previously heard of her. She was the woman with whom David was infatuated. I could see why, too. Marisa was nothing short of stunning—with long blonde hair, brown eyes, and a t-shirt with a picture of a pig that said, "Friend, Not Food."

Marisa pointed sternly at David. "You'd better eat the rest of that sandwich, David, I'm telling you..." David had been about to throw a quarter of a tuna melt in the trash. "Those tuna fish died for your sandwich. Do not waste them!"

Who was this woman? "Jazz, this is Marisa," David said, a few minutes after finishing his lunch. "She's that vegan friend I told you about." David tried to hide a conspiratorial smile.

A month later, I ran into Marisa in the packed waiting room at an audition for an Off-Off Broadway play. We chatted momentarily, both of us relieved to see a familiar face in a sea of nervous actors. After getting about 15 seconds into my monologue before the director said, "Thank you for coming. Next!" I left the audition and walked through Times Square, thinking about the fact that Marisa was vegan. "How extreme that is," I said to myself, "how radical of her..." Yet at the same time, I found myself—for the first time ever—giving thought to the ethical implications of the dairy and eggs that I consumed regularly. I had been a vegetarian for years, but I had never given any thought to animal products besides flesh.

Marisa and I became friendlier, and, at some point, even wound up in an ill-fated weekly "knitting circle" where I quickly learned that I was terrible at knitting. (I was, however, remarkably astute at creating large knots). Meanwhile, Marisa took any opportunity to eagerly explain why she was vegan. I listened intently and thoughtfully, yet somehow got it in my mind that the word "vegan" was something that defined the *other*—certainly not me. The internal conversation I was having about the label "vegan" was very similar to the one I'd had (and was still having) about the label "gay." It was something another person was, not something that belonged to me. The weight the label carried was too grandiose and too limiting. I shook off these thoughts.

A few days later, I attended a screening Marisa was hosting of a new film that focused on factory farming. I went with Owen, the guy I was fleetingly dating. Owen and I held each other for dear life and watched as tiny birds' beaks were cut off by searing hot irons without anesthesia, a standard practice for the production of egg-laying hens (performed so they don't peck each other when they are crammed into small cages with up to a dozen other birds). We watched in horror as dairy cows gave birth to their babies, then bellowed as the babies were ripped from them immediately—the boys sent to a horrific life in the veal industry, the girls fated to their mothers' existence as dairy cows: routinely forcibly inseminated so they would produce milk that humans would take, though it was meant for their calves. The contraptions these cows were attached to, I learned, were named—by the dairy industry itself—"rape racks."

Rape Racks!
My own experience five years prior came flooding back to me. Memories of meeting Joe at the bookstore. At his house, on his couch. Shouting "no." Feeling him inside me, over me, on top of me. The anger in his eyes, the reality sinking in. Staggering to the door, to my car, to my life that had suddenly erased me.

Owen held me closer as tears streamed down my face. I watched the screen and saw the cows bellowing as their newborns were torn away from them. I watched pigs scream as a bolt gun, intended to render them unconscious, didn't do the job. I watched as newly-hatched male chicks were suffocated in garbage bags.

It was all against their will. I wondered for a moment if these animals who were born as prisoners even *had* a will. I shook my head at myself; *of course they had a will.* These animals had a will to survive! That's why they had to be pushed, forced, prodded—all while adamantly protesting—to meet their horrid fate.

I squinted to look more closely at the screen, which now showed a farm animal sanctuary. Farm animals were being given a second chance at a life of peace and dignity.

My tears were replaced by a fierce determination. Suddenly, it all made sense.

What made it okay for me to consume dairy and eggs? What had made it acceptable to consume the flesh of animals? Why was I, why was anyone, able to get away with not thinking about it?

What made it okay for Ryan White to be expelled from his middle school because he had AIDS?

Why is it that every two minutes, someone in the United States is sexually assaulted? Why is it that, like my rapist, 97% of the attackers will never spend a day in jail?[4]

What made it okay for the students at the schools where I had taught to get a lesser education than I had received?

The answer, I realized, was that the same mindset leads to every one of these injustices. In each example, the marginalized group—be they people of color, LGBTQ folks, women, or yes, even animals—was "put there" by the same rationalization. "They" are less than me, beneath me. "They" are different from me. "I" am the status quo because I have the blessing of God, or because I need to take care of my own, or, at its simplest, because I have the power. "I" can do whatever I want to "them."

The film was over, but I couldn't move. "You coming?" Owen asked in a gravelly voice, clearly also affected by the film.

"Yeah, sure," I managed, acting as normal as I could, yet knowing that things would never be the same again.

A New Vegan?

A few days later, at a small party at Marisa's apartment, she introduced me as "a new vegan."

"Oh shit," I thought. Though I had internally decided I would no longer consume animal products—and I had, in fact, given my kitchen cabinets a "cruelty-free" makeover—I was still resistant to officially labeling myself as "vegan." But it looked like Marisa had just done it for me.

It was not even a matter of weeks before I was out on the street distributing "Say No to Factory Farming" leaflets, and attending protests against fur. Within a year of going vegan, I began to co-lead workshops with Marisa at community centers and colleges in New York on going vegan and becoming an animal activist. Both coming from a background in theatre, we incorporated skits, improv, interactive games, and prizes into our workshops. Our audiences grew, and even the press took notice. I went back to school and became a holistic health counselor, opening my own business that specialized in helping people make the transition to veganism. That certificate program led me to pursue a Master's Degree in Health and Healing, where, again, my focus became veganism.

Finally, I felt I had purpose. I had learned that there was an enormous world of suffering out there, a universe of misery hidden behind closed doors but happening all the time. And coming to terms with the fact that I was blind to this issue, and that I must constantly be open to learning what other issues I might be blind to, is something that at first deflated me, but ultimately strengthened and inspired me. It reminds me of the unjust power I have, and the fact that it is therefore up to me—and all of us—to advocate for those who have no voice.

I also came to realize how vital finding and fostering community was to me in my vegan and activist journey, and that part of that is understanding that animal rights and veganism do not stand apart from other efforts to improve the world. Aside from the direct links between animal agriculture, human hunger, and environmental devastation, there are countless other connections to human rights as well. It's important to understand that the movement to improve the lot of animals is, in very many ways, the same as the movements to end racism, homophobia, violence—any and all kinds of bigotry. The idea that life is a zero sum game with only so much compassion to go around—which we therefore must save for those who are like us—is, bottom line, the attitude that is destroying the world. Understood like this, our veganism, and our attitudes toward animals, become not something that separates us from other people, but something that potentially links us to all the people who are trying to rectify any injustice. And that is a very fine group of people to be linked to.

Coming Out and Falling In

When I was 27, while I was writing an article for a social justice magazine *Satya* exploring the connections between animal rights and gay rights, a woman came into my life. I had a fast and furious love affair with this woman, who was much older and more experienced than I was, and had been deeply involved in social justice issues for years. As is common with fast and furious affairs, it ultimately faded, but only after I had come out as a lesbian, finally accepting and embracing my true self.

When some of my friends doubted my newfound lesbianism ("Surely you'll sleep with men again at some point," one asserted), I realized the importance of officially "coming out." They needed to accept my gayness just as the world needed to accept that gayness exists.

"I'm a lesbian," I asserted, "and I feel fantastic. So the best thing you could do is accept that and be happy for me."

This experience was reminiscent of "coming out" as vegan a few years earlier, and the many times since then—at restaurants, social events with new people, weddings, first dates—when I've had to come out as vegan and been met with skepticism. Peoples' reactions imply that the societal norm—heterosexuality, meat-eating—is the only way worth pursuing, and that following a different path—homosexuality, veganism—merits an eye-roll, concern, and doubt.

In the late 1960s and on into the 1970s—a decade I was born at the tail-end of—coming out was an absolutely necessary step toward normalizing being gay. The LGBT revolution began with individuals having the courage to come out, with their allies standing proudly beside them.

Similarly, if vegans don't seize every opportunity to come out and show those around us that veganism is a viable, healthy, delicious, attainable, and affordable way of life, and let people know about the horrific violence that they are supporting by not being vegan, then veganism—and thus animals—will continue to be marginalized.

My Year of Vegan Love

Age 27 had yet another surprise in store. While attending a meeting about a campaign to end foie gras production, which was coincidentally being held at a rented room in The Gay and Lesbian Center, I noticed an attractive woman—I described her to myself then as a "professor-type"—sitting by herself. One of the organizers of the event approached her and introduced her to someone else. "This is Mariann Sullivan," he said.

Mariann Sullivan...Mariann Sullivan...Now why did I know that name? She had wavy brown hair that fell over her eyes, and something about her struck me as reminiscent of Diane Keaton, or at least a character Keaton would play.

It hit me. I had interviewed Mariann via email for the article about gay rights and animal rights, yet, embarrassingly, her quote—which, admittedly, was brilliant—became a casualty of my word count and landed on the cutting room floor. I introduced myself anyway.

In the following weeks and months of getting to know Mariann, I discovered that she was a lawyer who had been involved with animal law for many years, and sat on the boards of several animal rights organizations. She lived in a tiny apartment in Soho with her rescued pit bull, Rose. Mariann was brilliant, and looked at the world with an intensity and unique hopefulness that opened my heart and sharpened my drive. I developed a huge, otherworldly crush on her, and began to seek any excuse I could to find myself in her neighborhood, where I would always drop by with something I knew she'd like. I would frequently bring her a big chunk of watermelon, which was—I see now, in retrospect—my pathetic attempt to woo her.

It worked. Seven years later, I have learned and grown more from my relationship with Mariann than I ever could have imagined. It was not long before that tiny Soho apartment was my home, and sweet Rose became my dog too. And, in 2013, Mariann and I even took an early morning jaunt to City Hall to tie the knot, surprising our friends and family—and proving to each other that even the most unlikely of couples can find lifelong partnership in a shared worldview, a powerful determination, and what has turned out to be a deep and abiding romance.

Our Hen House

In January 2010, after a stint working as the campaigns manager for the farmed animal protection organization Farm Sanctuary, I joined forces with Mariann in starting a non-profit, Our Hen House (http://www.ourhenhouse.org), a multimedia hub of opportunities to change the world for animals. We saw a need for more independent media, and better use of online outlets, to help everyone who cares about animals to become activists in ways that work for them.

We called our organization Our Hen House for two reasons: One was because it is not mine and not Mariann's—rather, it is *all of ours*, a community we can each tap into, a positive resource for anyone who has awakened to animal issues to start changing the world. And two, we used "hens" because they are among the absolute underdogs of animal exploitation, comprising over 9 of the 10 billion land animals killed for food in the United States each year.[5] These birds can be brave, social, funny, and, of course, beautiful. The plight of hens is not only a feminist issue (egg production embodies one of the ultimate exploitation systems of female reproductive organs), but given just how many are bred and killed for human consumption, in so many ways, when you speak of *animal rights*, you are speaking of *chickens*. About 269 of them are killed every second in the United States alone.[6] Knowing about that scale of suffering and choosing not do something about it is immoral and, to me, inexcusable.

What began with a simple "Let's start a podcast!" quickly took on a life all its own. That was in January 2010, and we have since produced an episode every single week without fail. We receive emails daily from listeners who, when hearing us ramble about veganism and other social justice issues, feel as though they are finally understood.

We also produce an online magazine with new content added every day, highlighting ways for everyone to get involved with changing the world for animals, and we have a video production arm featuring activists who are doing just that. Our e-book publishing arm is a new addition to our multimedia platform, and we are regularly adding additional multimedia projects, all with the goal of having Our Hen House act as a clearinghouse of reliable, accessible, and fun inroads for each of us to create a new world for animals.

A year into starting Our Hen House, we wanted to do something to explore the connections between gay rights and animal rights. That motivated our trip to Chicago to film Nathan Runkle. The video that resulted from that trip is one that I frequently revisit because it refocuses and invigorates me.

Here is one of my favorite passages:

Equality and fairness and kindness and compassion—that's really what I think all rights movements are based on. It's just extending our circle of compassion beyond a certain sexual orientation or beyond a certain species or nationality. Whatever our background is, the animals need us to speak up and say no to their exploitation and oppression. It's really speaking truth to power and taking the side of the weak against the strong.[7]

These days, Mariann and I spend a great deal of our time traveling around the country giving workshops on activism, veganism, and animal law. Yet the subject we are asked to speak on the most is the commonality of oppression, the links between animal rights and various other social justice issues. The fact that people are not only waking up to these connections, but are thirsty for workshops and articles on them, is a huge leap forward from even eight years ago, when I wrote my first published article on the subject, the one for *Satya*, entitled "Coming Out for Animal Rights."

The Lucky Ones

I cannot and should not ignore that I am one of them, the lucky ones. Though there were bumps along my path, I have always been remarkably privileged, in ways that I am constantly trying to recognize. But I'm sure there are many aspects of my privilege I still don't see. I can't forget that I used to be blind to my unwarranted power as a member of the human species, as a person who received an advanced education, and as the recipient of so many other advantages I was given that others weren't. Bearing that in mind is a reminder to frequently ask myself, "In what ways am I still blind?"

The question lingers: were there specific events that led me down this path? If I try, I could trace my interest in social justice to so many things: my date rape, my long-suppressed sexuality, my experience teaching children in underserved communities...

In the "Gay Animal" video I made of Nathan, he stated that those who have been oppressed by society have a predisposition to empathizing with the underdog, i.e., animals. He explained:

> Our community understands oppression and we understand being the center of unjustified hate and intolerance, and being treated as different because people perceive us as being different from them. And I think that animals are oftentimes subject to oppression and exploitation because people consider them very different from us, even though in many important ways, they're very much like us, and they deserve the same consideration.[8]

It is true that those who have been marginalized by society often have a soft spot, a natural "way in" when it comes to fighting for social justice. Yet at the same time, understanding the importance of standing up for equality is clearly not limited to people who have been oppressed.

For me, AIDS-awareness activism came first, then came animal rights. After coming out as a lesbian, then reading *The Sexual Politics of Meat* by Carol J. Adams, I began to identify as a feminist. And I continue to learn about previously unknown social injustices. The Food

Empowerment Project, founded by lauren Ornelas, taught me about slavery in chocolate production. Then I learned about the orangutan habitat destruction inherent in palm oil production. The list goes on.

But the important thing to recognize is that these are all, at their roots, the same problem. Understanding and continuing to dissect the connections, based on the mindset of the particular oppressor at hand, is crucial. It is also a remarkably important way not only to foster allies and activists who care about animal rights, but to embrace other social justice issues that are new to us.

Yet, for each of these industries I learn about, and for each of the products I boycott, I have found a more satisfying and ethical alternative. My life is in no way about deprivation. It is abundant, delicious, and it allows me to live in harmony with my ethical beliefs.

For us, the lucky ones, to use our lives for anything besides fighting for social justice is, I believe, irresponsible. Boycotting cruelty in whichever ways are feasible—which for those of us in Western society absolutely includes promoting veganism—is the only ethically sound way to live. And then taking that personal boycott of cruel industries and practices (including animal agriculture) one step further and proactively fighting for those who are less fortunate than we are—is the only way to move forward. Given the web of social justice, and the many interconnections among these movements, picking a place on that web and jumping in to whatever issue calls to you, is not only simple, it's vital.

Like me, and like so many others, perhaps along the way you will also receive the added benefit of finding and embracing your true self. ✆

Notes

1 Jasmin Singer, "The Gay Animal: Natahn Runkle," Vimeo video, 4:57, uploaded by "Our Hen House," http://vimeo.com/21624081.

2 Shannan M. Catalano, *Criminal Victimization, 2005*, NCJ 214644 (Washington, DC: US Department of Justice, Bureau of Justice Statistics, 2006), revised June 16, 2011, http://www.bjs.gov/content/pub/pdf/cv05.pdf.

3 Rape, Abuse & Incest National Network (RAINN), "Effects of Rape," RAINN, 2009, https://rainn.org/get-information/statistics/effects-of-rape.

4 US Department of Justice, Bureau of Justice Statistics, *National Crime Victimization Survey*, reports 2008-2012.

5 Harish, "How Many Animals Does a Vegetarian Save?" *Counting Animals* (blog), last updated February 22, 2012, http://countinganimals.com/how-many-animals-does-a-vegetarian-save/.

6 Ibid.

7 See note 1 above.

8 Ibid.

Animal Rights as a Social Justice Issue

by Gary Smith

It's easy for most of us to recognize that LGBTQ rights, women's rights, rights of people with disabilities, and civil rights for minorities, for example, are issues of social justice. What is less obvious is that the rights of nonhuman animals belong in this category of social justice issues too, which is an understatement if ever there was one.

Not only are the rights of nonhuman animals largely ignored by both the public and those who profess a progressive or spiritual philosophy when it comes to the rights of humans, but there also tends to be a scoffing or outright adversarial attitude towards the idea of justice for other animals.

I suppose we should start by defining what exactly a social justice issue is. According to Appalachian State University professor Matthew Robinson, social justice is, "'promoting a just society by challenging injustice and valuing diversity.' It exists when 'all people [including nonhuman animals] share a common humanity [or sentiency] and therefore have a right to equitable treatment, support for their human [or essential] rights, and a fair allocation of community resources.'"[1]

It is a stretch for someone who has never considered other animals to be worthy of moral consideration to recognize animal rights as a social justice issue. Quite frankly, it would be difficult for someone to come to this conclusion given all the talk about various hot topics like Meatless Mondays, cage-free eggs on university campuses, harm reduction, larger cages, celebrities playing at eating a plant-based diet, promoting the consumption of cows' meat over chickens' meat, and finding more humane ways to exploit and kill other animals to assuage guilt. With so little focus, even from the vegan community, on the rights of nonhuman animals to be free from human exploitation, it is understandable there might be confusion about the goals of the animal rights movement.

Nonhuman animals should be included in any discussion of social justice because just like humans, nonhuman animals are sentient: they experience and feel pain, suffer, and experience joy. In addition, they have deep emotional lives, have a desire to continue living, and create and form bonds with members of their communities. Like us, they should have the right to control their bodies and fulfill their lives free from of confinement, mutilation, forced impregnation, and other forms of abuse. Our ability to eat and use other animals doesn't trump their right to not be used or eaten by us.

There is a single reason that animals are not considered in the moral discussion: speciesism, the prevailing belief that other animals are less than humans, that their bodies, their freedoms, their needs, their rights, are inferior or nonexistent compared to those of humans. And since they are less than humans, we can exploit and oppress them for food, clothing, entertainment, "scientific research," and as pets. It is this form of bigotry that allows us to kill them to the tune of more than 60 billion land animals globally for our food preferences each year.[2]

I do not want to minimize human social justice struggles and histories in the least, but if we are going to have a serious discussion about animal rights, we have to acknowledge that the violence and exploitation of nonhuman animals really has no equal, in terms of both sheer numbers and severity, in the human rights arena. That 60 billion number occurs each and every year, and does not even include the trillions of aquatic animals who die after they are violently removed from oceans. Hundreds of millions of other animals in public and private laboratories—be they dogs, cats, nonhuman primates, rats, or mice—are tortured and killed each year. Millions of cows, sheep, minks, coyotes, and other animals are exploited and killed on farms and in the wild for their skin and fur every year. Elephants, tigers, bears, horses, greyhounds, dolphins, orcas, and others are brutally beaten and asked to race or do tricks for our entertainment. And companion animals, confined and used for breeding, live in squalor in puppy mills.

Associated with the multiple billions of animals who are exploited each year for human tastes, traditions, and enjoyment, is the egregious exploitation of humans. It's impossible to exploit other animals without exploiting millions and possibly billions of humans, which also makes animal rights a uniquely complicated social justice issue.

In both factory farms and slaughterhouses, workers are exploited for their labor. Many workers are people of color living in low-income communities where there are few options for employment. Many are undocumented, and as such, are underpaid and have little to no labor rights governing their pay, personal safety, work hour demands, break times, physical output, and more. In the United States alone, 500,000 people work in slaughterhouses and "meat" processing plants—enduring some of the highest rates of work-related injuries in the country.[3]

As production demands increase, so do the expectations placed on workers to carve apart animals (sometimes while they are still conscious) at even more unsafe speeds. In factory farms, workers are kicked, scratched, and otherwise harmed by the animals they are exploiting. Can you blame the prisoners for defending themselves?

I don't think we can talk about these workers without mentioning they are repeatedly tail docking, de-beaking hens, grinding alive male chicks, de-toeing and de-snooding turkeys, removing piglets' scrotums and tails, raping female animals with foreign objects to impregnate them, ejaculating male animals for sperm, thumping (slamming piglets heads into the concrete to "euthanize" them), and performing other violent, inhumane jobs. These practices take an emotional and psychological toll on workers as well as the animals being abused. Too often these workers become violent, unfeeling beings. Sociologists note high crime rates in neighborhoods surrounding animal slaughter and processing facilities. Typical symptoms and side effects of this work include domestic violence, social withdrawal, drug and alcohol abuse, and severe anxiety.[4]

Humans are also harmed by starvation and food scarcity issues caused by the exploitation of animals for food. The Food and Agriculture Organization of the United Nations estimates that nearly 842 million people globally (one in eight), were suffering from chronic undernourishment in 2011–2013.[5] Over three million children under five die from starvation every year.[6] What does this have to do with nonhuman animals? According to Dr. Richard Oppenlander, we produce enough grain to feed twice as many human beings as currently live on the planet, but 77% of all coarse grains (corn, oats, sorghum, barely, etc.) and more than 90% of all soy grown globally are fed to livestock instead of hungry humans.[7]

Clearly it's not as simple as everyone going vegan immediately and redistributing the food that is currently funneled to animals whom we eat. Issues of food production and distribution are complex and layered. Animal agriculture also impacts humans—the poor disproportionately, who live next to these animal factories—by increasing air and water pollution near factory and so-called family farms, causing water shortages (animal agriculture uses many orders of magnitude more of water than for plant crops), and other environmental harms that in turn affect the health of humans' bodies and communities.

We can also add the chronic diseases that plague humans all over the developed world that are the direct and indirect results of consuming animal flesh and their secretions. Links have been made to heart disease, type 2 diabetes, obesity, liver and kidney diseases, hypertension, strokes, and various cancers. Not only are people dying and suffering immeasurably, but it also costs the US trillions of dollars in health care each year, which means skyrocketing health insurance costs to those of us privileged enough to afford insurance. All these chronic diseases would be improved, if not reversed, by leaving animal exploitation out of our diets.

While the food industry is the biggest violator of human rights, of course many workers are harmed and killed in other animal exploitation industries such as entertainment (look no further than the marine "abusement" park workers killed by frustrated captive orcas), "scientific research," animal skinning and tanning, and companion animal production as well.

We like to believe that we are nonviolent beings who use violence only under extreme duress or when it is absolutely necessary. Yet we participate in violence when we eat; every time we purchase leather, wool, silk, and fur; purchase cosmetics and household products tested on animal victims; pay to visit a circus, zoo, horse race, or dolphinarium; or buy a dog or cat rather than adopting one from a shelter or rescue. We are constantly participating in violence, and some of our greatest minds have opined that until we cease participating in the daily violence against other animals, we will never experience anything remotely like world peace. Is it any wonder we have been enmeshed in constant wars for the past 10 thousand years, since the beginning of animal agriculture?

We also like to believe that our deepest values include justice, compassion, fairness, and equality. But how can we live and achieve those values when we participate in this exploitation? We cannot. We will not reflect those values until we choose to be vegan, and work for the rights of other animals.

I am not sure that there has ever been a social justice movement that affected so much—health, the environment, different sectors of business, the government, as well as unimaginably vast numbers of nonhuman animals. We cannot promote a just society while billions of nonhuman persons are being exploited for reasons that are wholly unnecessary. The simple choice of going vegan, removing oneself from these systems of exploitation, and spreading the word to others, has the potential to change the direction of the world. ✍

Notes

1 Matthew Robinson, "What is Social Justice?" Department of Government and Justice Studies, Appalachian State University, quoting from Toowoomba Catholic Education (2006), accessed August 24, 2014, http://gjs.appstate.edu/social-justice-and-human-rights/what-social-justice.

2 Compassion in World Farming, *Strategic Plan 2013-2017: For Kinder, Fairer Farming Worldwide* (Surrey, UK: Compassion in World Farming, 2013), 3, http://www.ciwf.org.uk/includes/documents/cm_docs/2013/c/ciwf_strategic_plan_20132017.pdf.

3 "Slaughterhouse Workers," Food Empowerment Project, accessed August 24, 2014, http://www.foodispower.org/slaughterhouse-workers/.

4 Jennifer Dillard, "A Slaughterhouse Nightmare: Psychological Harm Suffered by Slaughterhouse Employees and the Possibility of Redress through Legal Reform," *Georgetown Journal on Poverty Law & Policy* XV, no. 2 (Summer 2008), published electronically September 24, 2007 as forthcoming, Social Science Research Network, http://ssrn.com/abstract=1016401.

5 Food and Agriculture Organization of the United Nations (FAO), International Fund for Agricultural Development (IFAD), and World Food Programme (WFP). *The State of Food Insecurity in the World 2013: The Multiple Dimensions of Food Security* (Rome: FAO, 2013), http://www.fao.org/docrep/018/i3434e/i3434e.pdf.

6 "Hunger Statistics," World Food Programme, accessed August 24, 2014, http://www.wfp.org/hunger/stats.

7 Richard Oppenlander, *Food Choice and Sustainability: Why Buying Local, Eating Less Meat, and Taking Baby Steps Won't Work* (Minneapolis: Langdon Street Press, 2013), 41.

Confronting the Saboteur Within:
Advancing a Consciousness of Compassion

by Jo Stepaniak

Remarkably, I've never encountered any friends, acquaintances, or strangers who don't think of themselves as compassionate people, regardless of how they actually behave. I'd venture to say that even many of the most hardened and heinous criminals alive believe they are capable of compassion. And if that's true, it would appear, then, that what we call "compassion" is a quality intrinsic to *all* people, regardless of gender, age, origin, or background, and regardless of whether that quality is ever actualized.

Some of the dictionary definitions of compassion include "a deep awareness of and sympathy for another's suffering," "the humane quality of understanding the suffering of others and wanting to do something about it," and "a spiritual consciousness of the personal tragedy of others and a selfless tenderness directed toward it." Therefore, to not have compassion would mean that we're heartless, unfeeling, and uncaring, and it seems few people consider themselves to be that way, even if their behavior belies such a notion.

Despite this amazing ability we have for caring about others, the human species has, throughout its history, frequently undermined and repressed this inherent characteristic, at times viewing it as a sign of weakness and at other times viewing it as simply pointless. In some ways, both of these viewpoints are accurate. Compassion indeed means letting down our guard, opening our hearts, and softening the protective barriers around our feelings. And by definition, compassion isn't self-serving; it's selfless. So people who consider it pointless might do so under the pretext that "there's nothing in it for me." And from that perspective, they'd be right, because compassion focuses on others, not on oneself.

Nevertheless, there are far-reaching beneficial side effects to compassion, especially from an anthropological vantage point. Our species wouldn't have survived and evolved if we hadn't exercised compassion in various ways and circumstances over time, because humans don't and can't live in a vacuum. We *need* each other. We *depend* on each other. And because of this thing called compassion, we *help* each other.

But therein lies the quandary. Although there's no question that we, as a species, help others, there's also no question that when we're divided into groups (by nation, ethnicity, politics, sex, age, religion, values, beliefs), we apply our compassion quite selectively. Our opinions—that quirky compilation of judgments, prejudices, likes, and dislikes unique to each individual and group—smother our predisposition for compassion. In other words, we each randomly decide that some beings are deserving of our compassion and others are not, and in doing so, we may put not only the quality of their lives at risk, but also their very existence.

The need for survival can certainly impede our compassion, as self-preservation is a basic drive among all life forms. Ensuring our own survival typically takes precedence over ensuring the survival of others. But when survival isn't at stake, and our impetus instead is based on greed or power or lust or pleasure, compassion inevitably becomes a casualty. On a certain level, we all acknowledge this basic law of nature, and yet we tend to act in ways that disregard it.

Our beliefs are often too intoxicating, too addictive, and too beguiling to ignore, so we mindlessly follow them or let them drive our decisions and choices. Consequently, we may come to think of our assumptions as gospel rather than merely concepts we created to insulate our feelings and justify our desires. When compassion is forsaken for baser inclinations, the fallout from that loss is immense.

It results in a life without conscience, a species without remorse, a world where anything goes because no one cares about the repercussions of their actions. Deconstructing our beliefs to separate truth from fiction, illusion from fear, and necessity from desire is the task of a lifetime, and yet it's the single most important objective for anyone concerned about advancing a more compassionate world.

Just as we withhold compassion from certain groups that don't fit our definition of "deserving," we extend compassion to groups that do. For people who have difficulty relating to other people, the object of their compassion might take the form of "the earth," "the environment," or, in particular, other species. In fact, it's relatively effortless to care about nonhuman beings who demand so little of us. Our companion animals, for instance, typically provide unconditional love, a listening ear, gratitude and appreciation, and enduring friendship, essentially asking nothing in return. Conversely, relationships with our fellow humans are generally messy, complicated, loaded with expectations, and charged with high emotion. It's often just cleaner and simpler to deal with other animals than with human ones.

For that reason, I consider the barometer of true compassion to be how we interact with the most aggravating, infuriating, formidable, and threatening of our own kind. Can we extend compassion to those we find horribly disagreeable, repellent, or even repulsive? Can we embrace those who won't, or can't, embrace us back? Can we love those we consider unlovable? Can we forgive acts we consider unforgivable? Can we break through the blockades of supposition and opinion to recognize and accept the similarities that unite us all while respecting the differences that make us unique?

While there are many noble activities that we might engage in or aspire to, such as being vegan or taking action on behalf of animals, people, or the environment, these compartmentalized actions don't, in and of themselves, define anyone as wholly compassionate. There are many self-serving reasons that people perform good deeds or make seemingly benevolent choices. And there are many kind and generous people who engage in activities that we might find abhorrent or that make our skin crawl. What separates the self-serving individuals from the compassionate ones? In a word, intention.

If our intent is to reap benefits from our good deeds or behavior, even if that intent is just to feel good about ourselves, our actions may be born of ego, not compassion. If we try to change people's minds to make them believe as we do, no matter how righteous or virtuous we believe that attempt is, our actions may be born of delusion. If we pity someone and are grateful that we're not in the same position, our actions may be born of embarrassment or guilt. The outcome of what we do is less significant than the motivation behind it, because without selfless intention, we are only feeding our vanity and promoting a sense of moral superiority. In fact, if at any time we actually do believe that we (or the group we belong to) are morally superior, we've simply proved the opposite.

Connecting the dots of compassion demands that we let go of egoism and pride and instead adopt a mind-set of openness and humility. In terms of compassion, it isn't important that others are unlike us, have contrary values, or engage in behavior we consider harmful or wrong. What matters is whether we can care about and accept them just as they are, in spite of our differences, and consider them our spiritual equals. There is something of value for us to learn from even the most contemptible among us. Unless we truly believe that, we are only dabbling in compassion, giving lip service to something we'd like to believe about ourselves that just isn't true yet.

Even if we preach kindness to all, if we're still delegating our compassion, guarding it jealously, or judiciously doling it out in bits and pieces to the "deserving" few, then our words are empty vessels and the compassion we eloquently tout is illusory. However, for those who strive to be wholly compassionate, who are brave enough to take on the challenge of connecting the dots, you can begin right now, starting with the one person who understands you better than anyone else—yourself.

Life has taught me that it's impossible for me to feed others if I'm hungry and my own cupboard is bare. Similarly, before we can fully extend compassion to all, it's valuable to take a critical look at where we're personally in need of compassion. Taking care of ourselves (physically, intellectually, emotionally, and spiritually), nurturing ourselves, and treating ourselves gently, like a good friend, provide the psychic sustenance that's necessary for us to offer that same solace to others, helping them to become fulfilled and able to pay that compassion forward.

For the process of self-compassion to be thorough, introspection must accompany one's self-nurturing. It's essential that we look inward and explore the history that gave birth to the set of beliefs we carry, because these beliefs are what formed and now frame our opinions and preconceptions. They are composed of all the hurts and joys we've had since childhood, all the sentiments, suppositions, values, and ideals that were imposed on us by our parents or caregivers and championed by the social complex in which we live. Everywhere we go, we lug these beliefs, like a backpack filled with rocks. They have become such an integral part of who we think we are that most of us can no longer differentiate between what we've absorbed from our culture and our own authentic thoughts and feelings.

It can be painful to acknowledge that the assumptions and distortions we've been clinging to as truth may be false prophets. It can be frightening to delve below the surface to find their origins so we can move beyond them. And yet it is extraordinarily liberating to let go of past hurts, disappointments, and regrets, and realize that our biases, fears, and preferences are generally based on our own limited experiences, which realistically can't be extrapolated to life as a whole.

The more tightly we cling to our beliefs—whether they're true or false, right or wrong—the more tightly we bind our hearts, leaving no room for compassion to enter. The first and most important step toward universal, rather than selective, compassion is cultivating this self-awareness. The second step is conceding our limited knowledge—of life, of others, of the world in general. The third step is accepting that what we know (or think we know), what we've experienced, and what we believe are illusory. At the center of our being is a never-changing spiritual nucleus that exists independent of these external influences. That spiritual nucleus is the essence of our true selves, the seat of the soul, if you will, the source of true compassion.

When we put down our sack of beliefs and remove our cloak of self-righteousness, we will perceive and recognize that spiritual nucleus. Then the dots of understanding will miraculously connect themselves, without our even trying, and a consciousness of compassion will be inevitable.

Is this level of compassion really achievable during our lifetimes? Possibly. But whether or not we succeed, it's the vision, effort, and practice that ultimately make our lives fulfilling and meaningful. In the end, what matters most isn't what we accomplish in this life but rather the legacy of love we leave for those from whom we've asked nothing. ✆

Unrecognized Roots of Injustice and the Vegan Transformation

by Will Tuttle

Social injustice, war, hunger, environmental degradation, and the other problems we're facing are the direct result of our cultural attitudes and practices. Is there an idea that could transform the roots of our culture and create a solid foundation for peace, abundance, and sustainability? I believe there is, and that it has to do with questioning the pervasive influence of animal agriculture. Our culturally mandated daily food choices drive an industrialized killing machine of epic proportions that reaches its damaging tentacles into every cranny, not just of our Earth, but of our culture, our bodies, and the inner landscape of our attitudes, beliefs, assumptions, thoughts, and feelings. Both our outer world and our inner mentality reflect the food choices that are instilled in us from infancy.

Our most immediate and socially significant connection with the larger order is through eating food. Our food choices are a surprising and overlooked key to understanding our culture and ourselves, and to transforming our world toward harmony and freedom. The ripples of our mistreatment of animals for food are vast. The essential dot-connecting we are called to make today is between our routine abuse of animals and virtually all of the crises we face, both collectively and individually. In many ways, this is our basic intelligence test and, though it's obvious we've been flunking it for quite a while, it appears that the tide may be turning. We may be emerging from the culturally inflicted trauma we've endured, and from the psychological numbing and trancelike consensus that keeps us oblivious to the programming that violates us from early childhood. This desensitization turns us into perpetrators, propelling us to indirectly (and often directly) attack nonhuman animals, the Earth, each other, and ourselves.

We were all born into a culture that forced us, virtually from birth, to eat the flesh and secretions of certain animals who are bred, confined, attacked, and killed for this purpose. Early on, we are injected with the habit of disconnecting the reality that is on our plate from the reality required to get it onto our plate. I believe there is no greater taboo in this culture than honestly discussing this, and the pervasive negative ramifications of using animals for food and other products. The reason it is such a potent taboo is that, in our hearts, we yearn to live in a world of kindness and respect for all life, and we know better. We naturally feel a kinship with nonhuman animals, so we repeat to each other many hollow and inaccurate official stories to justify our relentless mistreatment of animals for food, such as the protein story, the calcium story, the taste story, the no-soul story, and the life-feeds-on-life story, but the main weapon in our ongoing oppression of animals is our learned disconnectedness: we simply turn away, focus elsewhere, and numb our feelings. All the primary institutions in our culture (religion, science, media, family, government, business, and education) cooperate to keep our catastrophic abuse of animals well hidden, ignored, trivialized, and accepted.

And catastrophic it is. Not just to the animals and ecosystems, but to us, as well. Wherever we turn, we see the chickens of our mistreatment of animals coming home to roost. First, let's look briefly at some aspects of the external devastation caused by eating animal-sourced foods.

External Consequences of Animal Agriculture
Predictably, the most forcibly ignored cause of climate destabilization is eating meat and dairy products. As several writers in this volume discuss, breeding millions of cows, sheep, pigs, and other animals for food is the greatest source of both nitrous oxide and methane, which

are many times more powerful than carbon dioxide as greenhouse gases. The science on this is unequivocal and, in fact, a study by the WorldWatch Institute concluded that livestock production is responsible for a shocking 51% of greenhouse gas emissions by all human activity, including energy production, transportation, and industry.[1]

Eating animals requires massive amounts of fossil fuel inputs, directly pumping carbon dioxide into the atmosphere. In the West, we transport over 70% of our corn, soybeans, alfalfa, oats, and other grains to animal confinement operations, pump water to irrigate these fields, manufacture millions of pounds of fossil fuel-based fertilizers and pesticides, and house and slaughter billions of animals yearly. The end result of all this is that while it takes only about 2 calories of fossil fuel to produce 1 calorie of protein from soybeans, and 3 calories for wheat and corn, it takes roughly 54 calories of fossil fuel to produce one calorie of protein from beef. We waste huge amounts of petroleum for our meat and cheese, destabilize and overthrow foreign governments, and send our children to war to ensure the supply.

On top of this, the primary driving force behind deforestation is cattle grazing and clearing land to grow soybeans and cereal grains to feed farmed cows, chickens, pigs, and fish. This is a further major contributor not just to world hunger, global warming and climate destabilization, but also to the destruction of genetic diversity. By conservative estimate, we are destroying roughly an acre per second of Amazonian rainforest for animal agriculture,[2] and this is not just cutting down trees but destroying complex ecosystems and habitat that took millions of years to evolve. Because of eating animal foods, we are in the midst of the most devastating mass extinction of species in 65 million years. According to biologists, we are driving an average of between 50 and 300 species into extinction every day,[3] and the driving force behind this is our collective action of taking out our wallets and paying for millions of pounds of meat, fish, dairy products, and eggs daily.

Two thirds of our fish are now factory-farmed, causing severe water pollution and decimating wild fish populations. Our seemingly limitless appetite for fish for feeding not just ourselves but farmed fish, birds, and mammals as well has brought our oceans to the brink of collapse. Dairy cows, for example, consume enormous quantities of fish, added as fishmeal to "enrich" their feed in order to increase milk and fat output. And it takes 3 to 5 pounds of caught fish to make one pound of farmed salmon. We have exterminated fishes, turtles, and marine mammals and birds so completely that jellyfish are now taking over large areas of the oceans, and fishing vessels have to go out so far that they use unsustainable amounts of diesel fuel.[4] A study published in the prestigious *Lancet* medical journal concluded that the only effective way to reduce greenhouse gasses is to reduce human consumption of animal foods.[5]

This is just the tip of the iceberg. Converting precious land, water, petroleum, and grains to animal fat, protein, and sewage is extravagantly wasteful, and is also the main driving force behind water pollution, topsoil loss, and habitat destruction. Eating animal-sourced foods is also inherently elitist. With our higher incomes, we buy grain and feed it to animals whose flesh and secretions we eat, driving up the price of grain on world markets so that those less affluent and in less industrialized countries suffer malnutrition and starvation. Thich Nhat Hanh has summed it well: "Every day, forty thousand children die in the world for lack of food. We who overeat in the West, who are feeding grains to animals to make meat, are eating the flesh of these children."[6]

The information is available, and if we're interested, we can do the research and discover that a diet based on animal foods is responsible for the most serious environmental problems we face, and that it also devastates our personal environment as well as our social environment. The largest human nutrition study to date, the Cornell-Oxford study, concluded, "Our study suggests that the closer one approaches a total plant-based diet, the greater the health benefit."[7] Animal fat, animal protein, and cholesterol are directly implicated in the diseases that are epidemic in Western cultures such as heart disease, diabetes, obesity, strokes, kidney, liver, and gall bladder disease, breast, prostate, and colon cancer, arthritis, diverticulitis, autoimmune diseases, dementia, and so forth.

Internal and Historical Consequences of Animal Agriculture

Eating animal foods also devastates our social, psychological, and spiritual environment, because it fosters an attitude of reductionism, domination, disconnectedness, and exclusiveness. It is forced on us from infancy and is based, at its living core, on viciously dominating the reproductive cycles of female mammals, birds, and fishes. It requires a merciless exploitation of what we know in our bones is the most sacred dimension of life: mothers giving birth, nurturing, and protecting their offspring. Female animals are virtually always impregnated with sperm guns and restraining devices, their babies stolen from them and killed, and the mothers (mere "breeders") are also killed for their flesh after a few years of cruel exploitation. We drug them, we rape them, we terrorize them, we sicken them, we oppress them, we imprison them, we torture them, we break their families, and we wonder why we find pandemics of drugs, rape, terror, disease, oppression, incarceration, torture, and family breakdowns in our human world. As we sow, we reap. And we employ whole armies of our brothers and sisters to do the horrific work of confining, mutilating, and killing billions of hapless animals, work that brings out the worst in them. Slaughterhouse and animal farm workers have the highest rates of worker-related injuries, as well as of suicide, drug addiction, alcoholism, spousal abuse, and violence. If we are ordering, buying, and eating these foods of death and despair, we are responsible. We forget what Martin Luther King, Jr., taught us—that injustice anywhere is a threat to justice everywhere. We are all connected.

From its beginnings about ten thousand years ago, animal agriculture has been a war against animals, nature, each other, and our basic wisdom and kindness. As free-living sheep, goats, and later cows, pigs, and other animals began to be enslaved and killed for food, other free-living animals began to be viewed as mere pests that potentially threatened the enslaved animals. Animals and nature were gradually reduced to commodities, and an insatiable demand for land, water, and food for the herds caused relentless and savage conflict among herders. A wealthy elite class emerged of the men who owned the most livestock, leading to the first full-scale wars, which were then, as they still are today, driven by the desire of the elites for more wealth and power. The first word for war that we know of, the ancient Sanskrit "gavyaa," means literally "the desire for more cows."

The unfortunate losers of these first wars became the property of the victors, and so animal agriculture not only led to widespread warfare by herders against each other and against non-herders who were gardeners and gatherers. It also led to human slavery as well. Just as they impregnated female animals against their will to maximize their holdings and wealth, and castrated male animals to keep them docile, they learned to do the same to the human slaves they owned in order to maximize wealth and control.

The emergence of the practice of animal agriculture, which I refer to as the herding revolution in *The World Peace Diet*, is by far the most significant and devastating development in human history and prehistory, and yet it remains essentially invisible and unrecognized to this day. It occurred gradually over thousands of years, and it was a revolution of reductionism: reducing beings to the status of things. It required men whose innate sense of mercy and kindness was suppressed by routinely abusing nonhuman animals. Men are the natural role models for boys, traumatized by being forced to mutilate animals to become the hard, tough men. Women were increasingly viewed as mere breeders to be impregnated and used by men, just like livestock, and the fascination among elites with bloodlines and the emergence of a rigidly hierarchical, patriarchal, and bellicose culture dominated by a few spread gradually throughout the Mediterranean, central Asia, Europe, and from there to the Americas, Africa, and virtually the entire planet today. It is the culture all of us are born into, and is at its core a herding culture. A competitive economic system based on ownership of capital (capital meaning "head" in ancient Latin, as in head of livestock), capitalism has encouraged the elite land- and livestock-owning class to control virtually every major institution in the warrior society that exists to this day, including government, media, religion, education, science, and business.

This system is a war against virtually all cultures, and all of us as individuals have been and continue to be traumatized by it. For example, as infants, we are forced not just to witness everyone around us eating the flesh of enslaved animals, but also to eat this ourselves and to betray our natural affection for animals. We are traumatized by the pervasive need to compete, and by being forced to witness violence in the media and often in our families, and to be routinely abused by the desensitized adults and by the culture into which we're born. Because we've been traumatized and thus numbed to violence, we willingly participate in systems of structural violence that inevitably traumatize nonhuman animals, ecosystems, and other people. This ongoing trauma leads to rampant social injustice and diminishes our natural capacity to create a world of equality, freedom, abundance, and sustainability.

Structural Violence, Institutionalized Injustice, and Attitudes of Domination

Structural violence leads to institutionalized injustice and internalized attitudes of domination. For example, the arising of the structural violence of animal agriculture led to the reduction of nonhuman animals to mere commodities to be owned, killed, and eaten, and fostered the justifying mentality of speciesism: that humans are inherently superior to animals.

Animal agriculture led directly to war, which led to the establishment of human slavery, as the victors, typically of a different ethnicity, tribe, and/or race than the vanquished, enslaved both the humans they defeated and their livestock. It is sobering to contemplate the basic truth that whatever we've done to animals, we've also eventually done to each other. Thus, the structural violence of animal agriculture and war led to the structural violence of slavery, which led to the practice of domination and exploitation of people of other ethnicities and the justifying mentality of racism. Animal agriculture also directly led to the domination of the feminine as explained earlier, because female animals, particularly their reproductive organs and cycles, came under complete domination by male pastoralists, leading to the devaluation and exploitation of women who also eventually were seen as mere breeders to be used sexually and as property. The justifying mentality of sexism is the ongoing result of this institutionalized repression of females and the feminine, as required by animal agriculture. Similarly, animal agriculture requires boys to emulate the role model of the tough, hard, emotionally disconnected man, and the structural violence of socializing boys to be competitive and cruel towards other boys and animals and to use girls for sexual pleasure creates rigidity, harshness, and also mistrust and persecution of gay people and those who are "different" or less able to compete, and the resultant justifying mentalities of heterosexism and ableism.

Additionally, animal agriculture has always engendered an elite class of land and capital owners, and this structural violence leads to gross inequity in wealth and power, with the corresponding mentalities of classism, elitism, privilege, and entitlement. People who have less wealth and power suffer disproportionately from environmental degradation such as polluted and scarce water, air pollution, climate destabilization, and soil erosion, as well as from hunger, war, trafficking, and disease. Even more exploited are the free-living animals who are hunted, trapped, trafficked, and forced into starvation and extinction.

Animal agriculture is the unrecognized spinning fury at the core of both the outer and inner domains of exploitation, traumatizing the Earth, other species, our culture, and the inner landscape of our emotions and attitudes. It reaches also into plant agriculture as well. Because animal agriculture has completely insinuated its norms into our lives, we engage in plant agriculture—which is essentially harmonious and working with the bounty of seeds, gardens, and life-affirming abundance—the way we engage in animal agriculture, which is essentially about enslaving, killing, and dominating by force. So we see the perverse deployment of GMO crops, toxic pesticides and chemical fertilizers, monocropping, and other practices that turn plant agriculture into a war against nature and an effort to dominate the Earth and the feminine, conducted in the same way we engage in animal agriculture. In every other arena, the same mentality is applied. Another obvious example is health care, which in the dominant medical paradigm is seen as a war against nature, bacteria, and viruses using weapons and technologies of violence, rather than seeing our health as a reflection of our feelings, attitudes, and relationships with nature and each other.

Over the past 20 years or so, it has become clear that children who are traumatized, and who cruelly practice torturing and killing animals, are likely to become dangerous to other people as they get older. It's now well understood that serial killers practice first on animals. We live in a culture that similarly practices first on animals. As we work to heal the many social justice issues we face, it is incumbent upon us to look deeply into the roots of our violence toward each other, and to question both the practice and the mentality required by animal agriculture. It's well understood now that one of the worst things we can do to a child is to let him or her get away with cruelty toward animals. The same is true of ourselves. Working for peace, justice, sustainability, and equality without questioning animal agriculture is addressing symptoms while ignoring the underlying cause.

The Cultural Transformation is at Hand
Veganism—striving to minimize our violence and injustice toward others—is indeed an idea whose time has come. The beauty of veganism is that it reflects our true nature, and it is not just a philosophy, but also requires a basic transformation in our way of living. Veganism is nothing to be proud of. It is simply our true human eyes looking out and seeing beings to be respected rather than commodities to be manipulated and used for selfish purposes. The motivation underlying veganism is compassion and justice for all, and as each of us awakens to the power of this idea and begins to live it, we directly reduce animal cruelty and suffering. We bless the world by dramatically reducing our abuse of the Earth, other humans, other species, our loved ones, and ourselves. Our physical, psychological, social, and spiritual health are all connected, and they can flourish when we understand and live this understanding.

Strong diseases demand strong medicine. Veganism, properly understood, is that medicine, and it can be practiced by any one of us, starting right this minute. Authentic vegan living fundamentally questions and rejects the deep-seated, culturally-mandated attitudes of exclusivism, reductionism, and disconnectedness that generate our unyielding dilemmas. It replaces them with inclusion, compassion, respect, and awareness. Our culture will go vegan, transform, and flourish, or it will continue brutalizing animals, humans, and the earth to its self-destruction. We are not the only species on this planet, and we cannot continue to usurp the wisdom of the web of life here.

I have sketched just the briefest of outlines in this short piece. Today, perhaps more than ever before, we are in a position to recognize, understand, and discuss at a global level the devastating role animal agriculture plays in our lives, and to transform both our individual and collective lives with this understanding and discussion. Imagining a vegan world is imagining a completely different reality, immeasurably more sane, just, and in harmony with our true nature.

To understand the deep structure of our culture and the big picture in more detail, please read, explore, study, and ask questions. Each of us can change, and we are each called to be, as Gandhi said, the change we would like to see in the world. This is our vision and its message and power. ✆

[1] Robert Goodland and Jeff Anhang, "Livestock and Climate Change," *World Watch* 22, no. 6 (2009): 10-19, http://www.worldwatch.org/files/pdf/Livestock%20 and%20Climate%20Change.pdf.

[2] Editorial Board, "Losing Ground in the Amazon," *The New York Times*, April 15, 2014, http://www.nytimes.com/2014/04/16/opinion/losing-ground-in-the-amazon.html?_r=1.

[3] S.L. Pimm, G.J. Russell, J.L. Gittleman, and T.M. Brooks, "The Future of Biodiversity," *Science* 269 (1995): 347–350.

[4] Elizabeth Kolbert, "Is there Any Hope for our Overfished Oceans?" *The New Yorker*, August 2, 2010.

[5] The Canadian Press, "Eat Less Meat, Reduce Global Heat, Says Study," *CBCNews*, September 13, 2007, http://www.cbc.ca/news/technology/ eat-less-meat-reduce-global-heat-says-study-1.644769.

[6] Thich Nhat Hanh, *Creating True Peace* (New York: Simon & Schuster, 2003), 77.

[7] Colin Campbell, interview 1994, cited in Andrea Wiebers and David Wiebers, *Souls Like Ourselves* (Rochester, MN: Sojourn Press, 2000), 51.

The MOGO Principle for a Peaceful, Sustainable, and Humane World

by Zoe Weil

In my talks and workshops as a humane educator, I often ask people to participate in a guided visualization that asks them to imagine that they're very old, at the end of their life, sitting on a park bench in a now healthy, safe, restored, and peaceful world. Not a perfect world, but one in which we have solved the great challenges that we faced at the beginning of the 21st century. A child comes along, and sits down too. Having learned in history lessons about the terrible problems we once faced, this child asks, "What role did you play in creating the good world we have today?" I invite the participants to imagine what they would like to be able to say.

I know it's a stretch for many people to imagine a world in which we've truly solved such problems as global warming, poverty, genocide, warfare, pollution, high rates of species extinction, institutionalized animal cruelty, resource depletion, overpopulation, etc., but if we don't envision the world we want and identify the part we will play in its unfolding, it's much harder to achieve peace, sustainability, and a humane world.

When we do imagine such a world, single issues generally fade away. A human rights activist has no problem embracing the vision of a world without animal cruelty, just as an animal rights activist readily embraces a world without child abuse. An environmentalist dreams of peace, just as a peace activist dreams of clean rivers.

In recent years, winners of the Nobel Prize have included economist Mohammad Yunus, whose microcredit movement has lifted millions of people out of poverty, and environmentalist Al Gore and scientists on the Intergovernmental Panel on Climate Change, who work to prevent global warming and its resulting planetary disasters. These people did not receive the Nobel Prize for economics or any of the sciences, however. Rather, they received the Nobel Peace Prize. This is because solving poverty and preventing ecosystem collapse bring peace. It is because we understand the relationship between hunger and war, and between environmental destruction and international conflict.

The MOGO Principle

When people participate in the guided visualization above, and answer the child's question in their minds, they are called upon to make connections between their lives and choices, and the world that they wish to help create. In my life, I try to make choices that do the most good and the least harm toward everyone—all people, animals, the environment, and myself. I call this the MOGO principle, short for "most good," and I believe that if all of us endeavor to live by this principle—through our daily choices, our acts of citizenship, our communities, our work, our volunteerism, and our interactions—we will not only create systemic changes that solve our entrenched, interconnected problems, but will also significantly enrich our own lives.

For over 25 years, I have been teaching people of all ages about the interrelated issues of human rights, environmental preservation, and animal protection in an effort to offer information, tools, and motivation for conscious and positive choice-making and committed change-making in whatever careers, work, and volunteer efforts they choose. I came to adopt the MOGO principle after many years of asking students, "What does the most good and the least harm?" I would compare a Styrofoam cup to a ceramic mug; bottled water to a refillable, stainless steel bottle with tap water (filtered if necessary) inside; an afternoon at the mall with an afternoon spent volunteering, and so on. Eventually, this question turned into my own life philosophy, but I came to realize it was far more complex than simply bringing a canvas bag to the supermarket and eschewing paper or plastic.

Although we sometimes have easy and inexpensive MOGO alternatives that we can adopt readily once we've taken the time to learn, we often don't because of destructive, inhumane, and entrenched systems in our society. And sometimes we do have MOGO options, but our desire for un-MOGO choices eclipses our values. So while the MOGO principle is quite simple in theory, it can be quite challenging in practice.

My Laptop

For example, I'm writing this essay on my laptop. My computer is filled with toxic metals, mined in an unsustainable manner, that cause significant pollution and environmental destruction, not to mention endangering miners. My computer was assembled overseas by people who may have been working under unhealthy, sweatshop conditions. Some chemicals used in its manufacture were likely tested on animals, force-fed to them in quantities that kill, dripped into their eyes, and rubbed onto their abraded skin. All these animals would then have been killed upon completion of the tests.

My computer will have a brief life, and I will likely need to replace it after about five years. If I do the "right" thing, I will pay for it to be recycled, and it may wind up overseas again, being disassembled by children who will be exposed to the toxins within it. If I do the "wrong" thing and throw it away at our local transfer station, it will be incinerated, releasing airborne toxins into the atmosphere. I could donate it to an individual or school, if it is still working and useful, but this would simply delay its eventual disposal.

My computer is also one of the best tools I have for helping to create a better world. Through it, I am able to communicate across the globe easily and quickly; to train people to be humane educators and offer the MOGO principle through distance learning programs and courses; to acquire the information I need to teach as well as to promote better systems, and to reduce my travel, thus reducing my environmental footprint and contribution to climate change and pollution.

I have barely touched the surface of the effects, negative and positive, of my laptop, but as you can see, there are many questions we can and should ask and answer in our quest for MOGO living. And because I don't want us to get stuck on computers, I feel compelled to briefly explore two other ordinary items. Let us draw connections among their effects so that when we try to ask and answer important questions about choosing humane and sustainable lifestyles and changing entrenched systems, we will be looking at the big picture and thinking and choosing comprehensively and holistically.

Fast Food Cheeseburgers
Each day, millions of people eat fast food cheeseburgers, potentially damaging their health, since these foods are associated with heart disease, various cancers, strokes, diabetes, obesity, bacterial contamination, and more.

Meanwhile, millions of cows in the dairy industry are impregnated annually, their calves removed at birth so we can take their milk. Cows will often bellow out for days when their young are taken from them, and the male calves often wind up confined in stalls so small they can't move, in order to keep their flesh tender for the veal market. Engineered and given hormones to increase their milk production, about half of dairy cows will suffer from mastitis, a painful udder infection, necessitating antibiotics in their feed, which sometimes wind up in dairy products, as well as in water through the cows' waste. When cows' milk production wanes, they're slaughtered, and their bodies are turned into meat, usually hamburgers.

As for the environmental impact, the United Nations has noted that animal agriculture is a primary contributor to global warming. Additionally, such agricultural systems deplete topsoil, drain aquifers, pollute rivers and oceans, rely upon monoculture, make crops pesticide-dependent, and destroy habitats.

The labor impacts of fast food are tremendous as well. Slaughter-house work is the most dangerous employment in the United States, often relying upon undocumented workers who have no health insurance or access to healthcare when they are injured. Most fast food businesses also prevent unionizing, so work in these franchises is often low paid, with few or no benefits.

In an even more ironic twist, we exploit, sometimes quite cruelly, and then kill animals in laboratories to find cures for the diseases we cause by eating unhealthy foods.

What's good about fast food cheeseburgers? They're inexpensive, convenient, relatively tasty, and ubiquitous. If you're hungry when you're on the road, there's quick, cheap food readily available. Such food is so cheap because it's subsidized by taxpayers and because agricultural systems favor it, and this also means that fast food burgers are difficult to avoid for many people, especially those with children whose school teams stop at fast food restaurants as a matter of course, and who may be invited to many a birthday party that includes McDonald's. Thus, even if you want to avoid such food, current systems make it challenging to do so. They beckon, and we enthusiastically buy.

Cotton T-Shirts

Cotton is the world's most heavily pesticide-sprayed crop, accounting for approximately 10% of global pesticide use.[1] These include highly toxic chemicals that wind up in waterways, poisoning fishes and affecting the entire food chain, including humans. The cotton that is produced in Asia is often grown, sprayed, and picked by children who are not only exposed to these dangerous toxins, but who also suffer extreme deprivation and abuse. Cotton is also a crop that requires significant irrigation and is highly energy-intensive in its production.

Cottonseed oil, a by-product of the cotton industry, is used in a variety of foods, most notably in snack foods, even though cotton is not regulated as a food crop and is heavily sprayed with fungicides and insecticides.

Once the cotton is harvested and woven into fabric, it is usually dyed using textile dyes that are known to be hazardous substances. A large percentage of the dye (which does not adhere to the cotton) is carried off into the wastewater stream.

More often than not, conventional T-shirts are sewn together in factories that are not required to follow fair labor laws. This means that in many factories, workers, including children, may: be paid less than their country's minimum wage; work under extremely unhealthy and often dangerous conditions; receive none of the benefits common among factory workers in richer countries; be unable to form unions and are fired for trying to do so, and work excessively long hours.

The finished T-shirts are exported, often across the globe, using significant amounts of fossil fuels. They are then displayed in stores that we each travel to, usually using more fossil fuels, in order to buy them. As is with fast food, systems are in place to make energy-intensive, sweatshop-produced, chemical cotton cheap and ubiquitous.

Cotton is a great fabric. It's biodegradable. It breathes. It's easy to clean. It's soft and comfortable. And while there are healthy and humane alternatives to "chemical" cotton, sustainable and naturally dyed organic cotton T-shirts made closer to home are far more expensive and difficult to find than their "conventional" counterparts.

Why Do We Create Such Problematic Products?

Three items: computer, cheeseburger, T-shirt. What questions should we ask about their systems of production and disposal so that we can connect the dots and work to not only make MOGO purchasing choices, but also change systems so that they are more sustainable and humane? Let's begin with the question why:

- Why is my computer full of toxins and produced in ways that are exploitative, unjust, and destructive?
- Why have we created a system of agriculture and food procurement that is cruel, unhealthy, and unsustainable?
- Why do we create clothes that poison our planet, exploit other people, and use undue amounts of resources?

The answer to these "why" questions could comprise several dissertations, but I will outline a few, overarching reasons:

- *Disconnection, ignorance, and negative impulses and qualities*: Individuals tend not to demand changes to these unhealthy, unjust, and inhumane systems because we usually do not make the connections between our food, our products, and our clothing with their effects on others. It takes effort to pursue knowledge about these connections, and it's not in the best interests of the media to reveal them, since the media is dependent upon the advertising dollars that these industries generate. Therefore, consumers don't press for change, because they are largely unaware. Additionally, greed, apathy, and myopia all contribute to our failure to create better systems.

- *Election financing*: Because corporations, industries, and special interest groups donate huge sums to candidates and then lobby them, legislators who rely on corporate and special interest money to finance their elections (virtually all of them) lose their capacity for true independent judgment and decision-making that would require changes in current systems. For example, because of lobbying and industry dollars, the Farm Bill is always passed, even though it perpetuates destructive and cruel agricultural practices.

- *Poorly regulated capitalism*: Capitalism's goals are to maximize immediate profits and minimize expenses, not to balance profit-making with long-term health. Without constraints applied equally to all, poorly-regulated capitalism rewards those who find the most cost-effective methods to produce monetary wealth, even if that means outsourced labor that is inhumane, destructive environmental practices, planned obsolescence, human and animal cruelty, and shifting of pollution overseas.

- *Corporate charters*: Corporations have the rights of persons without the concomitant responsibilities. Therefore, corporations avoid responsibility for the harm they cause. In some cases, laws exclude certain industries from culpability for actions that individuals would be prosecuted for. For example, laws exclude farm animals from state anti-cruelty statues. Thus, while pressing a hot iron into the flesh of your dog or cutting off half of your parakeet's beak would be illegal, these are normal and legal practices when done to cows (branding), and chickens and turkeys (debeaking).

- *True costs are displaced*: The systems that perpetuate these problems succeed in large part because they keep our food, clothing, and electronics cheap, displacing the true costs elsewhere. So while we may collectively pay for ill health, pollution, oil-generated wars and political unrest, and climate change through our tax-subsidized programs in defense, environmental clean-up, healthcare, etc. (along with our own individual increased costs of personal health insurance that includes covering the uninsured and the rising costs of our own healthcare), we do not perceive these as real costs. We still think we're getting cheap goods, even though we're paying the true costs through our taxes and other personal expenses.

How Do We Change These Systems and Solve These Challenges?
Knowing some of the "whys" is very important. It allows us to determine how to change these systems so that they become healthy, just, sustainable, and humane. As enormous as these problems are—as seemingly intractable as they appear—there are, in fact, solutions to each of them that will enable us to live more fully aligned with the MOGO principle. Here are just a few hows to answer the whys above:

- *Educate for a sustainable, peaceful, world*: The most important and overarching solution to all our challenges is humane education. It is far better to prevent cruelty, destruction, war, sickness, climate change, etc., than it is to try to fix these problems once they've occurred. I realize that they are already occurring, but the longer we wait to embrace humane education fully and comprehensively, the less likely we will be in successfully solving our entrenched problems and averting catastrophes (e.g., those that may be caused by global warming, species extinction, and depletion of resources). I've identified five elements that comprise quality humane education and which can, if implemented in all educational settings, transform our world in a generation. They include:

1. Providing accurate information about the interrelated challenges of our time by drawing connections between human rights, environmental preservation, animal protection, and systemic change-making
2. Fostering the three Cs: curiosity, creativity, and critical thinking
3. Instilling the three Rs: reverence, respect, and responsibility
4. Offering positive choices and the tools for problem-solving
5. Inspiring people to be lifelong learners who employ the three Is: inquiry, introspection, and integrity

Humane education cannot rid us of negative qualities such as greed and apathy, but it can cultivate our commitment to acting from our best qualities, including our compassion, wisdom, and integrity; by drawing connections between our choices and their effects; engaging our commitment to positive change, and supporting the development of compassionate communities. Inadequate (and sometimes destructive) education lies at the root of all our problems, and a commitment to make living sustainably, peaceably, and humanely the highest purpose of education would produce a generation that has the skills and motivation necessary to tackle all our existing problems.

- *Transform the financing of elections*: During almost every election cycle, we hear the call for campaign finance reform. We have even seen some efforts in the US Congress and the passage of some legislation. Yet true campaign finance reform has yet to happen, and the Supreme Court has reversed the positive trend with its Citizens United decisions. This underlying problem is pivotal to creating systemic changes that prevent the problems described above with our products, foods, and clothes. True campaign finance reform would represent a systemic change in and of itself. Plus, once we tackle this root problem, we will be able to more easily and effectively create the other changes that will solve so many of our production challenges.
- *Reform capitalism*: Peter Barnes has written an excellent book, *Capitalism 3.0*, that offers a realistic and reasonable solution to

some of capitalism's failures. The founder of Working Assets, Barnes is pro-capitalism with *caveats*. He puts forth a plan to prevent capitalism's negative effects while preserving its successes in creating prosperity by calling for the protection of the commons, which we all share. Paul Hawken, in his book *Natural Capitalism* (among others), offers other practical and visionary perspectives on reforming capitalism. Many other authors, economists, and thinkers are contributing to such solutions as well.

- *Change corporate charters*: Robert Hinkley, a corporate lawyer turned corporate reformer, has proposed adding 28 words to corporate charters. In his proposed code of conduct, corporations will continue to pursue profit, "but not at the expense of the environment, human rights, public health or safety, welfare of the communities in which the corporation operates, or dignity of its employees."[2] If such a code were adopted nationally (and many are actively working to add such codes to state corporate charters), as well as internationally, the playing field for corporations would remain even while ensuring that we stop the outsourcing of harm, pollution, and destruction.

- *Add true costs to price tags*: As we infuse humane education into all levels of society, and focus on true campaign finance reform so that legislators are not beholden to their corporate funders, it will become easier to change corporate charters, to reform capitalism, and to put the true costs of products, foods, and clothing (among other things) where they belong—with the producer. The producer will, of necessity, add these costs to the price the consumer pays. Chemist Michael Braungart and architect William McDonough, authors of *Cradle to Cradle*, a book about the production of healthy, restorative goods, emphasize that accounting for true costs will improve our economies and our lives. The costs of healthy products, buildings, electronics, vehicles, etc., will be dramatically lower since they will not incur, and therefore pass on, the high negative costs of pollution, climate change, defense needs, and ill health to their consumers. Once true costs are added to products, those products that are safe and nourishing will be significantly cheaper than those that are not, reversing the existing paradigm.

Keys to Change

Now that I've outlined some broad categories examining why we're in the predicaments we're in, and how to create systemic change, it's time to turn to you. What can you do to create change and solve these interconnected problems? How can you personally be part of the solutions described above? How can you make MOGO choices in your life?

I've written a book to answer these questions, *Most Good, Least Harm: A Simple Principle for a Better World and Meaningful Life*, and I'll share the seven keys that I've identified that help people put the MOGO principle into practice. They are [as paraphrased and modified descriptors from the book]:

1. *Live your epitaph*: When we ponder our desired epitaph, imagining what we would want said about us when we die, we gain the opportunity to actually live that epitaph now, each day of our lives. Doing this may be one of the most liberating and meaningful choices we can make, setting us on a path of purpose and integrity that brings inner peace while contributing to outer peace in the world.

2. *Pursue joy through service*: I conducted an unscientific survey asking a couple of hundred people, "What brings you joy?" Over and over people wrote about service to others, whether to other people, animals, or the earth. No one wrote about a new house or car or designer clothes. So often it was in giving that people repeatedly spoke of experiencing joy. It's crucial to find the right forms of service, however. I know that when I am asked to be of service in an area that doesn't appeal (baking cookies for a fundraiser, for example), I may do so out of guilt and feel no joy. But when I give in ways that utilize my passions and skills (like volunteering to teach humane education

classes) I am able to give a significant amount of time (enough to bake many hundreds of cookies) with joy in service.

3. *Make connections and self reflect*: It takes effort to make connections between our choices and their effects. Doing so may appear at first glance to be onerous and guilt-inducing, yet ignorance doesn't actually serve us. When we are ignorant of the effects of a fast food cheeseburger, it doesn't mean that we won't suffer the health consequences of such a dietary choice; the community consequences of strip malls with ugly fast food franchises marring our landscape; the climate change consequences; the tax consequences, etc. It just means that we won't realize that our choices contribute to our own and others' harm. So making connections may entail some work and efforts at inquiry, but it is ultimately rewarding because it provides the opportunity to make different, healthier, and more enlivening choices. Once we have made connections and gained information, it's important to self reflect to see where the confluence of new knowledge and our values lies. Our introspection results in our commitment to make new and better choices.

4. *Model your message and work for change*: Mahatma Gandhi was once asked by a reporter, "What is your message?" He responded, "My life is my message." The truth is that each of our lives is our message; it cannot be otherwise. So we must ask ourselves: is my life the message I want it to be? Living your life in such a way that you model the message you intend means living with integrity. But in today's world, with all its inhumane and destructive systems, it's not enough. I don't model the message I want with my computer, because there is no computer that models my intended message. Thus, this key requires that we work for change and engage in efforts to create better systems. Then we can better model the message we want. Modeling your message and working for change are two sides of the same coin. Those who say our individual choices don't matter are wrong. They may not create significant

change in and of themselves, but they matter because they demonstrate our integrity and commitment, and can have meaningful effects. And those who say that it's enough to live a humane and sustainable life individually are wrong, too. In a world in which so many pervasive problems require systemic change, it's simply not enough. We must engage politically and through our communities, volunteerism, and work to create new and healthy systems.

5. *Find and create community*: Committing to the MOGO principle generally takes us out of the mainstream. As I alluded to earlier, McDonald's is mainstream; organic veggie burgers aren't. Conventional cotton T-shirts are ubiquitous and often cheap; organic, US-made ones are hard to find and often expensive. If you are the only person you know trying to make changes, you may feel disenfranchised, lonely, and sometimes even hopeless. It's critical to find or create a community of people who share your values and want to work toward a better world, too. This community can start small, with a single friend or family member, or person you connect with at an online group such as Meetup.com, but the goal is to create a vibrant community that empowers you as you empower others.

6. *Take responsibility*: The word responsibility often sounds burdensome. You may feel tired just reading this key. Yet responsibility carries with it profound freedom. When you take responsibility for your actions and choices, aligning them with your deepest values, you are free from the insidious effects of lack of self-esteem, peer pressures, keeping up with the Joneses, and advertising messages that make you feel inadequate and wanting more. By taking responsibility, we become liberated, no longer victims, but actors in the fabulous drama of creating both a better world and an engaged, joyful life.

7. *Strive for balance*: Living your epitaph, making connections, modeling your message, taking responsibility—these take effort. The effort is rewarding and meaningful, but it isn't easy.

Given that there are so many systems in place that need changing and that diminish our current capacity to live as MOGO as we want, it's critical not to burn out, but rather to maintain balance. We want others to join us so that together we can create peace and health. That means we must strive for balance so that we model peace and health. There is no single way to be MOGO, no perfect path, no absolute. We must each find our way joyfully and with commitment, balancing our needs with those of others.

When people imagine embracing the MOGO principle, they sometimes find it daunting and overwhelming. Some recoil at the weight of responsibility and the sorrow and fear that they know may come with exposing themselves to painful and threatening knowledge. But being a humane educator and adopting the MOGO principle has personally brought me, and many others, profound joy and a deep sense of purpose. Those of us on this path find ourselves surrounded by incredible people who inspire us daily. While there's no doubt that it's challenging to use the three Is of inquiry, introspection, and integrity, it is deeply fulfilling. With all the forces in society that perpetuate short-term thinking and the fulfillment of every desire—to the great detriment of our world and all who reside here—it can be a relief to have a path that helps one to live with integrity, generosity, and self-respect.

It is absolutely possible to create a peaceful, sustainable, humane world. And you are a necessary part of this great journey to create it. ☙

Notes

[1] "Cotton," Pesticide Action Network, accessed October 4, 2014, http://www.panna.org/resources/cotton.

[2] "The Code for Corporate Citizenship," Time to Change Corporations, accessed October 4, 2014, http://timetochangecorporations.com/the-code-for-corporate-citizenship/.

Conclusion: Going Forward

by Will Tuttle

Though we find ourselves now at the conclusion of this volume, we are also at the beginning of an effort to help create a more broadly inclusive vision of social justice work. It's a vision that specifically includes nonhuman animals within our sphere of concern, and as we've seen, there are many reasons for this. One of the most striking is that vast numbers of animals suffer terribly at our hands, and their suffering is as significant to them as ours is to us, so we have absolutely no logical or ethical basis to discount it. A further significant reason is that in many crucial ways, our mistreatment of nonhuman animals is the core injustice that creates the basic structural context in our culture that makes the many faces of social injustice to humans inevitable. It is the *ur*-injustice, so to speak. Animal agriculture and exploitation desecrate animals as they also devastate ecosystems and pervert human relationships, creating both the outer conditions for chronic war, hunger, injustice, and inequity, as well as the internal attitudes that propel these afflictions, and reduce our capacities and awareness.

Going forward, it's helpful to bear in mind that our colleagues who work in particular arenas of social injustice, working for example to overcome sexism, racism, child abuse, or global warming, may understandably resist the idea that our culturally mandated mistreatment of animals is the primary injustice. They may also resist the idea that they would be more effective in their work if they would make an effort to include the rights of animals as essential to progress in their movements, and to live this understanding as well, for example, by going vegan and encouraging others to do so as part of their activism. Fortunately, the evidence continues to mount, and the curtain hiding our culture's routine mistreatment of animals continues to be pulled back. This makes it increasingly difficult to ignore the empowering insights that emerge when we more fully understand the intersections between our cultural injustice toward animals and other people.

It's helpful to realize that we've all gone through stages in our understanding and in our commitment to the causes that are important to us. As my understanding deepens, my motivation deepens, and so I'd like to close this volume with an encouragement to continue the effort to deepen our level of understanding. Given the massive resources of the industries that profit from war, ecocide, disease, animal abuse, and social inequity, we have all been forced to ingest a lot of misinformation in our lives, and also to function in a social context that reduces our intelligence and empathy, and makes us pliant consumers and workers in a system that benefits few at the expense of many.

When it comes to veganism, for example, I think that there are at least several stages that we pass through on our journey. In the beginning, our understanding is typically quite shallow, and we have gone vegan usually either because we became aware of the terrible cruelty to animals through an online video or a book, or we have learned about the health benefits of ditching meat and dairy, or perhaps, more rarely, for concerns about our environment. We discover that although we're now vegan, most people, even friends and family, are resistant to exploring veganism themselves or becoming vegan. We also often run into strong resistance from healthcare providers who may warn us of the presumed nutritional risks of being vegan. Due to the strong negative social pressure, as well as internal doubts, lack of nutrition information, and a shortage of understanding on the underlying issues and support from other vegans, a fairly large number of us who self-identify as vegan for a while may slide back to being more socially and medically acceptable, and we may forsake (hopefully temporarily) vegan living.

If we're able to progress past these initial pitfalls in our vegan journey and are successfully eating a healthy plant-based diet for ethical reasons, we may find ourselves at the stage where we become chronically angry at others for continuing to support animal cruelty by eating animal foods, and frustrated and grief-stricken just knowing about the immense suffering that no one seems to care about. This is the angry vegan stage, and it's a difficult place to be. In a sense, we've gone beyond the shallow veganism of being only concerned about our health, or the knee-jerk reaction of going vegan because of being traumatized by watching an undercover video. But now we're feeling angry and hurt, and are perceived by others as being judgmental, moody, unhappy, and condescending. Because the angry vegan stage is so stressful, some of us avoid this by moving into the closet vegan stage, where we just don't talk about it with anyone anymore. We go ahead with our private vegan life, but we're in the closet about it because we don't like to argue or be seen as different or negative. Both the angry vegan stage and the closet vegan stage are understandable responses to our culture's hostility to having its basic premise questioned, but they are unsatisfying and disempowering, and keep us relatively ineffective in our efforts.

Fortunately, we can move beyond these middle stages on the vegan journey, and there are many more stages of progress as we develop our experience and understanding. Deep veganism arises in us as a heart-felt aspiration to embody lovingkindness in all of our relations with others, both human and nonhuman. It emerges as a sense of vast inclusivity. We realize that people who are not yet vegan have been wounded by pervasive cultural programming that has in many ways shut down their natural wisdom and compassion from infancy. We see that we have all been wounded by the meal rituals and our culture's food program that desensitizes us and breeds exclusivism, elitism, disconnectedness, injustice, competition, and self-centeredness. Deep compassion begins to grow in our hearts for all living beings and our interconnected suffering. We begin to yearn more than anything to embody the liberating truth-essence of veganism in every thought, word, and action.

As long as we see veganism as merely a reaction to the violence inherent in our culture, we will be caught in the shallows, and somewhat ineffective as individuals and as a movement. As we go deeper and realize that veganism—the compassionate and utterly transformative alternative to the status quo—is our future beckoning, we will be able, like the caterpillar, to open to a deep change in our way of being and relating to others. Awakening fully from the consensus trance, coming out of the closet, and transmuting our anger into joyful, creative, and liberating action on behalf of others is the beckoning future for us as individuals and as a culture. We see that activism is sacred action, and that authentic inner work is required to be effective as agents of positive social change.

Even though we may be vegan in our outer lives and choices, veganism, we begin to realize, is far more than consumer choices, talking points, and animal rights campaigns. Veganism demands us to question absolutely everything in us that has been modeled by our cultural programming, and to bring our thoughts and deeds into alignment with a radically more inclusive ethic that calls for respect and kindness for all beings, including our apparent opponents. We see that veganism, as boundless inclusiveness, is the essence of all social justice movements, and that it is the antidote to what ails our world.

There is a spiritual dimension to this process as well, in the sense that our culture, as organized around animal exploitation and killing, is profoundly materialistic, reducing animals to commodities, and ecosystems to resources, and humans also to mere material objects that are born, that die, and that compete to pass on genes. The pervasive practice of literally reducing beings to things for many generations has desacralized our view of the world and stripped our culture of wisdom. All of us are injected with the toxic and completely erroneous program that sees nature, animals, and ourselves as mere physical entities. Every meal is a ritual enactment of desecrating nature and animals, and literally eating the primary cultural teaching that beings are mere pieces of meat, without inherent worth, dignity, and interests, and undeserving of respect, kindness, and moral consideration. Industrial exploitation of markets, animals, people, ecosystems, and future generations are the inevitable result of this food practice and its consequent mentality.

Deep veganism is actively questioning this materialistic program in the nitty-gritty of our daily lives. It is making an effort to treat all beings with compassion, to create a new social matrix founded on justice for all, and to directly experience the deeper truth that what we are is essentially eternal consciousness that was never born and will never die. We are profoundly related to all expressions of this consciousness; we are all related in the timeless source of all living beings, and are called to realize the deeper truths that our culture tricks us into ignoring so that we remain trapped in slavery, enslaving others. Veganism is a call to spiritual awakening and to cultural transformation. It is unyielding in its demands that we take the great adventure of liberation, self-discovery, and transformation to its complete conclusion.

Social injustice arises from the delusion of materialism and ignorance of the true nature of what we actually are. Learning to look beyond the outer material forms—the species, race, ethnicity, gender, sexual orientation, economic class, age, abilities, and so forth—of other beings and to see, recognize, appreciate, respect, and address the light of consciousness that is their true nature: this is a practice that liberates not only others, but ourselves too from the materialist delusion propagated by and reinforcing the inherent violence in our herding culture. As each of us taps the yearning to fulfill our potential for freedom, justice, and being part of an awakening of human consciousness, we increasingly embody vegan values, and we no longer convince by our arguments, but by our presence.

Thank you for taking this journey with us, which is just beginning. If there were certain authors whose essays touched a chord in you, please consider exploring their other writings and materials. We all have a part to play, and as we deepen our understanding, our light gets brighter and we can help each other more, sending ever-greater ripples of compassion and freedom through the web of our shared life. ✆

Author Profiles

Carol J. Adams is author of the influential book *The Sexual Politics of Meat*, as well as *Living Among Meat Eaters; The Pornography of Meat;* and *The Inner Art of Vegetarianism*. She has edited several books, including *Ecofeminism and the Sacred* and *Animals & Women*, and is co-author of *Never Too Late to Go Vegan*. She lectures on the intersectionality of oppression and is a frequent speaker at college campuses.

David Cantor, a full-time animal advocate since 1989, founded Responsible Policies for Animals in 2002 and serves full-time as its director. RPA promotes equal autonomy, ecology, and dignity rights of all animals and campaigns to break the grip of animal-abuse industries on the public mind. RPA is preparing the first guide to accurate and truthful news reporting on animals. Cantor also contributed chapters to *A Primer on Animal Rights; The Great Ape Project;* and *Voices from the Garden: Stories of Becoming a Vegetarian*.

Angel Flinn is director of outreach for Gentle World, an intentional community and educational organization whose core purpose is to help build a more peaceful society by educating the public about the reasons for being vegan, the benefits of vegan living, and how to go about making the transition.

Katrina Fox is a writer, publisher, speaker, and media coach. A journalist for fifteen years, her work has appeared in media internationally, and she is the co-author and editor of books on varied topics including sexual diversity, hypnosis, and self-help. She is the founder and editor-in-chief of *The Scavenger*, an online alternative media hub, and is associate editor of *Ethical Futures* digital magazine for senior executives. Originally from the UK, Katrina now lives in Sydney, Australia.

Beatrice Friedlander is an animal advocate, attorney, nonprofit manager, and hands-on volunteer at several cat shelters. She is a board member of the Animals and Society Institute, having served previously as its Acting Executive Director. She is a founding and current member of the Animal Law Section of the State Bar of Michigan, and Michigan Attorneys for Animals. She also has a Certificate in Nonprofit Sector Studies from Wayne State University.

Lori B. Girshick is a sociologist, writer, and activist. She works with battered women, people who are homeless, individuals who are transgender, and cats who need homes. She has written four books and numerous articles.

Rachel Alicia Griffin is an assistant professor in Communication Studies at Southern Illinois University and is cross-appointed in Africana Studies and Women, Gender, and Sexuality Studies. As a critical intercultural scholar, her research interests span social justice in general and black feminist thought, critical race theory, gender violence, and education. Most recently, Dr. Griffin has published in *Critical Studies in Media Communication; International Journal of Qualitative Studies in Education;* and *The Howard Journal of Communications*. She is a frequent guest speaker at college campuses.

Robert Grillo is the founder and director of Free from Harm, a nonprofit animal rescue, education, and advocacy organization. Free from Harm specializes in online activism, publishing content that serves activists as well as the general public. Grillo has a professional background as a creative consultant, integrating twenty years of marketing and design experience into his animal advocacy strategy.

Melanie Joy is a professor of psychology and sociology at the University of Massachusetts, Boston, and is the founder and president of the Carnism Awareness and Action Network. Dr. Joy is the author of *Why We Love Dogs, Eat Pigs, and Wear Cows*. She also authored *Strategic Action for Animals* and has written a number of articles on psychology, animal protection, and social justice. Dr. Joy was the eighth recipient of the Institute of Jainology's Ahimsa Award, and she also received the Empty Cages Prize.

Lisa Kemmerer has worked on behalf of the environment, nonhuman animals, and disempowered humans for nearly thirty years. A graduate of Reed, Harvard, and Glasgow (Scotland), she is the author/editor of *Eating Earth: Dietary Choice and Planetary Health; Animals and World Religions;* and *Sister Species: Women, Animals, and Social Justice.* Dr. Kemmerer is currently a philosopher-activist at Montana State University in Billings.

Rita Laws is a Choctaw living in Oklahoma with the youngest of her children plus two dogs. She holds a PhD and MS in psychology and a BA in education. Dr. Laws has been a freelance writer since the 1980s when she left teaching to stay home with her family that was growing rapidly through adoption. She writes primarily for parenting and hobby magazines and has written several books.

Keith McHenry is an artist and author who helped start Food Not Bombs in 1980. He has recovered, cooked, and shared food with the hungry with Food Not Bombs for over thirty years. Keith was arrested "for making a political statement" in San Francisco, spent two years in jail, and faced twenty-five years to life in prison. He wrote and illustrated *Hungry for Peace: How You Can Help End Poverty and War with*

Food Not Bombs. Keith spends his winters in California and summers at the Food Not Bombs Free Skool in Taos, New Mexico.

Christopher-Sebastian McJetters is a social justice advocate who divides his time between New York City and Charlotte, North Carolina. He is a professional copyeditor and a staff writer at Vegan Publishers. In his spare time, he organizes events and discussions relative to exploring the intersectionality of veganism and other movements for social justice including the LGBT community and people of color.

Dawn Moncrief is the founding director of A Well-Fed World, a Washington DC-based hunger relief and animal protection organization that partners with and financially strengthens vegan feeding programs for people in need; farm animal care and rescue efforts; and pro-vegan outreach campaigns. She holds two master's degrees from The George Washington University: one in international relations, the other in women's studies—both with a focus on economic development. She speaks internationally about the negative impact of animal agriculture on global hunger and climate change.

David Nibert, a former tenant organizer and community activist, is now an award-winning writer and professor at Wittenberg University in Springfield, Ohio, where he teaches courses on Animals and Society, Global Change, and Social Stratification. He is the author of *Animal Rights/Human Rights: Entanglements of Oppression and Liberation* and *Animal Oppression & Human Violence: Domesecration, Capitalism and Global Conflict*, as well as numerous book chapters and journal articles. Dr. Nibert co-organized the section on Animals and Society in the American Sociological Association.

Anthony J. Nocella II, award-winning author, community organizer, and educator, is a senior fellow of the Dispute Resolution Institute at the Hamline Law School and is editor of the *Peace Studies Journal*. Dr. Nocella is executive director of Save the Kids, a national grassroots organization dedicated to creating alternatives to youth incarceration. He is also executive director of the Institute for Critical Animal Studies, the first center dedicated to intersectional social justice scholarship-activism centered on animal advocacy. He has a doctorate in social science and has published more than twenty books; some of his most recent include *Earth, Animal, and Disability Liberation: The Rise of the Eco-ability Movement; Terrorization of Dissent: Corporate Repression, Legal Corruption, and the Animal Enterprise Terrorism Act;* and *Defining Critical Animal Studies: An Intersectional Social Justice Approach for Liberation.*

Richard Oppenlander is a sustainability consultant, researcher, and author of *Food Choice and Sustainability: Why Buying Local, Eating Less Meat, and Taking Baby Steps Won't Work,* and also of *Comfortably Unaware.* Dr. Oppenlander lectures nationally on food choice and how it relates to sustainability, and serves as an advisor to world hunger projects in developing countries. He has spent forty years studying the environmental effects of food choices. He is founder of an organic plant-based food production company, co-founder of an animal rescue sanctuary, and founding president of the nonprofit organization Inspire Awareness Now.

lauren Ornelas is the founder/director of the Food Empowerment Project, a vegan food justice nonprofit seeking to create a more just world by helping consumers recognize the power of their food choices. FEP works in solidarity with farm workers and focuses on increasing access to healthy foods in low-income communities. As the director of Viva!USA, Ornelas investigated factory farms and ran consumer campaigns. She also served as campaign director with the Silicon Valley Toxics Coalition for six years. She has presented a TEDx talk on "The Power of Our Food Choices."

Colleen Patrick-Goudreau is a thought leader on the topics of food ethics, animal protection, and compassion, and is an award-winning author of six bestselling books, including *The Joy of Vegan Baking* and

The 30-Day Vegan Challenge. She is a regular contributor to National Public Radio and has appeared on the Food Network and PBS. She holds a master's degree in English literature.

Sailesh Rao is executive director of the nonprofit Climate Healers. An electrical engineer with a PhD from Stanford University, Dr. Rao founded Climate Healers to reforest land to help neutralize human carbon dioxide emissions. Among its projects, Climate Healers partners with NGOs, tribal villages, and school clubs to help low-income areas in India use solar stoves. He was selected as a Karmaveer Puraskaar Noble Laureate by the Indian Confederation of NGOs and is author of *Carbon Dharma: The Occupation of Butterflies.*

Anteneh Roba is board-certified in emergency medicine and aesthetic medicine, and has a private practice in Fairfax, Virginia. He is president and co-founder of the International Fund for Africa (IFA), an international non-governmental organization dedicated to helping both human and nonhuman animals in Africa. Through his organization, he has worked to improve healthcare for children in Ethiopia and is involved in the struggle to make medical care more accessible to the people of rural Ethiopia. Dr. Roba works to improve the condition of homeless dogs, equines, and other working animals in Ethiopia, and to promote the adoption of a plant-based diet. Dr. Roba has been featured on National Geographic, ABC, CBS, NBC, and FOX News.

Marla Rose is an award-nominated journalist, author, event planner, and activist based in Chicago. As co-founder of the popular Chicago VeganMania festival, she works to spread the message of compassionate living, and is co-founder of VeganStreet.com, which is dedicated to creating and providing innovative stories, images, and tools to help build a more kind and just world.

Ruby Roth is the world's leading author and illustrator of vegan and vegetarian books for children. The first of their kind in children's literature, today Roth's books have been translated into multiple languages. She has received international attention for her sensitive yet frank advocacy of a vegan diet and lifestyle, and her work has been featured on CNN, FOX, Today, and other major media outlets. Complementing her degrees in art and American studies, Roth has been researching animal agriculture, health, nutrition, and the benefits of a plant-based diet for over a decade.

Richard H. Schwartz is the author of *Judaism and Vegetarianism; Judaism and Global Survival; Who Stole My Religion? Revitalizing Judaism and Applying Jewish Values to Help Heal our Imperiled Planet;* and *Mathematics and Global Survival,* as well as over 200 articles and twenty-five podcasts at JewishVeg.com. Dr. Schwartz is president emeritus of Jewish Vegetarians of North America (JVNA) and president of the Society of Ethical and Religious Vegetarians (SERV). He is associate producer of the 2007 documentary *A Sacred Duty: Applying Jewish Values to Help Heal the World.* His latest project involves working to restore and transform the ancient Jewish holiday New Year for Animals.

Kim Sheridan, author and filmmaker, is founder of Compassion Circle, as well as Go Green Already! (which spreads the message of environmental responsibility), and EnLighthouse Entertainment. She is the author of the award-winning book *Animals and the Afterlife* and co-author of *Uncooking with Jameth and Kim.* With a background as a naturopath, Kim is the co-founder of HealthForce Nutritionals and founder of Healthy Chick and Healthy Hunk, helping people take charge of their health. Kim has been listed in *Who's Who in Executives and Professionals, 2,000 Notable American Women,* and *Great Minds of the 21st Century.*

Jasmin Singer is the Executive Director of Our Hen House, a multimedia hub of opportunities to improve conditions for animals. She is the co-host of the Our Hen House podcast and the Our Hen House TV show. Jasmin has appeared on The Dr. Oz Show, HuffPost Live, and in the documentaries *Vegucated* and *The Ghosts In Our Machine*. Most recently, she published chapters in *Defiant Daughters* and in *Running, Eating, Thinking*.

Gary Smith is co-founder of Evolotus, a public relations agency working for a better world. Evolotus specializes in nonprofits, documentary films, animal advocacy campaigns, health/wellness, natural foods, and socially beneficial companies. Gary blogs at The Thinking Vegan and has written for *Elephant Journal, Jewish Journal, Mother Nature Network*, and other publications. He lives in Sherman Oaks, California.

Jo Stepaniak has been involved with compassion-related issues for nearly five decades. She has authored and co-authored seventeen books on compassionate living and vegan cuisine, and has been a contributing author to many other books, articles, and national publications. Since the 1990s, through her online advice column, she has responded to many hundreds of questions related to compassionate living. She is the senior editorial director at Book Publishing Company, an ethics-based publishing house. In addition, she is a community and victim-offender mediator and an international business dispute-resolution specialist and arbitrator.

Will Tuttle, educator and activist, lectures widely throughout North America and internationally. Author of the best-selling *The World Peace Diet*, which was translated and published in over a dozen languages worldwide, he is a recipient of the Courage of Conscience Award, as well as the Empty Cages Prize. The creator of several wellness and advocacy training programs, Dr. Tuttle is a frequent radio, television, and online presenter and writer. His PhD from the University of California, Berkeley, focused on educating intuition and altruism in adults, and he has taught college courses in creativity, humanities, mythology, religion, and philosophy. A former Zen monk, he has created eight CD albums of original piano music.

Zoe Weil is president of the Institute for Humane Education, which offers MEd, MA and PhD programs in comprehensive Humane Education linking human rights, environmental preservation, and animal protection. IHE also offers online programs and workshops for teachers, parents, and change agents. In 2016, IHE will be opening the world's first preK-12 Solutionary School in New York City. Zoe has given many TEDx talks including her acclaimed TEDx talk "The World Becomes What You Teach," and is the author of Nautilus silver medal winner *Most Good, Least Harm*, as well as *Above All, Be Kind*, and Moonbeam gold medal winner *Claude and Medea*. She is the recipient of the Unity College Women in Environmental Leadership award and was a subject of the "Americans Who Tell the Truth" portrait series.